MANHEIMER'S
CATALOGING AND
CLASSIFICATION

ADDITIONAL VOLUMES IN PREPARATION

MANHEIMER'S
CATALOGING AND
CLASSIFICATION

FOURTH EDITION, REVISED AND EXPANDED

JERRY D. SAYE

School of Information and Library Science
University of North Carolina at Chapel Hill
Chapel Hill, North Carolina

with April J. Bohannan

School of Library and Information Studies
Texas Woman's University
Denton, Texas

MARC formatting with the assistance of Terri O. Saye

Kathrine R. Everett Law Library
University of North Carolina at Chapel Hill
Chapel Hill, North Carolina

MARCEL DEKKER, INC.   NEW YORK · BASEL

Library of Congress Cataloging-in-Publication Data

Saye, Jerry D.
    Manheimer's cataloging and classification / by Jerry D. Saye; with April J. Bohannan. — 4th ed., rev. and expanded.
        p. cm. — (Books in library and information science; v. 59)
    Includes bibliographical references.
    ISBN 0-8247-9476-1 (alk. paper)
    1. Cataloging—United States Problems, exercises, etc. 2. Classification—Books Problems, exercises, etc. I. Bohannan, April. II. Title. III. Series.
        Z693.S28 2000
        025.3'076—dc21   99-38007
                                                                                    CIP

Examples of bibliographic and authority records in the OCLC/MARC format are used with the permission of OCLC Online Computer Library Center, Inc.

Microsoft® and PowerPoint® 97 are registered trademarks of Microsoft Corporation.

Marcel Dekker, Inc., and the author make no warranty with regard to the accompanying software, its accuracy, or its suitability for any purpose other than as described in the preface. This software is licensed solely on an "as is" basis. The only warranty made with respect to the accompanying software is that the diskette medium on which the software is recorded is free of defects. Marcel Dekker, Inc., will replace a diskette found to be defective if such defect is not attributable to misuse by the purchaser or his agent. The defective diskette must be returned within 10 days to: Customer Service, Marcel Dekker, Inc., P.O. Box 5005, Cimarron Road, Monticello, NY 12701, (914) 796-1919.

Comments regarding the software may be addressed to the author: Jerry D. Saye, Associate Professor, School of Information and Library Science, CB # 3360, The University of North Carolina at Chapel Hill, Chapel Hill, NC 27599-3360. email: saye@ils.unc.edu, telephone: 919-962-8073, fax: 919-962-8071.

This book is printed on acid-free paper.

Headquarters
Marcel Dekker, Inc.
270 Madison Avenue, New York, NY 10016
tel: 212-696-9000; fax: 212-685-4540

Eastern Hemisphere Distribution
Marcel Dekker AG
Hutgasse 4, Postfach 812, CH-4001 Basel, Switzerland
tel: 41-61-261-8482; fax: 41-61-261-8896

World Wide Web   http://www.dekker.com

The publisher offers discounts on this book when ordered in bulk quantities. For more information, write to Special Sales/Professional Marketing at the headquarters address above.

Current printing (last digit):

10 9 8 7 6 5 4 3

PRINTED IN THE UNITED STATES OF AMERICA

In memory of

Martha L. Manheimer

teacher, colleague, and dear friend.

NOTE TO INSTRUCTORS AND STUDENTS

The CD-ROM that accompanies this text is designed to be used by students for individual use on a PC. One does not need to own the PowerPoint software in order to use these graphics. The graphics on it are in Microsoft PowerPoint 97 format. A free copy of the Microsoft PowerPoint Viewer 97 for Windows 95/98/NT is available for downloading at:

http://officeupdate.microsoft.com/downloadDetails/ppview97.htm

These graphics can also be used by instructors to prepare transparency masters and, in some situations, for computer projection. Experience has shown that the graphics on this CD-ROM do not work well with all computer projectors due to the lower resolution of some projectors compared to that of computer monitors and laser printers.

If these graphics don't project well and you desire to use computer projection, or if you would like an expanded version of the graphics that includes the other illustrations in the text, an enhanced set of the graphics is available free to instructors. These graphics have been enlarged for clarity while remaining identical to the examples in the text and the CD-ROM. Copies of these PowerPoint files are available by FTP and also on disk from the author at cost. Given the file sizes only ZIP disks have sufficient capacity to hold these files.

To obtain the address and password for FTP access or information on obtaining the files on disk please call or write:

Jerry D. Saye, Associate Professor
School of Information and Library Science
CB# 3360
The University of North Carolina at Chapel Hill
Chapel Hill, North Carolina 27599-3360

Telephone: (919) 962-8073
Fax: (919) 962-8071
email: saye@ils.unc.edu

PREFACE

The concept and structure of this book follows those developed by Martha L. Manheimer for the 1975 first edition. I have been assisted in this revision by Dr. April Bohannan who reviewed the exercises for the chapters on the Dewey Decimal Classification and Library of Congress Subject Headings and who provided much valuable consultation on the revision of the other parts of this book. Terri O. Saye assisted in the OCLC/MARC formatting of the catalog and name authority records and provided that valuable "cataloger's eye" for detail.

Changes in this edition reflect the 1998 revision of the *Anglo-American Cataloguing Rules, Second Edition* and the use of developmental order in the examples for descriptive cataloging, choice of access points, and headings. The most notable change in this edition is the inclusion of MARC formatting as implemented by OCLC. The cataloging examples have been changed significantly and expanded from those in the third edition to cover more fully descriptive cataloging and heading work. The exercises that support access point and heading work have been thoroughly revised to reflect that work in a machine-readable cataloging environment. The chapters on the Dewey Decimal Classification, Library of Congress Classification, and Library of Congress Subject Headings have been revised to reflect the most recent editions of those tools and to address some OCLC/MARC formatting issues.

The third edition of the book was the first to make readily available to instructors the graphics that support the examples in Chapters 1 through 5. With the fourth edition these graphics are now available with the text on CD-ROM for the use of both individual students and instructors. These graphics are identical to the examples in the text but add scans of the title page, title page verso and other features useful in illustrating the point at issue. When the items are in color the graphics are in color.

In addition to the extremely valuable contributions of April Bohannan and Terri Saye, thanks must go to the wonderful graduate assistants who have aided me in finding examples, carting books to and fro, scanning, proofreading and all the other tasks that helped make this book what it is. Special mention must go to Alenka Šauperl and Selden Durgom for their Herculean efforts over the past three years.

Jerry D. Saye
School of Information and Library Science
University of North Carolina at Chapel Hill
Chapel Hill, North Carolina

CONTENTS

INTRODUCTION

Since its first edition in 1975, this text has been used to support an introductory course in cataloging and classification. In order to be utilized to its fullest extent it should be used with the following texts:

> *Anglo-American Cataloguing Rules*, prepared under the direction of the Joint Steering Committee for Revision of AACR . . . [et al.]. 2nd ed., 1998 revision. Ottawa: Canadian Library Association; London: Library Association Publishing; Chicago: American Library Association, 1998. [AACR2R]

Additionally, this edition introduces for the first time MARC formatting of catalog records utilizing the conventions of OCLC: Online Computer Library Center. In those courses where MARC formatting will be introduced access to the following text will also be essential:

> OCLC. *Bibliographic Formats and Standards.* 2nd ed. Dublin, OH: OCLC Online Computer Library Center, 1996.

In order to be able to use the exercises in this book the following resources also should be available to the student in the classroom or the laboratory:

> Dewey, Melvil. *Dewey Decimal Classification and Relative Index.* Edition 21. Albany, NY: Forest Press, 1996.

> Library of Congress. *Classification.*

Class A	*General Works.* 1998 ed. (1998).
Class B-BJ	*Philosophy. Psychology.* 1996 ed. (1996).
Class BL, BM, BP, BQ	*Religion: Religions, Hinduism, Judaism, Islam, Buddhism.* 3rd ed. (1984).
Class BR-BV	*Religion: Christianity, Bible.* 3rd ed. (1987).
Class BX	*Religion: Christian Denominations.* 3rd ed. (1985).
Class C	*Auxiliary Sciences of History.* 1996 ed. (1996).
Class D-DJ	*History (General); History of Europe, Part 1.* 3rd ed. (1990).
Class DJK-DK	*History of Eastern Europe (General), Soviet Union, Poland.* 3rd ed. (1987).
Class DL-DR	*History of Europe, Part 2.* 3rd ed. (1990).
Class DS-DX	*History of Asia, Africa, Australia, New Zealand, etc.* 1998 ed. (1998).
Class E-F	*History: America.* 1995 ed. (1995).
Class G	*Geography. Maps. Anthropology. Recreation.* 4th ed. (1976).
Class H	*Social Sciences.* 1997 ed. (1997).
Class J	*Political Science.* 1997 ed. (1997).
Class K	*Law in General. Comparative and Uniform Law. Jurisprudence.* 1998 ed. (1998).
Class K Tables	*Form Division Tables for Law.* 1999 ed. (1999)

Class KD	*Law of the United Kingdom and Ireland.* 1998 ed. (1998).
Class KDZ, KG-KH	*Law of the Americas, Latin America and the West Indies.* (1984).
Class KE	*Law of Canada.* 1999 ed. (1999).
Class KF	*Law of the United States.* Prelim. ed. (1969).
Class KJ-KKZ	*Law of Europe.* (1988).
Class KJV-KJW	*Law of France.* (1985).
Class KK-KKC	*Law of Germany.* (1982).
Class KL-KWX	*Law of Asia and Eurasia, Africa, Pacific Area, and Antarctica.* (1993). 2 v.
Class KZ	*Law of Nations.* 1998 ed. (1998).
Class L	*Education.* 1998 ed. (1998).
Class M	*Music and Books on Music.* 1998 ed. (1998).
Class N	*Fine Arts.* 1996 ed. (1996).
Class P-PZ Tables	*Language and Literature Tables.* 1998 ed. (1998).
Class P-PM Supplement	*Index to Languages and Dialects.* 4th ed. (1991).
Class P-PA	*Philology and Linguistics (General). Greek Language and Literature. Latin Language and Literature.* 1997 ed. (1997).
Class PB-PH	*Modern European Languages.* (1933, reprinted 1966).
Class PG (in part)	*Russian Literature.* (1948, reprinted 1965).
Class PJ-PK	*Oriental Philology and Literature, Indo-Iranian Philology and Literature.* 2nd ed. (1988).
Class PL-PM	*Languages of East Asia, Africa, Oceania; Hyperborean, Indian and Artificial Languages.* 2nd ed. (1988).
Class PN	*Literature (General).* 1997 ed. (1997).
PQ	*French, Italian, Spanish, and Portuguese Literatures.* 1998 ed. (1998)
Class PR, PS, PZ	*English and American Literature. Juvenile Belles Lettres.* 1998 ed. (1998).
PT, Part 1	*German Literature.* 2nd ed. (1989).
PT, Part 2	*Dutch and Scandinavian Literatures.* 2nd ed. (1992).
Q	*Science.* 1996 ed. (1996).
R	*Medicine.* 1995 ed. (1995).
S	*Agriculture.* 1996 ed. (1996).
T	*Technology.* 1995 ed. (1995).
U-V	*Military Science. Naval Science.* 1996 ed. (1996).
Z	*Bibliography and Library Science.* 1995 ed. (1995).

Library of Congress. Office for Subject Cataloging Policy. *Subject Cataloging Manual: Classification.* 1st ed. Washington, DC: Cataloging Distribution Service, Library of Congress, 1992.

Library of Congress. Cataloging Policy and Support Office. *Subject Cataloging Manual: Shelflisting.* 2nd ed. Washington, DC: Library of Congress, Cataloging Policy and Support Office, 1995.

Library of Congress. Cataloging Policy and Support Office. *Library of Congress Subject Headings*. 22nd ed. Washington, DC: Library of Congress, Cataloging Distribution Service, 1999.

Library of Congress. Cataloging Policy and Support Office. *Subject Cataloging Manual: Subject Headings*. 5th ed. Washington, DC: Library of Congress, Cataloging Distribution Service, 1996.

This book is not intended to be a standalone text. Rather, it is designed to support lectures on cataloging, classification, and subject heading work as well as provide structured exercises in those areas. Ideally, this book will be used with one of the excellent introductory texts on cataloging and classification such as:

Chan, Lois Mai. *Cataloging and Classification: An Introduction*. 2nd ed. New York: McGraw-Hill, 1994.

or

Wynar, Bohdan S. *Introduction to Cataloging and Classification*. 8th ed. by Arlene G. Taylor. Englewood, CO: Libraries Unlimited, 1992.

The exercises are designed to be self-instructional for the student. It is anticipated that instructors may wish to supplement them with graded exercises developed locally. The coverage is general in that only situations commonly encountered are addressed. It is assumed that students interested in an in-depth coverage of cataloging, classification, and subject headings will have an advanced cataloging course and/or practicum later in their educational program.

Description of the Chapters

Chapter 1 covers the essential elements of the International Standard Bibliographic Description (ISBD) as presented in AACR2R Chapters 1 and 2 and also introduces the associated OCLC/MARC formatting tags, indicators and subfields as implemented by OCLC. Although presentation of the cataloging rules in this part is based upon the creation of catalog records for books using the MARC format, the principles are applicable to all types of documents and catalog types, including card catalogs. In the latter situation the instructor may choose to ignore the MARC coding and concentrate exclusively on the cataloging rules while introducing separately the style used to present cataloging information on catalog cards. This chapter is organized using a developmental approach. As a result, access points are not provided. This results in some of the OCLC/MARC formatting being incomplete for a field because an indicator or indicators for that field impact only on access decisions. This may also apply to a field number not being provided in its entirety because that full field number has access implications. This is particularly true for some uses of Field 246 and the 4xx fields. These access point issues are addressed in Chapter 2. This book allows students to check their own proficiency in descriptive cataloging by completing the descriptive cataloging exercise at the end of this chapter. Material covered in Chapter 1 can be reinforced by having the students catalog books from a practice collection.

Chapter 2 covers the choice of access points and corresponds to AACR2R Chapter 21. Only commonly encountered rules are exemplified. As in the chapter for description, OCLC/MARC formatting is also provided for these access points. The catalog records in this chapter and those that follow also serve as a review and continuation of the principles of descriptive cataloging. This chapter continues the developmental approach in that the catalog records in this chapter only indicate the access points that would be assigned and not their proper form. Form of headings is covered in succeeding chapters. At the end of Chapter 2 is an exercise that calls for students to identify and tag the access points for the catalog record examples in Chapter 1.

Chapters 3, 4, and 5 cover forms of headings and correspond to AACR2R Chapters 22, 24, and 25 and provide OCLC/MARC formatting for each heading. If a name in a heading appears in the Library of Congress Name Authority File and has been established under AACR2, that form has been used in the examples. Name forms established by LC as "AACR2 Compatible" have not been used. Instead, the form prescribed by AACR2R is used. References for the type of heading addressed in that chapter are illustrated for each heading requiring a reference through the use of an OCLC/MARC format name authority record using the OCLC style of name authority display. Whenever appropriate, Library of Congress name authority records have been provided. The name references used in this text are selective rather than providing all the name references LC has used. Continuing the developmental order used in other chapters, the chapter dealing with personal name headings does not have corporate name headings in their proper form because those rules have not been addressed yet. Similarly, only the examples in Chapter 5 (Uniform Title) use uniform title headings. Within these three chapters, however, developmental order has not been adhered to; thus, in the chapter for personal name headings, dates are given with names whenever appropriate, rather than only after the rule for dates has been encountered. At the end of Chapters 3, 4, and 5 are exercises calling for students to develop personal and corporate name headings, uniform titles and their references to access points assigned to the examples in Chapter 2.

There has been no consistent attempt in this work to conform to all Library of Congress Rule Interpretations (LCRIs) for description, access points or form of headings. Rather, in limited cases, particularly in descriptive cataloging, some LCRIs have been used when they provide useful guidance to the application of a particular rule and reflect expected standardization of form. In all other cases, the catalog examples represent a catalog record as called for by AACR2R. In no cases are LCRIs used when they contradict rules in AACR2R, unless this use is clearly indicated by a comment to the example.

Chapters 6 and 7 introduce the student to the two classification systems predominantly in use in American libraries -- the Dewey Decimal Classification and the Library of Congress Classification. Each chapter consists of a brief review of the classification techniques used in the system, OCLC/MARC related issues and a series of exercises in their use. Normally, in the two steps of the classification process, a classifier first analyzes the document and its relationship to other documents in the field and in the library's collection. Secondly, the classifier translates this analysis into the paradigm of the class heading and deals with the mechanics of the classification scheme. The classification exercises deal only with the second part of the classificatory process. The titles presented reflect, unambiguously it is hoped, the subject specification of the classification scheme. All the student is expected to do is to manipulate the scheme to create the classification notation in a way that most precisely reflects the subject content of the work. The answers to the exercises in the appendices provide hierarchical development for each of the titles as well as significant commentary so that a student can analyze how the final call number was developed.

Chapter 8 addresses the provision of subject index terms through the assignment of subject headings from the 22nd edition of *Library of Congress Subject Headings* and LC's *Subject Cataloging Manual: Subject Headings* and OCLC/MARC issues. Accompanying exercises provide a structured approach to the use of topical subdivisions, geographical subdivisions, free-floating and pattern headings. In the last exercise, subject headings are assigned to some of the titles already used in the Library of Congress Classification Exercise to allow for a comparison of the subject analysis provided by classification and alphabetical subject indexing.

The Accompanying CD-ROM

The CD-ROM that accompanies this book presents an exact copy of the examples used to illustrate Chapters 1 through 5. Additionally, it provides a scanned copy of the title page (or its substitute), the title page verso, and other elements in the work that help illustrate the point being addressed by the example. As is true for most monographs the sources used for examples are primarily in black and white, but when there is a color aspect to them the graphic is in color. All the presentations use using Microsoft PowerPoint 97 for Windows. See the "Note to Instructors and Students" earlier in this text for instructions on how to obtain a free copy of the PowerPoint 97 Viewer.

MARC Formatting Conventions

The MARC formatting conventions used for the examples are the OCLC variation of the MARC format. OCLC's approach is very compatible with those used by other bibliographic utilities and vendors but does have some unique characteristics that may not be common to all. Below are some of the differences.

Fixed Field: The labels for the elements of the fixed field may differ from those used by other bibliographic utilities.

Subfield delimiter: The subfield delimited used by OCLC is "‡". Other bibliographic utilities may use a "$" or some other convention.

Subfield code "a":   OCLC does not use a subfield delimiter and subfield code "a" when that subfield is the first element in a field. Other systems may still require this coding of the initial "a" subfield.

Additionally, a unique convention is used in this text for the blank (b̷) symbol. Although this symbol does not display on most, if not all, screen displays, it is used in some instances in the examples. Where that symbol has a meaning, e.g., "No information provided," then the blank symbol appears in the record. However, when the blank symbol indicates that the field is "undefined" the blank symbol is not used.

Part I

CATALOGING

CHAPTER ONE

Rules for Description

Suggested Lecture Outline

A. Catalog Cards, MARC Records and Online Catalogs

B. AACR2R and Related MARC Fields, Indicators and Subfields

    1. Rule 1.0/2.0   General Rules

    2. Rule 1.1/2.1   Title and Statement of Responsibility Area

    3   Rule 1.2/2.2   Edition Area

    4. Rule 1.4/2.4   Publication, Distribution, Etc., Area

    5. Rule 1.5/2.5   Physical Description Area

    6. Rule 1.6/2.6   Series Area

    7. Rule 1.7/2.7   Notes Area

    8. Rule 1.8/2.8   Standard Number and Terms of Availability Area

C. Fixed-Field Elements

D. Additional Variable Fields

Readings: *Anglo-American Cataloguing Rules.* 2nd ed., 1998 revision. Ottawa: Canadian Library Association; London: Library Association Publishing; Chicago: American Library Association, 1998. (AACR2R)[*]
        General Introduction, p. 1-4;
        Introduction, p. 7-9;
        Chapter 1, General Rules for Description, p. 11-59;
        Chapter 2, Books, Pamphlets, and Printed Sheets, p. 60-85.

---

[*] In this text all references to AACR2R refer to the 1998 revision of the *Anglo-American Cataloguing Rules*, 2nd ed.

Refer also to:
Appendix A, Capitalization, p. 563-599;
Appendix B, Abbreviations, p. 600-610;
Appendix C, Numerals, p. 611-614;
Appendix D, Glossary, p. 615-624.

Resources: Library of Congress. *Library of Congress Rule Interpretations.* 2nd ed. Washington, DC: Library of Congress, Cataloging Distribution Service, 1989-

OCLC. *Bibliographic Formats and Standards.* 2nd ed. Dublin, OH: OCLC Online Computer Library Center, 1996.

Saye, Jerry D. and Vellucci, Sherry L. *Notes in the Catalog Record: Based on AACR2 and LC Rule Interpretations.* Chicago: American Library Association, 1989.

N.B. The level of description used in this text, except where noted otherwise, is the second level. The examples in this chapter illustrate only descriptive cataloging elements. The selection of access points, their proper formatting, and the assignment of call numbers and subject headings are treated in the chapters that follow.

Library of Congress Policy: In some examples Library of Congress practices have been employed that are not specifically called for by AACR2R. These policy decisions have been taken from the Library of Congress Rule Interpretations. When these practices have an effect on the rule being illustrated a comment has been made following the example.

Rule Citations. Provided with each catalog record that follows is the AACR2R rule number and rule caption the example is intended to illustrate. Catalog records illustrating general rules for description have the relevant rule numbers from Chapter 1. For examples illustrating situations covered by rules in both the general chapter for description (Chapter 1) and in the chapter for books (Chapter 2), reference is made only to the rules in Chapter 2 unless the rule in Chapter 2 only refers the cataloger back to the general rule.

OCLC/MARC Formatting. In the examples that follow, an underline "_" is used in the first and second indicator positions for some fields to show that an indicator would be used with that field but not revealing what that indicator value would be. This is done when the indicator value would be inappropriate in this chapter addressing description because the indicator is related to access point or form of heading decisions. Similarly, 4__ is used for the series field because the use of 440 and 490 fields are access point decisions. For fields where an indicator value has been defined, and the appropriate value for the indicator in the example is a blank, that value is represented by the "ʬ" symbol.

Catalog Card Format. Since the late 19th century, the card catalog has been the dominant format for library catalogs. The following example is a typical catalog card record created using AACR2R:

Catalog Card

```
HF        Kriegel, Robert J.
5386           If it ain't broke--break it! : and other unconventional wisdom
.K855     for a changing business world / Robert J. Kriegel and Louis
1991      Patler. -- New York : Warner Books, c1991.
               xix, 284 p. ; 24 cm.

               Includes bibliographical references (p. 278-284).
               ISBN 0-446-51539-6


               1. Success in business. 2. Job stress. 3. Organizational
          change. I. Patler, Louis. II. Title.
```

It includes the call number identifying the subject of the document and its shelving location, information used to describe the document as well as an indication of the points of access by which this catalog record could be retrieved in the card catalog. These include the name "Kriegel" which is termed the main entry as well as access points called added entries. These added entries appear at the bottom of the card preceded by roman numerals. Additionally, the three subject access points for this catalog record also appears at the bottom of the card each preceded by an arabic numeral.

MARC Format. In the late 1960s the Library of Congress introduced the MARC (Machine-Readable Cataloging) format. Its adoption in modified form internationally as a communication standard for the transmission of cataloging data and the increased use of computers in library operations made the use of online catalogs in libraries an increasing reality beginning in the 1980s. Today, although many libraries still retain some form of card catalog, an increasing number are using online catalogs as either their primary or sole tool to inform users of the holdings of the library.

The MARC bibliographic record consists of a number of fields containing cataloging data. These fields are of two types: fixed and variable length. The cataloging data typically recorded on catalog cards appears in the variable fields of the MARC record. These variable fields consist of a three-digit "tag" also called a "field number," up to two single digit "indicators," and one or more "subfields." This example illustrates the variable fields of a MARC record as they would be displayed by the OCLC system. It contains the same cataloging data that appeared on the preceding card example.

OCLC/MARC Record

020		0446515396
050	0 0	HF5386 ‡b .K855 1991
100	1	Kriegel, Robert J.
245	1 0	If it ain't broke--break it! : ‡b and other unconventional wisdom for a changing business world / ‡c Robert J. Kriegel and Louis Patler.
260		New York : ‡b Warner Books, ‡c c1991.
300		xix, 284 p. ; ‡c 24 cm.
504		Includes bibliographical references (p. 278-284).
650	0	Success in business.
650	0	Job stress.
650	0	Organizational change.
700	1	Patler, Louis.

Areas of Description. In AACR2R, the elements of the description are divided into eight areas, each associated with a number. This area numbering has a direct relationship in the numbering of the rules in the chapters for description. The following example illustrates the elements in each area for a second level description of a book for both a catalog card and an OCLC/MARC record.

Rule 1.0B1   Areas of description

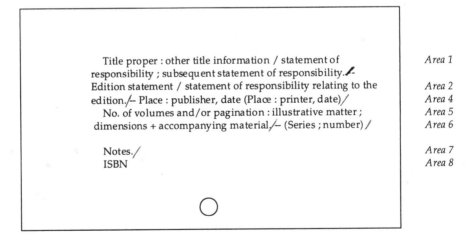

Title proper : other title information / statement of responsibility ; subsequent statement of responsibility. /-	*Area 1*
Edition statement / statement of responsibility relating to the edition. /- Place : publisher, date (Place : printer, date) /	*Area 2* *Area 4*
No. of volumes and/or pagination : illustrative matter ; dimensions + accompanying material, /- (Series ; number) /	*Area 5* *Area 6*
Notes. /	*Area 7*
ISBN	*Area 8*

Rule 1.0B1   Areas of description

020	ISBN	*Area 8*
245 _ _	Title proper : ‡b other title information / ‡c statement of responsibility ; subsequent statement of responsibility.	*Area 1*
250	Edition statement / ‡b statement of responsibility relating to the edition.	*Area 2*
260	Place : ‡b publisher, ‡c date ‡e (Place : ‡f printer, ‡g date)	*Area 4*
300	No. of volumes and/or pagination : ‡b illustrative matter ; ‡c dimensions + ‡e accompanying material.	*Area 5*
4_ _ _	Series ; ‡v number	*Area 6*
5_ _	Notes.	*Area 7*

Levels of Description. Prior to the publication of AACR2 in 1978, national cataloging codes had provided a standard for description, which, in general, met the more demanding description needs of academic and research libraries. AACR2 and its revision (AACR2R) provided catalogers with a cataloging code that allows for the description of documents using different levels of detail. AACR2R Rule 1.0D identifies three levels of detail. For each level, the elements stated are the minimum requirements for that level, provided that those elements are appropriate to the document being described. Additional descriptive elements can be added at a library's option to augment the description without rising to the requirements of the next higher level of description. It should be noted that variation in the information recorded in a description can affect the provision of access points for the document. The three examples that follow illustrate the differences in description for the same document at each of the levels of description in both the catalog card format and the OCLC/MARC format. Only the elements of description are presented. Subject and non-subject access points are not covered by the levels of description.

Rule 1.0D1   First level of description

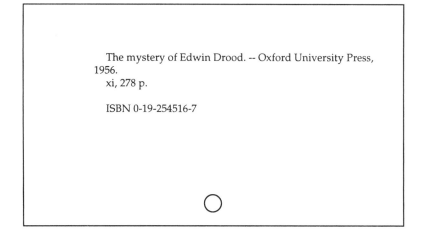

The mystery of Edwin Drood. -- Oxford University Press, 1956.
    xi, 278 p.

    ISBN 0-19-254516-7

Rule 1.0D1   First level of description

```
020       0192545167
245 _ _   The mystery of Edwin Drood.
260       ‡b Oxford University Press, ‡c 1956.
300       xi, 278 p.
```

Rule 1.0D2   Second level of description

> The mystery of Edwin Drood / by Charles Dickens ; with
> twelve illustrations by Luke Fildes and two by Charles Collins ;
> and an introduction by S.C. Roberts. -- Oxford ; New York :
> Oxford University Press, 1956.
>   xi, 278 p. : ill. ; 19 cm. -- (The Oxford illustrated Dickens)
>
> Prior to 1966 the series had the title: The illustrated Dickens.
> ISBN 0-19-254516-7

Rule 1.0D2   Second level of description

```
020       0192545167
245 _ _   The mystery of Edwin Drood / ‡c by Charles Dickens ; with
          twelve illustrations by Luke Fildes and two by Charles Collins ;
          and an introduction by S.C. Roberts.
260       Oxford ; ‡a New York : ‡b Oxford University Press, ‡c 1956.
300       xi, 278 p. : ‡b ill. ; ‡c 19 cm.
4 _ _  _  The Oxford illustrated Dickens
500       Prior to 1966 the series had the title: The illustrated Dickens.
```

Rule 1.0D3　　Third level of description

The mystery of Edwin Drood [text] / by Charles Dickens ;
with twelve illustrations by Luke Fildes and two by Charles
Collins ; and an introduction by S.C. Roberts. -- Oxford ; New
York : Oxford University Press, 1956. (1978 printing)
xi, 278 p. : ill. ; 19 cm. -- (The Oxford illustrated Dickens)

Prior to 1966 the series had the title: The illustrated Dickens.
ISBN 0-19-254516-7

Rule 1.0D3　　Third level of description

020	0192545167
245 _ _	The mystery of Edwin Drood ‡h text / ‡c by Charles Dickens ; with twelve illustrations by Luke Fildes and two by Charles Collins ; and an introduction by S.C. Roberts.
260	Oxford ; ‡a New York : ‡b Oxford University Press, ‡c 1956 ‡g (1978 printing)
300	xi, 278 p. : ‡b ill. ; ‡c 19 cm.
4_ _ _	The Oxford illustrated Dickens
500	Prior to 1966 the series had the title: The illustrated Dickens.

1.0　　GENERAL RULES

2.0B　　　Sources of information

1　　Rule 2.0B1　　Standard title page

020	0030476461
245 _ _	Nothing could be finer than a crisis that is minor in the morning / ‡c Charles Osgood.
250	1st ed.
260	New York : ‡b Holt, Rinehart and Winston, ‡c c1979.
300	xii, 202 p. ; ‡c 22 cm.

2   Rule 2.0B1   Facing title pages

020	0805039643 (alk. paper)
245 _ _	Lucy's bones, sacred stones, & Einstein's brain : ‡b the remarkable stories behind the great objects and artifacts of history, from antiquity to the modern era / ‡c Harvey Rachlin.
250	1st ed.
260	New York : ‡b H. Holt, ‡c 1996.
300	xii, 402 p. : ‡b ill. ; ‡c 24 cm.
504	Includes bibliographical references (p. [361]-382) and index.

3   Rule 2.0B1   Title page substitute

245 _ _	Carnegie Library of Pittsburgh : ‡b a brief history and description / ‡c by Ralph Munn.
260	[Pittsburgh] : ‡b The Library, ‡c [1968]
300	[10] p. ; ‡c 23 cm.
500	Cover title.
500	"May 1, 1968."

4   Rule 1.0H1   Multiple title pages. The first occurring is treated as the chief source of information

245 _ _	Seminary addresses & other papers / ‡c Solomon Schechter.
260	New York : ‡b Arno Press, ‡c 1969.
300	xiv, 253 p. ; ‡c 23 cm.
4_ _	Religion in America
500	Originally published: Cincinnati : Ark Pub. Co., 1915.

[The first title page also bears the latest date of publication, cf. Rule 1.0H1b.]

5   Rule 1.0H1a   Multiple title pages—different works with no title page pertaining to the whole item—the title pages of the works are treated as if they were a single chief source of information

245 _ _	Isn't that just like a man! / ‡c by Mary Roberts Rinehart. Oh, well, you know how women are! / by Irvin S. Cobb.
260	New York : ‡b G.H. Doran, ‡c c1920.
300	32, 32 p. ; ‡c 20 cm.

1.1   TITLE AND STATEMENT OF RESPONSIBILITY AREA
[Field 245 -- Title statement]

1.1B   Title proper
[Subfield a -- Title]

6   Rule 1.1B1   **Exact wording, order, and spelling but not necessarily punctuation and capitalization**

....

245 _ _   **The principles, origin and establishment of the Catholic school system in the United States** / ‡c by J.A. Burns.
260   New York : ‡b Benziger, ‡c 1912, c1908.
300   415 p. ; ‡c 20 cm.
504   Includes bibliographical references (p. [387]-399) and index.

7   Rule 1.1B1   **Accents and other diacritical marks present on the chief source of information**

....

245 _ _   **Deutsch für Amerikaner** / ‡c C.R. Goedsche, Meno Spann.
250   2. Aufl.
260   New York : ‡b American Book Co., ‡c c1964.
300   xiv, 466 p. : ‡b ill. ; ‡c 24 cm.
546   German and English.
500   Includes vocabularies and index.

8   Rule 1.0F1   **Inaccuracies**

[In this case, "relative" is simplified spelling. This rule applies because the word resembles an inaccuracy.]

....

245 _ _   **Decimal classification and relativ [sic] index** / ‡c by Melvil Dewey.
250   Ed. 14, rev. and enl.
260   Lake Placid Club, N.Y. : ‡b Forest Press, ‡c 1942.
300   2 v. in 1 : ‡b port. ; ‡c 26 cm.
500   Constantin J. Mazney, editor, Myron Warren Getchell, associate editor.

9   Rule 1.1B1   Alternative title

....

020	0894740121
245 _ _	**The fun book of fatherhood, or, How the animal kingdom is helping to raise the wild kids at our house** / ‡c by Jerry Cammarata with Frances Spatz Leighton.
260	Los Angeles : ‡b Corwin Books, ‡c c1978.
300	xiii, 303 p. : ‡b ill. ; ‡c 22 cm.
504	Includes bibliographical references (p. 301-303).

10   Rule 1.1B2   Statement of responsibility is an integral part of the title proper

....

020	0131282239
245 _ _	**Chaucer's major poetry** / ‡c Albert C. Baugh, editor.
260	Englewood Cliffs, N.J. : ‡b Prentice-Hall, ‡c c1963.
300	xlvii, 616 p. ; ‡c 26 cm.
504	Includes bibliographical references (p. xliii-xlv).

11   Rule 1.1B2   Publisher's name is an integral part of the title proper

....

020	0442214456 (cloth)
020	0442214464 (pbk.)
245 _ _	**Van Nostrand Reinhold manual of film-making** / ‡c Barry Callaghan.
260	New York : ‡b Van Nostrand Reinhold, ‡c 1974, c1973.
300	164 p. : ‡b ill. ; ‡c 25 cm.
504	Includes bibliographical references (p. 162) and index.

12   Rule 1.1B3   Title proper consists solely of the name of the person responsible for the item

....

020	0405119461
245 _ _	**William Alanson White** / ‡c William A. White.
260	New York : ‡b Arno Press, ‡c 1980, c1938.
300	xix, 293 p. : ‡b port. ; ‡c 21 cm.
4_ _	Historical issues in mental health
500	Originally published: Garden City, N.Y. : Doubleday, Doran, 1938.
504	Includes bibliographical references (p. 277-293).

13   Rule 1.1B10   **Chief source of information bears both the**
                     collective title and the titles of the individual works

....

245 _ _   **Three from the 87th** / ‡c Ed McBain.
260   Garden City, N.Y. : ‡b N. Doubleday, ‡c [197-]
300   470 p. : ‡b ill. ; ‡c 22 cm.
500   "Book club edition"—Jacket.
505 0 ƀ   **Hail, hail, the gang's all here — Jigsaw — Fuzz.**

1.1D   Parallel titles

[Subfield b -- Remainder of the title]

14   Rule 1.1D2   **Parallel title—Second level description**

....

020   8611140702
245 _ _   **Triglavski Narodni Park = ‡b Triglav National Park** / ‡c
              [besedilo] Janez Bizjak ; [fotografije] Stane Klemenc.
260   Ljubljana : ‡b Mladinska knjiga, ‡c 1994.
300   207 p. : ‡b col. ill., col. maps ; ‡c 31 cm.
546   Slovenian, English, German, and Italian.
500   Published in cooperation with the Triglav National Park Office.

15   Rule 1.1B5   **Word appears only once but is intended to be read**
                    more than once

....

020   8437810418
245 _ _   **Murallas de San Juan = ‡b Forts of San Juan.**
250   1st ed.
260   San Juan, P.R. : ‡b Escudo de Oro Caribe [distributor], ‡c 1984.
300   [34] p. : ‡b col. ill. ; ‡c 25 cm.
546   English, French, German, and Spanish.
500   Cover title.

1.1E   **Other title information**

[Subfield b -- Remainder of the title]

16   Rule 1.1E1   Other title information—Subtitle

020	0394412524
245 _ _	The wild boy of Burundi : ‡b **a study of an outcast child** / ‡c Harlan Lane & Richard Pillard.
250	1st ed.
260	New York : ‡b Random House, ‡c c1978.
300	xiv, 188 p., [8] p. of plates : ‡b ill., map ; ‡c 24 cm.
500	Foreword by B.F. Skinner.
500	Includes index.

17   Rule 1.1E5   Other title information transcribed following the title proper

---

020	0307136566
020	0307470024 (invalid)
245 _ _	Birds of North America : ‡b **a guide to field identification** / ‡c by Chandler S. Robbins, Bertel Bruun, and Herbert S. Zim ; illustrated by Arthur Singer.
260	New York : ‡b Golden Press, ‡c c1966.
300	340 p. : ‡b col. ill., col. maps ; ‡c 19 cm.
4xx _	Golden field guide series
504	Includes bibliographical references (p. 326-327) and index.

18   Rule 1.1D3   Other title information—Original title in the same language as the title proper and appearing on the chief source of information

---

020	044689429X
245 _ _	Gray lady down : ‡b a novel : **original title, Event 1000** / ‡c by David Lavallee.
250	Warner Books ed.
260	New York : ‡b Warner Books, ‡c c1971.
300	269 p. : ‡b ill. ; ‡c 18 cm.

19   Rule 1.1E3   Lengthy other title information abridged

- - - -

245 _ _   1066 and all that : ‡b a memorable history of England ... / ‡c by
            Walter Carruthers Sellar and Robert Julian Yeatman ; illustrated
            by John Reynolds.
260   New York : ‡b Dutton, ‡c c1931.
300   xii, 116 p. : ‡b ill. ; ‡c 20 cm.

1.1G   Items without a collective title

**20   Rule 1.1G2   Work lacking a collective title with no one work
                      predominating cataloged as a unit**

**Rule 1.1G3   Transcription of individual titles in the order in
                which they appear in the item**

- - - -

245 _ _   Solitaire ; ‡b &, Double solitaire / ‡c by Robert Anderson.
260   New York : ‡b Random House, ‡c c1972.
300   83 p. ; ‡c 22 cm.
500   Two plays.

1.1F   Statements of responsibility
[Subfield c -- Remainder of title page transcription]

**21   Rule 1.1F1   Statement of responsibility appearing prominently
                      in the item transcribed in the form in which it
                      appears there**

- - - -

020   0670805149
245 _ _   Lake Wobegon days / ‡c Garrison Keillor.
260   New York, N.Y. : ‡b Viking, ‡c 1985.
300   x, 337 p. : ‡b ill. ; ‡c 24 cm.
500   "Portions of this book appeared originally in The Atlantic
            monthly"—T.p. verso.

22   Rule 1.1F3   **Statement of responsibility precedes the title proper**
                        on the chief source of information transposed to its
                        required position

020   0670841153
245 _ _   Against the wind / ‡c **J.F. Freedman.**
260   New York : ‡b Viking, ‡c 1991.
300   vii, 423 p. ; ‡c 24 cm.

23   Rule 1.1F7   **Omission of titles, qualifications, etc.**

020   0688048838
245 _ _   "And I was there" : ‡b Pearl Harbor and Midway—breaking the
        secrets / ‡c **by Edwin T. Layton with Roger Pineau and John**
        Costello.
260   New York : ‡b W. Morrow, ‡c c1985.
300   596 p., [24] p. of plates : ‡b ill. ; ‡c 25 cm.
504   Includes bibliographical references (p. 570-581) and index.

24   Rule 1.1F7d   **Inclusion of a title of nobility or British term of**
                        honor

245 _ _   Digging up the past / ‡c **Sir Leonard Woolley.**
250   Rev. ed.
260   New York. : ‡b T. Y. Crowell, ‡c 1954.
300   xiii, 125 p., 32 p. of plates : ‡b ill. ; ‡c 20 cm.
500   Includes index.

        [For this person "Sir" is a British term of honor]

25   Rule 1.1F8   Addition of a short phrase to clarify the relationship between the title and the person or body named in the statement of responsibility

245 _ _	Famous speeches of the eight Chicago anarchists / ‡c [compiled by] Lucy Parsons.
246 _ 8	Speeches of the eight Chicago anarchists
260	New York : ‡b Arno Press, ‡c 1969.
300	121 p. : ‡b ports. ; ‡c 24 cm.
4 _ _	Mass violence in America
500	Originally published: 2nd ed. Chicago : L.E. Parsons, 1910. With new editorial note.
500	Speeches by August Spies, Michael Schwab, Oscar Neebe, Adolph Fischer, Louis Lingg, George Engel, Samuel Fielden and Albert R. Parsons.

26   Rule 1.1F14   Statement of responsibility transcribed even if no person or body is named in the statement

020	0874715008
245 _ _	A journal of the plague year : ‡b being observations or memorials of the most remarkable occurrences ... during the last great visitation in 1665 / ‡c written by a citizen who continued all the while in London.
260	London : ‡b W. Clowes ; ‡a Totowa, N.J. : ‡b Distributed in the USA by Rowman & Littlefield, ‡c 1974.
300	302 p. : ‡b facsim. ; ‡c 24 cm.
4 _ _	The Shakespeare Head edition of the novels & selected writings of Daniel Defoe
500	Originally published: Oxford : B. Blackwell, 1928.

27   Rule 1.1F13   Person associated with responsibility for the item is named in the title—no further statement is made relating to that name

020	0786863323
245 _ _	Red Lobster, white trash and the Blue lagoon : ‡b Joe Queenan's America.
250	1st ed.
260	New York : ‡b Hyperion, ‡c c1998.
300	194 p. ; ‡c 24 cm.
500	Includes index.

[Joe Queenan is the author.]

28   Rule 1.1F13   Person associated with responsibility for the item is
                     named in the title and also in a separate statement of
                     responsibility on the chief source of information

020   0517411393
245 _ _   The best of Robert Benchley / ‡c by Robert Benchley ; with
          illustrations by Peter Arno, Herbert F. Roese, Adam John Barth
          and others.
260   New York : ‡b Avenel Books, ‡c 1983.
300   353 p. : ‡b ill. ; ‡c 24 cm.

29   Rule 1.1F5   Single statement of responsibility names more than
                     three persons or corporate bodies performing the
                     same function

245 _ _   Outdoor education / ‡c Julian W. Smith ... [et al.].
260   Englewood Cliffs, N.J. : ‡b Prentice-Hall, ‡c 1963.
300   ix, 322 p. : ‡b ill. ; ‡c 24 cm.
504   Includes bibliographical references and index.

30   Rule 1.1F6   More than one statement of responsibility

020   0879720638
245 _ _   Irving Wallace : ‡b a writer's profile / ‡c by John Leverence ;
          with an introduction by Jerome Weidman ; an interview by
          Sam L. Grogg, Jr. ; and an afterword by Ray B. Browne.
260   Bowling Green, Ohio : ‡b Popular Press, ‡c 1974.
300   454 p. : ‡b ill. ; ‡c 24 cm.
4_ _   Profiles in popular culture ; ‡v no. 1
500   Includes index.

31   Rule 1.1G3   **Work lacking a collective title cataloged as a unit.**
                       Each work is by a different person

··

245 _ _   The rights of woman / ‡c Mary Wollstonecraft. The subjection
            of women / John Stuart Mill.
260   London : ‡b Dent ; ‡a New York : ‡b Dutton, ‡c 1929.
300   xxxix, 317 p. ; ‡c 18 cm.
4 _ _   Everyman's library ; ‡v no. 825. Science
500   Introduction by G.E.G. Catlin.
500   Wollstonecraft work was first published under the title: A
            vindication of the rights of woman.
504   Includes bibliographical references.

            [The introduction is for both works. The statement of responsibility
            for the introduction appears on the half title page.]

32   Rule 1.1F1   **Statement of responsibility from other than the**
                       chief source of information but from a prescribed
                       source of information for either area 1 or 2

··

245 _ _   Pictorial treasury of U.S. stamps / ‡c **[edited and published by**
            Collectors Institute ; editor, Elena Marzulla].
260   Omaha, Neb. : ‡b The Institute, ‡c c1974.
300   viii, 223 p. : ‡b col. ill. ; ‡c 29 cm.
4 _ _   Collectors Institute reference library
504   Includes bibliographical references (p. 218-219) and index.

1.2   EDITION AREA
            [Field 250 -- Edition statement]

1.2B   Edition statement
            [Subfield a -- Edition statement]

33   Rule 1.2B1   **Edition statement**

        Rule C.8A   **Ordinal numbers for English language items**

        Rule B.9   **Abbreviations (Roman alphabet)**

··

245 _ _   An introduction to historical bibliography / ‡c by Norman E.
            Binns.
250   **2nd ed., rev. and enl.**
260   London : ‡b Association of Assistant Librarians, ‡c 1962.
300   387 p. : ‡b ill. ; ‡c 23 cm.
504   Includes bibliographical references and index.

1.2C   **Statements of responsibility relating to the edition**
[Subfield b -- Remainder of edition statement]

34   **Rule 1.2C1**   **Statement of responsibility that does not relate to all editions**

---

245 _ _   Two thousand years of science : ‡b the wonders of nature and their discoverers / ‡c by R.J. Harvey-Gibson.
250   **2nd ed. / ‡b revised and enlarged by A.W. Titherley.**
260   London : ‡b A. & C. Black, ‡c 1931.
300   x, 508 p., [1] leaf of plates : ‡b ill. ; ‡c 22 cm.
500   Includes index.

1.4   **PUBLICATION, DISTRIBUTION, ETC., AREA**
[Field 260 -- Publication, distribution, etc. (Imprint)]

1.4C   **Place of publication, distribution, etc.**
[Subfield a -- Place of publication, distribution, etc.]

35   **Rule 1.4C1**   **Place of publication**

---

245 _ _   The happy critic and other essays / ‡c by Mark Van Doren.
260   **New York : ‡b Hill and Wang, ‡c c1961.**
300   xii, 177 p. ; ‡c 22 cm.
500   Includes index.

36   **Rule 1.4C3**   **Addition of a state name that did not appear in a prescribed source of information**

        Rule B.14A   **Names of certain countries, states, provinces, territories, etc.**

---

020   0838777538
020   0838776663 (pbk.)
245 _ _   Brian Friel / ‡c D.E.S. Maxwell.
260   **Lewisburg, [Pa.] : ‡b Bucknell University Press, ‡c c1973.**
300   112 p. ; ‡c 20 cm.
4_ _   The Irish writers series
504   Includes bibliographical references (p. 111-112).

37   **Rule 1.4C5**   **Multiple places with none given prominence—the first named place is in the country of the cataloging agency**

020   0672519909
245 _ _   Strictly speaking : ‡b will America be the death of English? / ‡c Edwin Newman.
260   **Indianapolis** : ‡b Bobbs-Merrill, ‡c c1974.
300   205 p. ; ‡c 24 cm.
500   Includes index.

38   **Rule 1.4C5**   **Multiple places with none given prominence—the first named place is not in the country of the cataloging agency**

020   0553050222
245 _ _   The 13th valley : ‡b a novel / ‡c by John M. Del Vecchio.
260   **Toronto ; ‡a New York** : ‡b Bantam Books, ‡c 1982.
300   606 p. : ‡b maps ; ‡c 24 cm.

39   **Rule 1.4C6**   **No place or probable place of publication known**

020   0550202323 (paper)
020   0550202331 (hardback)
245 _ _   Reading and reasoning / ‡c John Downing.
260   **[S. l.]** : ‡b Chambers, ‡c 1979.
300   192 p. : ‡b ill. ; ‡c 23 cm.
504   Includes bibliographical references (p. 174-183) and indexes.

> *[No place of publication is given in the work. No information was available in any reference held by the library of the cataloging agency. The author was affiliated with a Canadian university in 1979. The work was printed in Great Britain.]*

1.4D **Name of publisher, distributor, etc.**

[Subfield b -- Name of publisher, distributor, etc.]

40 **Rule 1.4D1** **Name of the publisher**

Rule 1.4D2 **Name of the publisher in the shortest form in which
it can be understood and identified internationally**

....

020	0393013359
245 _ _	Kennedy and Roosevelt : ‡b the uneasy alliance / ‡c Michael R. Beschloss ; foreword by James MacGregor Burns.
250	1st ed.
260	New York : **‡b Norton,** ‡c c1980.
300	318 p. : ‡b ill. ; ‡c 24 cm.
504	Includes bibliographical references (p. [281]-285) and index.

41 **Rule 1.4D4** **Publisher's name appears in a recognizable form in
Area 1 recorded in the shortest form possible in
Area 4**

....

245 _ _	Printed books, 1481-1900, in the Horticultural Society of New York / ‡c a listing by Elizabeth Cornelia Hall.
260	New York : **‡b The Society,** ‡c 1970.
300	xiii, 279 p. ; ‡c 24 cm.

42 **Rule 1.4D5** **Work with two publishers described in terms of the
first named**

....

020	0029250609
020	0029250617 (pbk.)
245 _ _	Secrecy and power : ‡b the life of J. Edgar Hoover / ‡c Richard Gid Powers.
260	New York : **‡b Free Press,** ‡c c1987.
300	x, 624 p., [16] p. of plates : ‡b ill. ; ‡c 24 cm.
504	Includes bibliographical references (p. 591-605) and index.

43   Rule 1.4D5d   Work with two publishers described in terms of both—the first named publisher is not in the country of the cataloging agency and a subsequently named publisher is

245 _ _   Rare, vanishing & lost British birds / ‡c compiled from notes by W.H. Hudson by Linda Gardiner ; with 25 coloured plates by H. Gronvold.
260   London : ‡b Dent ; ‡a New York : ‡b Dutton, ‡c 1923.
300   xix, 120 p., [25] leaves of plates : ‡b col. ill. ; ‡c 23 cm.
500   Enl. ed. of the author's Lost British birds. 1894.
504   Includes bibliographical references (p. 115) and index.

44   Rule 1.4D5a   Work with two publishers described in terms of both—the first and subsequently named entity are linked in a single statement

245 _ _   Raising laboratory animals : ‡b a handbook for biological and behavioral research / ‡c James Silvan.
250   1st ed.
260   Garden City, N.Y. : ‡b Published for the American Museum of Natural History [by] the Natural History Press, ‡c 1966.
300   viii, 225 p., [16] p. of plates : ‡b ill. ; ‡c 22 cm.
504   Includes bibliographical references (p. [209]-215) and index.

45   Rule 1.4D6   *Optionally,*
                   Name of the distributor when the first named entity is a publisher

020   067940693X
245 _ _   David Brinkley : ‡b 11 presidents, 4 wars, 22 political conventions, 1 moon landing, 3 assassinations, 2,000 weeks of news and other stuff on television and 18 years of growing up in North Carolina.
260   New York : ‡b Knopf : ‡b Distributed by Random House, ‡c 1995.
300   273 p. , [16] p. of plates : ‡b ill. ; ‡c 25 cm.

46   **Rule 1.4D6**   *Optionally,*
                        Place and name of the distributor when first named
                        entity is a publisher

---

020   188259312X (alk. paper)
245 _ _   Patty Jane's House of Curl : ‡b a novel / ‡c Lorna Landvik.
250   1st ed.
260   Bridgehampton, N.Y. : ‡b Bridge Works Pub. Co. ; **‡a Lanham,**
            Md. : ‡b Distributed in the U.S. by National Book Network, ‡c
            1995.
300   292 p. ; ‡c 22 cm.

47   **Rule 1.4D7**   Name of the publisher is unknown

      Rule 1.4G1   **Place and name of the manufacturer**
                        [Subfield e -- Place of manufacture]
                        [Subfield f -- Manufacturer]

---

245 _ _   Shipwrecks in Puerto Rico's history / ‡c by Walter A. Cardona
            Bonet.
250   1st ed.
260   San Juan, P.R. : ‡b [s.n.], ‡c c1989-   **‡e (Puerto Rico : ‡f Model**
            Offset Print.)
300   v. : ‡b ill. (some col.) ; ‡c 23 cm.
504   Includes bibliographical references.
505 0 ƀ   v. 1. 1502-1650.

1.4F   **Date of publication, distribution, etc.**
            [Subfield c -- Date of publication, distribution, etc.]

48   **Rule 1.4F1**   **Date of publication**

---

020   068911009X
245 _ _   Tunnel war / ‡c Joe Poyer.
250   1st ed.
260   New York : ‡b Atheneum, **‡c 1979.**
300   x, 339 p. : ‡b ill. ; ‡c 24 cm.

49   **Rule 1.4F5**   *Optional addition*
                          Date of publication and the latest copyright date differ

020	0846201305
245 _ _	Principles of bibliographical description / ‡c Fredson Bowers.
260	New York : ‡b Russell & Russell, **‡c 1962, c1949.**
300	xvii, 505 p. ; ‡c 25 cm.
504	Includes bibliographical references and index.

50   **Rule 1.4F6**   **Copyright date**

020	0871137194
245 _ _	Eat the rich / ‡c P.J. O'Rourke.
260	New York : ‡b Atlantic Monthly Press, ‡c **c1998.**
300	xviii, 246 p. : ‡b ill. ; ‡c 24 cm.

51   **Rule 1.4F7**   **Approximate date of publication**

245 _ _	Golden mists / ‡c by the author of Poppet, Too bad of him, Squabbles, A grass widow, &c.
260	London : ‡b William Stevens, **‡c [188-?]**
300	208 p. ; ‡c 20 cm.
4__	The Family story-teller

52   **Rule 1.4F8**   **Multipart work—Earliest and latest dates**

[Compare this record with Example 82 where volume 1 is cataloged separately.]

020	0835204898 (v. 1)
020	0835204979 (v. 2)
020	0835204987 (v. 3)
020	0835204995 (v. 4)
245 _ _	A history of book publishing in the United States / ‡c by John Tebbel.
260	New York : ‡b Bowker, **‡c 1972-1981.**
300	4 v. ; ‡c 26 cm.
505 0 ‡	v. 1. The creation of an industry, 1630-1865 — v. 2. The expansion of an industry, 1865-1919 — v. 3. The golden age between two wars, 1920-1940 — v. 4. The great change, 1940-1980.

53   **Rule 2.4G2**   *Optional addition*
               Date of printing differs from date of publication,
               etc.
               [Subfield g -- Date of manufacture]

---

020   0809424088
020   080942407X (lib. bdg.)
245 _ _   Doors and windows / ‡c by the editors of Time-Life Books.
260   Chicago, Ill. : ‡b Time-Life ; ‡a Morristown, N.J. : ‡b School and
               library distribution by Silver Burdett, **‡c c1978 ‡g (1980**
               printing)
300   128 p. : ‡b col. ill. ; ‡c 26 cm.
4_ _   Home repair and improvement
500   "Second printing. Revised 1980"—T.p. verso.
500   Includes index.

2.5   PHYSICAL DESCRIPTION AREA
[Field 300 -- Physical Description]

2.5B   Number of volumes and/or pagination
[Subfield a -- Extent]

Single volumes

54   **Rule 2.5B2**   **Last numbered page of each separately numbered**
               sequence

---

020   0446514241
245 _ _   Whose broad stripes and bright stars? : ‡b the trivial pursuit of
               the Presidency, 1988 / ‡c Jack W. Germond & Jules Witcover.
260   New York, N.Y. : ‡b Warner Books, ‡c c1989.
300   **xvi, 478 p.** ; ‡c 24 cm.
500   Includes index.

[The pages are numbered ix-xvi and 3-478.]

55   Rule 2.5B2   Last numbered leaf of each separately numbered sequence

245 _ _   Technical services : ‡b a syllabus for training leading to certification of library assistants / ‡c Bureau of Library Development, Pennsylvania State Library, Department of Education, Commonwealth of Pennsylvania.
260   [Harrisburg, Pa.?] : ‡b The Library, ‡c [197-]
300   96 leaves ; ‡c 27 cm.
504   Includes bibliographical references.

[The leaves are numbered 2-96.]

56   Rule 2.5B3   Unnumbered sequence includes pages referred to in a note

020   0192817876 (pbk.)
245 _ _   Daniel Deronda / ‡c George Eliot ; edited with an introduction by Graham Handley.
260   Oxford ; ‡a New York : ‡b Oxford University Press, ‡c 1988.
300   xxii, [3], 727 p. : ‡b facsim. ; ‡c 19 cm.
4 _ _   The world's classics
4 _ _   Oxford paperbacks
504   **Includes bibliographical references (p. [xxv]).**

57   Rule 2.5B7   Pages are unnumbered but the number of pages is readily ascertainable

020   067940676X
245 _ _   French for cats : ‡b all the French your cat will ever need / ‡c Henri de la Barbe (Henry Beard) ; text by Henry Beard and John Boswell ; illustrations by Gary Zamchick.
260   New York : ‡b Villard Books, ‡c 1991.
300   [87] p. : ‡b ill. (some col.) ; ‡c 16 cm.
500   "A John Boswell Associates book."

**58   Rule 2.5B7   Pages are unnumbered and the number of pages is
                      not readily ascertainable—estimated number of
                      pages recorded**

020   0030149061
245 _ _   The Doonesbury chronicles / ‡c G.B. Trudeau ; with an
           introduction by Garry Wills.
260   New York : ‡b Holt, Rinehart and Winston, ‡c [1975?]
300   ca. 200 p. : ‡b ill. (some col.) ; ‡c 29 cm.

**59   Rule 2.5B7   Pages are unnumbered and the number of pages is
                      not readily ascertainable**

[Library of Congress practice]

020   0815600682
245 _ _   Trees, shrubs and vines : ‡b a pictorial guide to the ornamental
           woody plants of the northern United States exclusive of conifers
           / ‡c Arthur T. Viertel.
260   Syracuse, N.Y. : ‡b Syracuse University Press, ‡c c1970.
300   1 v. (unpaged) : ‡b ill., map ; ‡c 26 cm.
504   Includes bibliographical references and index.

60   Rule 2.5B8c   Complicated or irregular paging

020   1556532172
245 _ _   OCLC communications & access planning guide.
250   1996 [ed.]
260   Dublin, Ohio : ‡b OCLC, ‡c c1996.
300   1 v. (various pagings) : ‡b ill. ; ‡c 28 cm.
500   Includes index and glossary.

           *[The pages are numbered: iii-viii, 1-47, A:1-A:9, B:1-B:10, C:1-C:6,
           I:1-I:5, G:1-G:12.]*

           *[Although in loose-leaf form, the document is not believed to be
           designed to receive additions.]*

61   Rule 2.5B9   Loose-leaf publication designed to receive additions

020	0844406392 (loose-leaf)
245 _ _	Library of Congress rule interpretations.
250	2nd ed.
260	Washington, D.C. : ‡b Cataloging Distribution Service, Library of Congress, ‡c 1989-
300	**1 v. (loose-leaf)** ; ‡c 30 cm.
500	Formulated by Office for Descriptive Cataloging Policy, Library of Congress.
500	Editor: Robert M. Hiatt.
500	Updated with quarterly supplements. Base text April 1989.
500	Includes index.

62   Rule 2.5B10   Pages of plates

020	0671250361
245 _ _	Lucy : ‡b the beginnings of humankind / ‡c Donald C. Johanson and Maitland A. Edey.
260	New York : ‡b Simon and Schuster, ‡c c1981.
300	409 p., **[8] p. of plates** : ‡b ill. (some col.) ; ‡c 25 cm.
504	Includes bibliographical references (p. 385-389) and index.

[The plates are on unnumbered pages located between pages 96 and 97.]

63   Rule 2.5B10   Leaves of plates

245 _ _	The makers of Florence : ‡b Dante, Giotto, Savonarola, and their city / ‡c by Mrs. Oliphant ; with portrait of Savonarola engraved by C.H. Jeens and illustrations from drawings by Professor Delamotte.
250	New ed.
260	London : ‡b Macmillan, ‡c 1881.
300	xx, 422 p., **[9] leaves of plates** : ‡b ill. ; ‡c 19 cm.
500	Includes index.

[The plates are on unnumbered leaves (i.e., illustrations on one side of the sheet of paper with the verso blank) located as the frontispiece, and between pages 102-103, 154-155, 204-205, 232-233, 272-273, 306-307 340-341 and 374-375.]

64   **Rule 2.5B10   Pages of plates not recorded**

*[In this instance, the rule does not apply because the plates fail to meet the
definitional requirement for plates in that they do "form part of ... the main
sequence of pages or leaves."]*

020   081281505X
245 _ _   Was this Camelot? : ‡b excavations at Cadbury Castle, 1966-1970
           / ‡c Leslie Alcock.
260   New York : ‡b Stein and Day, ‡c 1972.
300   224 p. : ‡b ill. (some col.) ; ‡c 26 cm.
4_ _   New aspects of archaeology
500   Report of research conducted by the Camelot Research
           Committee.
504   Includes bibliographical references and index.

*[The pages of illustrations are located on unnumbered pages
between pages 32-49, 56-61, 84-101, etc. Their presence is
accounted for by the gap in page numbering.]*

Publications in more than one volume

65   **Rule 2.5B17   More than one physical volume**

      Rule 2.5B20   Volumes are continuously paged

245 _ _   The complete works of O. Henry / ‡c foreword by Harry
           Hansen.
260   Garden City, N.Y. : ‡b Doubleday, ‡c c1953.
300   2 v. (xiii, 1692 p.) ; ‡c 22 cm.

[v.1: vi-xiii, 2-810 p.; v.2: 812-1692 p.]

66   **Rule 2.5B17   More than one physical volume**

      **Rule 2.5B21   *Optional addition*
                        Volumes are individually paged**

020   0124658016 (v. 1)
020   0124658024 (v. 2)
245 _ _   The organic chemistry of palladium / ‡c Peter M. Maitlis.
260   New York : ‡b Academic Press, ‡c 1971.
300   2 v. (xiii, 319; 216 p.) ; ‡c 24 cm.
4_ _   Organometallic chemistry
504   Includes bibliographical references and index.
505 0 b̸   v. 1. Metal complexes — v. 2. Catalytic reactions.

67   Rule 1.5B5   Multipart item not yet complete

[Compare this record with Example 52 where the multipart item is complete.]

245 _ _	West's New York digest, 4th.
260	St. Paul, Minn. : ‡b West Pub. Co., ‡c c1989-
300	**v. ; ‡c 27 cm.**
500	"Key number digest covers New York state and federal case law from 1978"—Pref.
500	Kept up-to-date by pocket supplements, cumulative supplements, revised volumes, and supplementary pamphlet which also updates the New York digest, 3rd and Abbott New York digest.

[AACR2R calls for the placement of 3 blank spaces preceding the "v." The OCLC-MARC format specifies that these spaces not be input, rather they are system supplied.]

68   Rule 2.5B19   Number of bibliographic volumes differs from the number of physical volumes

245 _ _	Russia under the autocrat, Nicholas the First / ‡c by Ivan Golovine.
260	New York : ‡b Praeger, ‡c 1970.
300	**2 v. in 1 : ‡b port. ; ‡c 22 cm.**
4_ _	Praeger scholarly reprints. ‡p Source books and studies in Russian and Soviet history
500	Translation of: La Russie sous Nicholas I.
500	Originally published: London : H. Colburn, 1846. With new introd.

[Special formats]

69   Rule 2.5B24   Large print intended for use by the visually impaired

020	0816154783 (alk. paper)
245 _ _	She walks in beauty / ‡c Sarah Shankman.
260	Boston : ‡b G.K. Hall, ‡c 1993, c1991.
300	**xxxix, 423 p. (large print) ; ‡c 25 cm.**
4_ _	G.K. Hall large print book series

2.5C   Illustrative matter
[Subfield b -- Other physical details]

70   **Rule 2.5C1   Illustrated matter**

---

020   0393024601
245 _ _   Burning down the house : ‡b MOVE and the tragedy of
            Philadelphia / ‡c John Anderson and Hilary Hevenor.
250   1st ed.
260   New York : ‡b Norton, ‡c c1987.
300   xv, 409 p. : **‡b ill.** ; ‡c 25 cm.
500   Includes index.

[The illustrations are reproductions of photographs.]

71   **Rule 2.5C2   *Optionally,***
            Specific type of illustration are considered to be
            important

       Rule 2.5C4   Number of illustrations readily ascertained

---

245 _ _   Why Wisconsin / ‡c by Francis Favill Bowman.
260   Madison, Wis. : ‡b F. F. Bowman, ‡c 1948.
300   210, vi p. : **‡b 1 map** ; ‡c 24 cm.
504   Includes bibliographical references and index.

72   **Rule 2.5C2   Only some of the illustrations in the work are**
            specific types of illustrations considered to be
            important

---

020   0030468019
245 _ _   Men of Dunwich : ‡b the story of a vanished town / ‡c
            Rowland Parker.
260   New York : ‡b Holt, Rinehart and Winston, ‡c 1979, c1978.
300   272 p. : **‡b ill., maps** ; ‡c 22 cm.
504   Includes bibliographical references (p. 267) and index.

[The illustrations are drawings and maps.]

73   Rule 2.5C3   Colored illustrations

020	0307102602
020	0307682609 (lib. bdg.)
245 _ _	The secret life of Walter Kitty / ‡c story and pictures by Joan Elizabeth Goodman.
260	New York : ‡b Golden Book, ‡c c1986.
300	[24] p. : **‡b col. ill.** ; ‡c 21 cm.
4 _ _	A big little golden book
520 ƀ	When unlawful badgers take over a city park, a young cat dons a mask and cape and becomes the super hero, Wonder Cat.

74   Rule 2.5C3   Some illustrations in color

245 _ _	Greek art / ‡c John Boardman.
250	Rev. ed.
260	New York : ‡b Praeger, ‡c c1973.
300	252 p. : **‡b ill. (some col.)** ; ‡c 21 cm.
4 _ _	Praeger world of art series
4 _ _	Books that matter
504	Includes bibliographical references (p. 238-241) and index.

[There are 219 illustrations in b&w and 30 in color.]

75   Rule 2.5C5   Work consists wholly of illustrations

245 _ _	Gods' man : ‡b a novel in woodcuts / ‡c by Lynd Ward.
260	New York : ‡b J. Cape and H. Smith, ‡c 1929.
300	[117] p. : **‡b all ill.** ; ‡c 22 cm.

[The work has no pages of text.]

2.5D   Dimensions
[Subfield c -- Dimensions]

76   Rule 2.5D1   Height of the item

020	068804333X
245 _ _	Sacred cows—and other edibles / ‡c Nikki Giovanni.
260	New York : ‡b Morrow, ‡c c1988.
300	**167 p. ; ‡c 25 cm.**
500	"Some of these articles have appeared in: The Boston globe, Essence magazine, Black women writers, 1950-1980 ... The crusader (Cincinnati), USA today, and Touchstone magazine.—T.p. verso.

[The book measures 24.3 cm.]

77   Rule 2.5D2   Width of the item is greater than its height

020	0895770105
245 _ _	Reader's Digest complete do-it-yourself manual.
260	Pleasantville, N.Y. : ‡b Reader's Digest Association, ‡c c1973.
300	**600 p. : ‡b ill. (some col.) ; ‡c 22 x 28 cm.**
500	Includes index.

[The book measures 21.7 cm high by 27.8 cm. wide.]

1.5E   Accompanying material
[Subfield e -- Accompanying material]

78   Rule 1.5E1d   Accompanying material—Number of physical units and the name of the accompanying material

Optional addition
Physical description of the accompanying material

[The physical description for the accompanying material was made according to Rule 2.5.]

020	0835966062
020	0835966070 (instructor's manual)
245 _ _	Records management : ‡b controlling business information / ‡c Irene Place, David J. Hyslop.
260	Reston, Va. : ‡b Reston Pub. Co., ‡c c1982.
300	**xi, 371 p. : ‡b ill. ; ‡c 24 cm. + ‡e 1 instructor's manual (84 p. : ill. ; 23 cm.)**
504	Includes bibliographical references (p. 348-353) and index.

**79   Rule 1.5E1d   Accompanying material—Number of physical units
and the name of the accompanying material**

Optional addition
Physical description of the accompanying material

*[The physical description for the accompanying material was made according
to Rule 9.5.]*

020	1856040860
245 _ _	Using the new AACR2 : ǂb an expert systems approach to choice of access points / ǂc David Smith ... [et al.].
250	Rev. ed.
260	London : ǂb Library Association Pub., ǂc 1993.
300	**xiii, 97 p. : ǂb ill. ; ǂc 26 cm. + ǂe 1 computer disk (3 ½ in.)**
500	Rev. ed. of: Using AACR2 : a step-by-step algorithmic approach. 1980.
500	"LA student textbook"—Cover.
500	Title on disk: AACR2Expert.
538	System requirements for computer disk: IBM PC or compatible; 512K; DOS 3.2 or higher.
504	Includes bibliographical references.

1.6   SERIES AREA

[Field 440 -- Series statement/added entry/title]
   or
[Field 490 -- Series statement]

1.6B   Title proper of series

[Subfield a -- Title]

80   Rule 1.6B1   Title proper of series

---

245 _ _	American railroads / ǂc by John F. Stover.
260	Chicago : ǂb University of Chicago Press, ǂc 1961.
300	x, 301 p. : ǂb ill. ; ǂc 21 cm.
4_ _	**The Chicago history of American civilization**
504	Includes bibliographical references (p. 272-281) and index.

1.6G   **Numbering within the series**
               [Subfield v -- Volume number/sequential designator]

        81   Rule 1.6G1   Numbering within series

               Rule B.9   Abbreviations

        ....

               020   0911216189
               245 _ _   Role of vitamin B6 in neurobiology / ‡c editors: Manuchair S.
                          Ebadi, Erminio Costa.
               260   New York : ‡b Raven Press, ‡c 1972.
               300   x, 238 p. : ‡b ill. ; ‡c 25 cm.
               4__   Advances in biochemical psychopharmacology ; ‡v v. 4
               504   Includes bibliographical references.

        **82   Rule 1.6G1   Numbering within series—Single item in a set
                              cataloged individually with the set title recorded as
                              the series title**

               [Compare this record with Example 52 where the set is cataloged together.]

        ....

               020   0835204898 (v.1)
               245 _ _   The creation of an industry, 1630-1865 / ‡c by John Tebbel.
               260   New York : ‡b Bowker, ‡c 1972.
               300   xvi, 646 p. ; ‡c 26 cm.
               4__   **A history of book publishing in the United States ; ‡v v. 1**
               504   Includes bibliographical references and index.

1.6F   **ISSN of series**
               [Subfield x -- International Standard Serial Number]

        83   Rule 1.6F1   ISSN of series

        ....

               020   1881094138 (alk. paper)
               245 _ _   Settlement and politics in three classic Maya polities / ‡c Olivier
                          de Montmollin.
               260   Madison, Wis. : ‡b Prehistory Press, ‡c c1995.
               300   xvii, 369 p. : ‡b maps ; ‡c 28 cm.
               4__   Monographs in world archaeology, **‡x 1055-2316** ; ‡v no. 24
               504   Includes bibliographical references (p. 343-369).

1.6E   Statement of responsibility relating to the series

84   Rule 1.6E1   Statement of responsibility relating to the series

245 _ _	The Fourth of July valley : ‡b glacial geology and archeology of the Timberline ecotone / ‡c by James B. Benedict.
260	Ward, Colo. : ‡b Center for Mountain Archeology, ‡c c1981.
300	viii, 139 p. : ‡b ill. ; ‡c 28 cm.
4__	Research report / **Center for Mountain Archeology** ; ‡v no. 2
504	Includes bibliographical references (p. 127-139).

1.6J   More than one series statement

85   Rule 1.6J1   More than one series statement

020	0934718563
245 _ _	The graffiti of Tikal / ‡c Helen Trik and Michael E. Kampen.
260	Philadelphia : ‡b University Museum, University of Pennsylvania, ‡c 1983.
300	v, 11 p., 105 p. of plates (1 folded) : ‡b ill. ; ‡c 29 cm.
4__	**Tikal report ; ‡v no. 31**
4__	**University Museum monograph ; ‡v 57**
504	Includes bibliographical references (p. 6).

1.6H   **Subseries**

[Field 440 -- Series statement/added entry/title]
[Subfield p -- Name of part/section of a work]

[The use of Field 440 is addressed in Chapter 2 of this text. That chapter deals with the provision of access points.]

86a   Rule 1.6H1   Subseries

....

245	_ _	The quintessence of Irving Langmuir / ‡c by Albert Rosenfeld.
250		1st ed.
260		Oxford ; ‡a New York : ‡b Pergamon, ‡c 1966.
300		369 p. : ‡b port. ; ‡c 20 cm.
440	_	The Commonwealth and international library. **‡p Selected readings in physics**
440	_	Men of physics
500		"Written to accompany The collected works of Irving Langmuir"—P. 9.
504		Includes bibliographical references (p. 331-336) and index.

[Other subseries in The Commonwealth and international library include: Higher mathematics for scientists and engineers; Mathematical topics; Programmed texts series.]

[Information about the second series appears on the front cover.]

or

[Field 490 -- Series statement]

[No subfield is used for the subseries with Field 490]

[The use of Field 490 is addressed in Chapter 2 of this text. That chapter deals with the provision of access points.]

86b   Rule 1.6H1   Subseries

....

245	_ _	The quintessence of Irving Langmuir / ‡c by Albert Rosenfeld.
250		1st ed.
260		Oxford ; ‡a New York : ‡b Pergamon, ‡c 1966.
300		369 p. : ‡b port. ; ‡c 20 cm.
490	_	The Commonwealth and international library. **Selected readings in physics**
490	_	Men of physics
500		"Written to accompany The collected works of Irving Langmuir"—P. 9.
504		Includes bibliographical references (p. 331-336) and index.

1.7   NOTE AREA
[Field 5xx -- ₁Notes₁]

[Field 246 -- Varying form of title]
[1st Indicator 0 or 1 -- Note]

1.7A   Preliminary Rule

87   **Rule 1.7A1   Punctuation**

Rule 1.7A3   Form of notes

Order of information

Rule A.10A   Capitalization of notes

020	0815194161 (alk. paper)
245 _ _	Michels retinal detachment / ‡c Charles P. Wilkinson, Thomas A. Rice ; art coordinator and medical illustrator Timothy C. Hengst ; assisted by Diane T. Hodgkins.
250	2nd ed.
260	St. Louis : ‡b Mosby, ‡c c1997.
300	xv, 1163 p. : ‡b ill. ; ‡c 29 cm.
500	**Rev. ed. of: Retinal detachment / Ronald G. Michels, Charles P. Wilkinson, Thomas A. Rice. 1990.**
504	Includes bibliographical references and index.

88   **Rule 1.7A3   Form of notes**

Quotations

020	0719557550
245 _ _	Victoria / ‡c Stanley Weintraub.
260	London : ‡b John Murray, ‡c 1996.
300	xi, 692 p., [20] p. of plates : ‡b ill., ports ; ‡c 24 cm.
500	First published: 1987.
500	**"Additions and revisions ... update this edition extensively, and add to its accuracy."—Pref.**
504	Includes bibliographical references (p. 644-670) and index.

[The quotation is not from the chief source of information.]

1.7B   Notes

[Field 5xx -- ₁Notes₁]

89   Rule 2.7B1   Nature, scope, or artistic form

[Field 500 -- General note]

[Subfield a -- General note]

---

245 _ _   Essay on rime / ‡c by Karl Shapiro.
260   New York : ‡b Reynal & Hitchcock, ‡c c1945.
300   72 p. ; ‡c 22 cm.
500   Verse.

90   Rule 2.7B2   Language of the item and/or translation or adaptation

[Field 500 -- General note]

[A translation/adaptations note is recorded in Field 500. A language of the item note is recorded in Field 546 (Language Note).]

---

020   0679739041 (pbk.)
245 _ _   Confessions of Felix Krull : ‡b confidence man : the early years / ‡c Thomas Mann.
250   1st Vintage International ed.
260   New York : ‡b Vintage International, ‡c 1992, c1955.
300   384 p. ; ‡c 24 cm.
500   Translation of: Bekenntnisse des Hochstaplers Felix Krull.
500   Originally published: New York : Knopf, 1955.

91   Rule 2.7B3   Source of title proper

[Field 500 -- General note]

[See also Rule 1.1B1.]

---

245 _ _   Greening the government : ‡b closing the circle : a guide to implementing executive order 12873.
260   [Washington, D.C.? : ‡b Office of the Vice President, ‡c 1996?]
300   ii, 97 p. : ‡b ill. ; ‡c 28 cm.
500   Cover title.

92   Rule 2.7B4   Variations in title
> [Field 246 -- Varying form of title]
> [1st Indicator 0 or 1 -- Note]
> [2nd Indicator 4 -- Cover title]
> [Subfield a -- Title proper/short title]

---

245 _ _   What you should know about selling and salesmanship / ‡c by Milton B. Burstein.
246 _ 4   Selling and salesmanship
260   Dobbs Ferry, N.Y. : ‡b Oceana Publications, ‡c 1969.
300   x, 85 p. ; ‡c 20 cm.
4_ _   Business almanac series ; ‡v no. 18
500   "Oceana book number 297-18"—T.p. verso.

> *[In addition to creating a note, the first indicator value in Field 246 would be either '0' or "1" depending or whether the cover title is to be made an access point in the catalog ('1") or not made an access point ("0"). The print constant "Cover title:" is provided when the 2nd indicator value of "4" is used.]*

93   Rule 2.7B5   Other title information
> [Field 246 -- Varying form of title]
> [1st Indicator 0 or 1 -- Note]
> [2nd Indicator ♭ -- No information provided]
> [Subfield i -- Display text]
> [Subfield a -- Title proper/short title]

[See also Rule 1.1E3.]

---

020   0133641821
245   Great men of American popular song / ‡c David Ewen.
246 _ ♭   ‡i Subtitle: ‡a The history of the American popular song told through the lives, careers, achievements, and personalities of its foremost composers and lyricists—from William Billings of the Revolutionary War through Bob Dylan, Johnny Cash, Burt Bacharach
250   Rev. and enl. ed.
260   Englewood Cliffs, N.J. : ‡b Prentice-Hall, ‡c c1972.
300   x, 404 p. ; ‡c 25 cm.

> *[Although it might appear that Subfield "b" (Remainder of title) should be used in this note, Subfield "i" must be followed by Subfield "a." OCLC will not validate the use of Subfield "b" in this situation.]*

94   **Rule 2.7B6   Statements of responsibility**
       [Field 500 -- General note]

       [See also Rule 1.1F2.]

---

020   0844406430
245 _ _   Classification. Class KJ-KKZ, law of Europe / ‡c Subject
           Cataloging Division, Processing Services, Library of Congress.
246 _ 4   Law of Europe
260   Washington : ‡b The Library, ‡c 1988.
300   xxxi p., 599 leaves ; ‡c 28 cm.
500   **"Prepared in the Subject Cataloging Division by Jolande E.**
           Goldberg"—P. iii.

95   **Rule 2.7B7   Edition and history**
       [Field 500 -- General note]

---

245 _ _   Foreign diplomacy in China, 1894-1900 : ‡b a study in political
           and economic relations with China / ‡c by Philip Joseph.
260   New York : ‡b Octagon Books, ‡c 1971.
300   458 p. : ‡b maps ; ‡c 23 cm.
500   **Originally published: London : Allen & Unwin, 1928.**
           (Studies in economics and political science ; no. 93)
504   Includes bibliographical references (p. [423]-426) and index.

           [Information about the reprint note taken from the half-title page,
           the title page verso and the catalog record for the 1928 ed.]

96   **Rule 2.7B9   Publication, distribution, etc.**
       [Field 500 -- General note]

---

245 _ _   Old Mr. Boston de luxe official bartender's guide / ‡c compiled
           and edited by Leo Cotton.
260   Hackensack, N.J. : ‡b Wehman Bros., ‡c c1970.
300   viii, 149 p. : ‡b ill. (some col.) ; ‡c 19 cm.
500   **Imprint from label on t.p. Imprint under label reads:**
           Published by Mr. Boston Distiller Corporation.
500   Includes index.

97   Rule 2.7B9   Publication, distribution, etc.—Transmittal date
  [Field 500 -- General note]

---

245 _ _   Defense Intelligence Agency : ‡b organization, mission and key
          personnel.
260   [Washington, D.C. : ‡b The Agency, ‡c 1987]
300   vi, 73 p. ; ‡c 22 x 28 cm.
500   Cover title.
500   "Prepared by the Directorate for Human Resources"—Pref.
500   "November 1987."
500   "DRS-2600-926-87."

98   Rule 2.7B11   Accompanying material
  [Field 500 -- General note]

---

245 _ _   Early Renaissance fifteenth century Italian painting / ‡c by
          C.H.M. Gould.
260   New York : ‡b McGraw-Hill, ‡c c1965.
300   47 p. : ‡b ill. ; ‡c 25 cm. + ‡e 24 slides (col.)
4_ _   _ Color slide program of the world's art
500   Slides mounted in pocket.

99   Rule 2.7B11   Accompanying material
  [Field 538 -- System details note]
     [Subfield a -- Systems details note]
  [Field 500 -- General note]

---

020   0670772895 (alk. paper)
245 _ _   The road ahead / ‡c Bill Gates with Nathan Myhrvold and
          Peter Rinearson.
260   New York : ‡b Viking, ‡c 1995.
300   xiv, 286 p. : ‡b ill. ; ‡c 24 cm. + ‡e with 1 computer laser optical
          disk (4 ¾ in.)
**538   System requirements for accompanying computer disk: PC
          with 486 SX or faster processor; 6 MB RAM, Microsoft
          Windows; VGA monitor with at least 256 colors; 2X CD drive;
          hard disk with 3 MB free.**
**500   Interview with Gates can be played on an audio compact disk
          player.**
**500   Disk in pocket. Disk contains the complete text of the book
          and several hundred hyperlinks.**
500   Includes index.

100   Rule 2.7B12   Series—Phrase naming an in-house editor or
another official of the firm
[Field 500 -- General note]

020   0151241554
245 _ _   Death of a schoolboy / ‡c Hans Koning.
250   1st ed.
260   New York : ‡b Harcourt Brace Jovanovich, ‡c c1974.
300   187 p. ; ‡c 21 cm.
500   "A Helen and Kurt Wolff book."

101   Rule 2.7B12   Series—Publisher's characterization of the work
[Field 500 -- General note]

020   0385470797
245 _ _   Bubba talks of life, love, sex, whiskey, politics, foreigners,
          teenagers, movies, food, football, and other matters that
          occasionally concern human beings / ‡c Dan Jenkins.
250   1st ed.
260   New York : ‡b Doubleday, ‡c 1993.
300   149 p. ; ‡c 21 cm.
500   "Main Street books."

102   Rule 2.7B17   Summary
[Field 520 -- Summary, etc. note]
[1st Indicator ♭ -- No information provided]
[Subfield a -- Summary, etc. note]

020   0590421441
245 _ _   Alexander and the terrible, horrible, no good, very bad day / ‡c
          Judith Viorst ; illustrated by Ray Cruz.
260   New York : ‡b Scholastic, ‡c 1989, c1972.
300   [32] p. : ‡b ill. ; ‡c 18 x 23 cm.
520 ♭   One day when everything goes wrong for him, Alexander is
consoled by the thought that other people have bad days too.

[The print constant "Summary:" is provided unless the 1st
indicator value of "8" is used. Bibliographic utilities other than
OCLC may give the choice of other print constants, e.g.,
"Annotation."]

103   Rule 2.7B18   Contents—Works by one author

[Field 505 -- Formatted contents note]
[1st Indicator 0 -- Contents]
[2nd Indicator ƀ -- Basic]
[Subfield a -- Formatted contents note]

020	0140131167
245 _ _	Rumpole and the age of miracles / ‡c John Mortimer.
260	New York : ‡b Penguin, ‡c 1989, c1988.
300	225 p. ; ‡c 18 cm.
505 0 ƀ	**Rumpole and the bubble reputation -- Rumpole and the barrow boy -- Rumpole and the age of miracles -- Rumpole and the tap end -- Rumpole and the chambers party -- Rumpole and Portia -- Rumpole and the quality of life.**

[The print constant "Contents:" is provided when the 1st indicator values of "0" or "1" are used. A 1st indicator value of "2" produces the print constant "Partial Contents:".]

104   Rule 2.7B18   Contents—Works by different authors

245 _ _	Shakespeare : ‡b lectures on five plays / ‡c by A. Fred Sochatoff ... [et al.].
260	Pittsburgh : ‡b Carnegie Institute of Technology, ‡c 1958.
300	83 p. ; ‡c 23 cm.
4 _ _	Carnegie series in English ; ‡v no. 4
505 0 ƀ	**Much ado about nothing / A. Fred Sochatoff -- Measure for measure / Robert C. Slack -- Antony and Cleopatra / Austin Wright -- Cymbeline / Neal Woodruff, Jr. -- The tempest / John A. Hart.**

105   Rule 2.7B18   Contents—Works by different authors
[Field 505 -- Formatted contents note]
  [1st Indicator 0 -- Contents]
  [2nd Indicator 0 -- Enhanced]
  [Subfield t -- Title]
  [Subfield r -- Statement of responsibility]

020   0881450375
245 _ _ Plays from the Circle Repertory Company.
246 _ 4 Plays from Circle Rep
260   NY, NY : ‡b Broadway Play Pub., ‡c c1986.
300   vii, 410 p. ; ‡c 23 cm.
505 0 0 ‡t The mound builders / ‡r Lanford Wilson-- ‡t The great-
         great grandson of Jedediah Kohler / ‡r John Bishop -- ‡t The
         Diviners / ‡r Jim Leonard, Jr. -- ‡t Snow orchid / ‡r Joseph
         Pintauro -- ‡t Knock knock / ‡r Jules Feiffer -- ‡t Down by the
         river where waterlilies are disfigured every day / ‡r Julie
         Bovasso.

106   Rule 2.7B18   Contents—Bibliography and index note
[Field 504 -- Bibliography, etc., note]

020   0415907284
020   0415907292 (pbk.)
245 _ _ Annoying the Victorians / ‡c James R. Kincaid.
260   New York : ‡b Routledge, ‡c 1995.
300   xi, 271 p. ; ‡c 23 cm.
504   Includes bibliographical references (p. [255]-268) and index.

        *[This is the format currently used by the Library of Congress. The
        format used for the examples in AACR2R would have resulted in
        two notes:*

            504   Bibliography: p. 72-74.
            500   Includes index.

107   Rule 2.7B19   Numbers
[Field 500 -- General note]

---

245 _ _   Internal Revenue Service : ‡b computer readiness for 1988 filing
             season : report to the Chairman, Joint Committee on Taxation,
             U.S. Congress / ‡c United States General Accounting Office.
260   Washington, D.C. : ‡b The Office, ‡c [1988]
300   12 p. ; ‡c 28 cm.
500   Cover title.
500   "March 1988."
504   Includes bibliographical references.
500   "GAO/IMTEC-88-31."

108   Rule 2.7B20   Copy Being Described
[OCLC Field 590 -- Local note]
[OCLC Subfield a -- Local note]

---

020   0027501426
245 _ _   A child's book of wildflowers / ‡c M.A. Kelly ; illustrated by
             Joyce Powzyk.
250   1st ed.
260   New York : ‡b Four Winds Press, ‡c c1992.
300   32 p. : ‡b col. ill. ; ‡c 29 cm.
520 ⱨ   Describes a variety of wildflowers, discussing their appearance,
             blooming season, and significance in history and folklore.
590   Library's copy bound upside down.

[Field 590 is not a MARC field but an OCLC defined field.]

109   Rule 2.7B20   Copy Being Described
[OCLC Field 590 -- Local note]

---

020   0948021357
245 _ _   Letter to Loren / ‡c Dylan Thomas ; with an introduction and
             notes by Jeff Towns.
260   Swansea : ‡b Salubrious Press, ‡c 1993.
300   63 p. : ‡b ill., facsims, ports. ; ‡c 27 cm.
500   "Limited to 200 numbered copies. A further twenty-six copies,
             hors commerce, were printed."—Colophon.
500   Includes glossary and notes.
590   This is copy no. 53.

*[The limited distribution statement and the copy number appear in
the colophon.]*

In addition to the note examples provided for Area 7 in this chapter, notes have been used on the catalog records for the examples for Areas 1 to 6. Additionally, some of the examples for Area 7 have notes which illustrate notes other than just the one being addressed by the rule in question. In the list below, following the rule number and the heading for the type of note, are the example numbers for the catalog record that used that type of note. Some very commonly used notes, e.g., bibliographical reference and index notes, have not been included in this listing due to their frequent use in the examples and the lack of variability in their format.

2.7B1	**Nature, scope or artistic form**	
	20, 67	
2.7B2	**Language of the item and/or translation or adaptation**	
	Other languages (Field 546): 7, 14, 15	
	Translation: 68	
2.7B3	**Source of the title proper**	
	3, 15, 107	
2.7B4	**Variations in title**	
	Cover title (Field 246): 94, 105	
	Spine title (Field 246): 25	
2.7B6	**Statements of responsibility**	
	8, 16, 25, 31, 61, 64, 97	
2.7B7	**Edition and history**	
	"Based on ...": 21	
	Edition: 13, 111	
	Numbered edition: 109	
	Originally published: 4, 12, 25, 26, 68, 90, 111	
	Previous title: 31, 43	
	Previously appeared in ...: 21, 76	
	Revision statement: 79, 87	
	Updates: 67	
2.7B9	**Publication, distribution, etc.**	
	Frequency: 61	
	Relationship of publisher to another body: 14	
	Revised printing: 53	
	Transmittal date: 3, 107	
2.7B11	**Accompanying material**	
	Accompanying work: 86a, 86b	
	System requirements: 79	
	Title differs: 79	
2.7B12	**Series**	
	Publisher's characterization: 57	
	Series-like statement: 79	
2.7B17	**Summary**	
	73, 108	
2.7B18	**Contents**	
	Formal contents: 13, 47, 52, 66	
	Informal contents	
	Glossary: 109	
	Vocabulary: 7	
2.7B19	**Numbers**	
	92, 97	

1.8   STANDARD NUMBER AND TERMS OF AVAILABILITY AREA
1.8B   Standard number

[Field 020 -- International Standard Book Number]
[Subfield a -- International Standard Book Number]

110   Rule 1.8B1   International Standard Book Number

Rule 2.8C1   *Optional addition*
Terms of availability

[Subfield c -- Terms of availability]

[The Library of Congress does not apply this optional addition. Accordingly, except for this and the next example, none of the examples in this chapter have the terms of availability given.]

---

020   0812926242 : ‡c $25.00
245 _ _ Hot air : ‡b all talk, all the time / ‡c Howard Kurtz.
250   1st ed.
260   New York : ‡b Times Books, ‡c c1996.
300   viii, 407 p. ; ‡c 25 cm.
504   Includes bibliographical references (p. 373-387) and index.

111   Rule 1.8B2   Multiple ISBNs

Optionally,
Other ISBNs

Rule 2.8D1   Qualifications

---

020   **0822959046 (pbk.) : ‡c $22.50**
020   **0822938286 : ‡c $49.95**
245 _ _ Andrew Carnegie / ‡c Joseph Frazier Wall.
250   [2nd ed.].
260   Pittsburgh, Pa. : ‡b University of Pittsburgh Press, ‡c c1989.
300   xiii, 1137 p., [16] p. of plates : ‡b ill. ; ‡c 25 cm.
500   2nd ed. contains "no additions, no deletions and no corrections" from the 1st ed.
500   Originally published: New York : Oxford University Press, 1970.
504   Includes bibliographical references and index.

[Library of Congress policy is to record as the first ISBN the ISBN for the item being described.]

FIXED-FIELD ELEMENTS

These fixed-field elements characterize the physical content or subject nature of a document, although most are, to a greater or lesser degree, related to document description. Except for the date information all the data are recorded using codes. Each element has a maximum length of from one to four characters. OCLC displays the field-field elements in a more human-readable form than the way they appear in two different fields in the MARC format. The fixed-field as it appears on an OCLC Books Format workform, absent OCLC control elements, is as follows:

```
Type: _   ELvl: _    Srce: _    Audn: _    Ctrl:  _    Lang: ___
BLvl: _   Form: _    Conf: _    Biog: _    Mrec: _    Ctry: ___
          Cont: ____  GPub: _    Fict: _    Indx: _
Desc: _   Ills: ____  Fest: _    DtSt: _    Dates: ____/____
```

The workform uses an abbreviation for the name of each element. The meanings of those abbreviations are:

Type	Type of Record	Ctry	Country of Publication, etc.
ELvl	Encoding Level	Cont	Nature of Contents
Srce	Cataloging Source Code	GPub	Government Publication
Audn	Target Audience	Fict	Fiction
Ctrl	Type of Control	Indx	Index
Lang	Language Code	Desc	Descriptive Cataloging Form
BLvl	Bibliographic Level	Ills	Illustrations
Form	Form of Item	Fest	Festschrift
Conf	Conference Publication	DtSt	Type of Date/Publication Status
Biog	Biography	Dates	Date 1 and Date 2
Mrec	Modified Record Code		

The following catalog record illustrates an OCLC record displaying both the fixed-field and variable fields related to description.

N.B. To aid readability in this and the next two examples displaying a fixed-field, the ƀ symbol has not been displayed but rather an underline to indicate that a blank value has been used for that element.

112   OCLC Fixed-Field

Type: a	ELvl: I	Srce: d	Audn:	Ctrl: _	Lang: eng
BLvl: m	Form: _	Conf: 0	Biog: c	Mrec: _	Ctry: nyu
	Cont: b___	GPub: _	Fict: 0	Indx: 1	
Desc: a	Ills: af__	Fest: 0	DtSt: r	Dates: 1995,1994	

020	0684804484 (pbk.)
020	0671642405
245 _ _	No ordinary time : ‡b Franklin and Eleanor Roosevelt : the home front in World War II / ‡c Doris Kearns Goodwin.
260	New York : ‡b Simon & Schuster, ‡c 1995, c1994.
300	759 p., [32] p. of plates : ‡b ill. ; ‡c 24 cm.
500	First published: 1994.
500	"A Touchstone book."
504	Includes bibliographical references (p. [715]-725) and index.

ADDITIONAL VARIABLE FIELDS

There are several variable MARC fields that provide additional descriptive information about an item. In some instances, these fields supplement descriptive information called for by AACR2R (e.g., Field 041) while in other instances they record cataloging data provided for by AACR2R (Fields 037, 074 and 086). The examples that follow illustrate several of these additional variable fields.

Languages

113 Multiple Languages and the Item is not a Translation
[Field 041 -- Language Code]
[1st Indicator 0 -- Item not a translation/does not include a translation]
[Subfield a -- Language code of text/sound recording]

[Note the relationship of the "Lang" element in the fixed-field and Field 041]

Type: a	ELvl: I		Srce: d	Audn: _	Ctrl: _	Lang: eng
BLvl: m	Form: _		Conf: 0	Biog: _	Mrec: _	Ctry: nyu
	Cont: ____		GPub:	Fict: 0	Indx: 1
Desc: a	Ills: ____		Fest: 0	DtSt: s	Dates: 1995,____

010	94-73692
020	0812090500
041 0	**englat** ◀
245 _ _	501 Latin verbs fully conjugated in all the tenses in a new easy-to-learn format alphabetically arranged / ‡c by Richard E. Prior, Joseph Wohlberg.
260	Hauppauge, NY : ‡b Barron's Educational Series, ‡c c1995.
300	ix, 548 p. ; ‡c 23 cm.
500	Rev. ed. of: 201 Latin verbs fully conjugated in all the tenses, alphabetically arranged / Joseph Wohlberg. 1964.
500	Includes indexes.

[Field 041 does not print on a catalog card from OCLC.]

114 Multiple Languages and the Item is a Translation
[Field 041 -- Language Code]
[1st Indicator 1 -- Item is or includes a translation]
[Subfield a -- Language code of text/sound recording]
[Subfield h -- Language code of original language and/or intermediate translations of text

[Note the relationship of the "Lang" element in the fixed-field and Field 041]

Type: a	ELvl: I		Srce: d	Audn: _	Ctrl:	Lang: eng
BLvl: m	Form: _		Conf: 0	Biog: _	Mrec: _	Ctry: ru_
	Cont: ____		GPub: _	Fict: 1	Indx: 0
Desc: a	Ills: ____		Fest: 0	DtSt: s	Dates: 1987,____

020	5050011280
041 1	**eng ‡h rus** ◀
245 _ _	Dead souls / ‡c Nikolai Gogol ; translated by Christopher English ; [edited by Olga Shartse].
260	Moscow : ‡b Raduga, ‡c c1987.
300	421 p. ; ‡c 21 cm.
4_ _	Russian classics

[Field 041 does not print on a catalog card from OCLC.]

Although Field 041 was not displayed on the MARC records for Examples 7, 14, 15, and 68, these records could also have used Field 041.

Numbers

115 Library of Congress Control Number
[Field 010 -- Library of Congress Control Number]
[Subfield a -- LC control number]

010	**96-5335**
020	0684874350
245 _ _	Angela's ashes : ‡b a memoir / ‡c Frank McCourt.
260	New York : ‡b Scribner, ‡c c1996.
300	364 p. : ‡b ill. ; ‡c 25 cm.

[Other national library or national bibliography control numbers can be recorded in Field 015 (National Bibliography Number) and Field 016 (National Library of Canada Bibliographic Control Number).]

116 Acquisition Information
[Field 037 -- Source of Acquisition]
[Subfield a -- Stock number]
[Subfield b -- Source of stock number/acquisition]

037	**001-001-00518-5 ‡b GPO**
074	0084
086 0	A 13.2:R 32/3
245 _ _	Revegetation equipment catalog / ‡c prepared for the Vegetative Rehabilitation and Equipment Workshop (VREW) by John E. Larson.
246 _ 4	Catalog, revegetation equipment
260	Missoula, Mont. : ‡b Forest Service, U.S. Dept. of Agriculture, Equipment Development Center, Fort Missoula ; ‡a Washington, D.C. : ‡b For sale by Supt. of Docs., U.S. G.P.O., ‡c [1980]
300	v, 198 p. : ‡b ill. ; ‡c 27 cm.
500	"February 1980."
504	Includes bibliographical references (p. 181-182).
500	"8042 2501"—Cover

["Stock Number" and "S/N" are not input.]

[Field 037 does not print on a catalog card from OCLC.]

117 GPO Item Number
[Field 074 -- GPO Item Number]
[Subfield a -- GPO item number]

074	0084
086 0	A 13.2:M52
245 _ _	Men who matched the mountains : ‡b the Forest Service in the Southwest / ‡c by Edwin A. Tucker and George Fitzpatrick.
260	[S.l.] : ‡b U.S. Dept. of Agriculture, Forest Service, Southwestern Region ; ‡a Washington, D.C. : ‡b For sale by the Supt. of Docs., U.S. G.P.O., ‡c 1972.
300	293 p. : ‡b ill. ; ‡c 24 cm.

[Field 074 does not print on a catalog card from OCLC.]

118 Government Document Classification Number
[Field 086 -- Government Document Classification Number]
[1st Indicator 0 -- Superintendent of Documents Classification Number]
[Subfield a -- Classification number

074	0086-C
086 0	**A 13.36/2:Ea 7/2**
245 _ _	Handbook for eastern timber harvesting / ‡c by Fred C. Simmons.
260	Broomall, Pa. : ‡b U.S. Dept. of Agriculture, Forest Service, Northeastern Area, State & Private Forestry ; ‡a Washington, D.C. : ‡b For sale by the Supt. of Docs., ‡c 1979.
300	180 p. : ‡b ill. ; ‡c 26 cm.
500	Rev. ed. of: Northeastern loggers' handbook. 1951. (Agriculture handbook ; no. 6)
504	Includes bibliographical references (p. 165).
500	"31"—Cover.
500	"NA-GR-2"—P. 4 of cover.

[Field 086 does not print as a note. If the SUDOCS number is to be a displayed as a note (Rule 2.7B19) the data would be entered as a 500 field instead of Field 086.]

500   Supt. of Docs. no.: A 13.36/2:Ea 7/2

There are two fields that appear in the variable field location on an OCLC record but actually record fixed-field data. These fields, 006 (Fixed Length Data Elements—Additional Material Characteristics) and 007 (Physical Description Fixed-Field) can be used to provide additional information about the characteristics of an item that could not be coded in the fixed-field. This includes data for additional physical description information for microforms, motion pictures, videorecordings, projected graphics, sound recordings, maps, globes, and computer files. Currently these two fields are seldom used for books but they may experience increased use in the future.

DESCRIPTIVE CATALOGING EXERCISE

Using the information from the title pages, title page versos, and the descriptive paragraph that follows them, descriptively catalog each of the following books (Areas 1 through 8 as needed) adding the appropriate OCLC/MARC formatting for the variable fields. In developing the answers, do not include any indicator values that are not related to the description of the item. Record the Field number for series as 4__. Answers to this exercise appear in Appendix A.

1.

Title page verso

Title page

HOUSE DESIGN
FOR
MODERN LIVING

by

ROBERT GROGAN

With Illustrations by
Patty Brown

Third Edition

ALBATROSS PRESS, INC.
New York   Chicago

1979

© 1979
by Albatross Press, Inc

No part of this publication may be reproduced, stored
in or introduced into a retrieval system, or transmitted,
in any form, or by any means (electronic, mechanical,
photocopying, recording, or otherwise), without the
prior written permission of the copyright owner.

1st Printing   1979
2nd Printing   1980

Library of Congress Card:
79-192064

ISBN 0-9876-4321-0

The book is 22 cm. high and 17 cm. wide. The first numbered preliminary page
is iii and the last numbered page is xii. The first numbered page of text is 1 and
the last numbered page is 306. The book is illustrated with black & white
reproductions of photographs and line drawings. There are 12 unnumbered
pages of colored illustrations appearing between pages 242 and 243.

2.

Title page verso

Title page

ENVIRONMENTAL EFFECTS
OF THE USE OF ASBESTOS

Horace Lemper, M.D.
Justine McCabe, Ph.D.

Introduction by
J. Wells Sinclair

Photographs by
Ann Reed & Ella Julianno

THE OSGOOD PUBLISHING COMPANY
LONDON   STOCKHOLM   NEW YORK

1972

©1969
Under
International Agreement

Second Revised Edition

Reprinted 1972

Printed in Stockholm

The first numbered preliminary page is i and the last numbered page is vi. The first page of text is numbered 7 and the last numbered page of text is 398. There are no pages intervening between the preliminary paging and the text. The book is 22.3 cm. high. The book has several tables and is illustrated with line drawings and black and white photographs. There is a bibliography that begins on unnumbered page 361 and continues through numbered page 388. There is an index beginning on page 389 and continuing to page 398.

3.

Title page

THE PROBLEMS OF EARTH

READINGS IN ECOLOGY

by

Adam Smith
Helen R. Roberts
John A. Kirschwin
A. N. Untermeyer

ECOLOGY ASSOCIATION PRESS
Bloomington, Indiana

© 1992

First Published 1993
Second Printing 1995
Third Printing 1997

NUMBER IX

Environmental Sciences Series

Series Editor:
Oscar W. Friedlander

ISBN 0-2345-9870-1
ISBN 0-2345-9871-2
(paperback)

The book is 24 cm. high.   The first numbered page of text is 1 and the last numbered page is 296, although the text continues for 5 more pages.   There is a bibliography at the end of each separately written section, on pages 73, 141, 212, and 296.   There are 12 pages of maps appearing between pages 170 and 183.   This is the hardcover edition.

4.

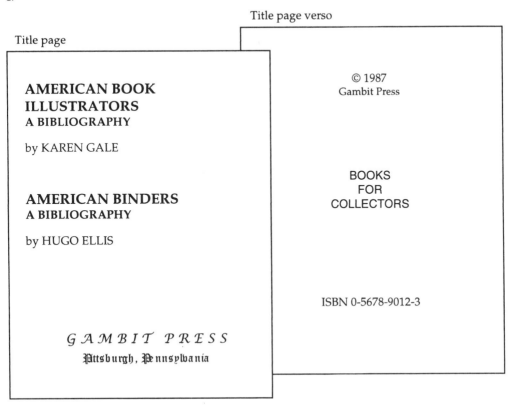

Title page verso

Title page

**AMERICAN BOOK
ILLUSTRATORS**
A BIBLIOGRAPHY

by KAREN GALE

AMERICAN BINDERS
A BIBLIOGRAPHY

by HUGO ELLIS

G A M B I T   P R E S S
Pittsburgh, Pennsylvania

© 1987
Gambit Press

BOOKS
FOR
COLLECTORS

ISBN 0-5678-9012-3

The book is 27.6 cm. high. The pagination is 1-116 and 1-125. The book is not illustrated, but at the back of the book are pockets containing 120 2x2 inch colored slides showing the work of illustrators and binders. There is a topical index to the slides at the end of the book. The title on the book's spine reads "American Illustrators and Binders."

5.

Page following the Table of Contents

Cover

Department of the Navy **Office of Retirement Affairs** **THE** **OFFICIAL GUIDE** **TO** **POST-SERVICE** **EMPLOYMENT OPPORTUNITIES** May 1996 ORA P-19913	A revision of *The Reference Guide to* *Post-Service Employment* *Opportunities for Naval Personnel* Compiled by Nelson F. Halleck

The book is 21.2 cm. high. There is no title page or title page verso. There are 3 unnumbered preliminary pages. The first numbered page begins with 1. The last numbered page is 96. The book is not illustrated, but does have bibliographic footnotes and an index. The binding is paperback. No place of publication is stated but one can assume it was published in Washington, D.C.

6.

Title page verso

Title page

The Feminist Struggle
Volume Seven

THE RIGHT OF WOMEN
Our Struggle for the Vote

by

Alice Faberman

A Susan Ebert / Karen Norris Book

Philadelphia
THE FEMINIST ISSUES PRESS
1995

FIRST EDITION

Limited to 500 copies
Copy **173**

Photo-offset reproduction of the
work originally published in
Philadelphia, Penn. By J. P.
Lippincott in 1911 from the copy
in the Van Pelt Library of the
University of Pennsylvania

The book is 23 cm. high. The pagination sequences begin with i and 1 and ends with xiii and 389 respectively. There are no illustrations other than a frontispiece portrait of the author that precedes the numbered preliminary pages (consider this a leaf). On the series title page, the series title reads: The Feminist Struggle Series, Volume Seven.

7.

Title page verso

Title page

Wilson's
History of Computer Processing

Cover designed by Gil Atkins

© All rights reserved
   Bull's Eye Book Company

Third Edition
revised by
B. Cameron
Distinguished Professor
Ohio Institute of Technology

ISBN 0-513-63499-1 (v. 1)
ISBN 0-513-63498-2 (set)

Volume 1
The Early Years

Printed by Oxford Craftsman
York, Pa.

New York
Bull's Eye Book Company
1996

10 9 8 7 6 5 4 3 2 1

The book is 27 cm tall. The preface indicates that this is the first of a planned
three-volume work. To date, this is the only volume that has been published. It
has preliminary pagination ending with page xi and a main sequence ending
with page 457. The work has 6 pages of black and white photographs occurring
between pages 262 and 263. The work has bibliographical references at the end
of most chapters and an index at the end of the book.

CHAPTER TWO

Choice of Access Points

Suggested Lecture Outline

A. Unit Records and Access Points in Card and Online Catalogs

B. Shelf lists

C. AACR2R and Related MARC Fields, Indicators and Subfields

WORKS THAT ARE MODIFICATIONS OF OTHER WORKS

Modifications of Texts

MIXED RESPONSIBILITY IN NEW WORKS

RELATED WORKS

13.   21.28   Related Works

ADDED ENTRIES

14.   21.29   General Rule

15.   21.30   Specific Rules

Readings: *Anglo-American Cataloguing Rules.* 2nd ed., 1998 revision.
                   Part II, Headings, Uniform Titles, and References:
                       Introduction, p. 305-306;
                       Chapter 21: Choice of Access Points, p. 307-358.

CARD CATALOGS

Format. Initially, catalog records for book and card catalogs utilized a form of presentation where one access point (the main entry) contained the complete description of the item. Often the cards for the other access points were less complete. This was a labor-saving approach when catalog records were produced by hand or typewriter. With the advent of printed catalog cards it became less costly to produce one complete catalog record (the unit card) in multiple copies to be used for each access point.

Main Entry Unit Card Format

Call   Main entry.
number   Title proper : other title information / statement of
               responsibility ; subsequent statement of responsibility. --
               Edition statement / statement of responsibility relating to the
               edition. -- Place : publisher, date (Place : printer, date)
                   number of pages : illustrations ; dimensions + accompanying
               material. -- (Series title proper ; number)

                   Notes.
                   ISBN

                   1. Subject added entries. I. Non-subject added entries.

When the title rather than a personal or corporate name was the main entry a slightly different style, called the "hanging indention," was used on catalog cards.

Title Main Entry Unit Card Format

Call number	Title proper : other title information / statement of responsibility ; subsequent statement of responsibility. -- Edition statement / statement of responsibility relating to the edition. – Place : publisher, date (Place : printer, date)
	    number of pages : illustrations ; dimensions + accompanying material. -- (Series title proper ; number)
	
	    Notes.
	    ISBN
	
	    1. Subject added entries. I. Non-subject added entries.
	
	                        ◯

Using the main entry unit card format the catalog record for the book *Making Sense of College Grades* at the second level of description would be as follows:

Main Entry Unit Card

LB2368
.M57
1986
	Milton, Ohmer.
	        Making sense of college grades / Ohmer Milton, Howard R. Pollio, James A. Eison ; foreword by Laura Bornholdt. -- 1st ed. – San Francisco : Jossey-Bass, 1986.
	        xxii, 287 p. : ill. ; 24 cm. -- (Jossey-Bass higher education series)
	
	        Half-title: Making sense of college grades : why the grading system does not work and what can be done about it.
	        Includes bibliographical references (p. 271-280) and index.
	
	        1. Grading and marking (Students). 2. College credits. I. Pollio, Howard R. II. Eison, James A., 1950- III. Title. IV. Series. ◯

Catalog Entries. For a card catalog the catalog entries for the book would have seven cards created and filed in a dictionary catalog as illustrated on the next page.

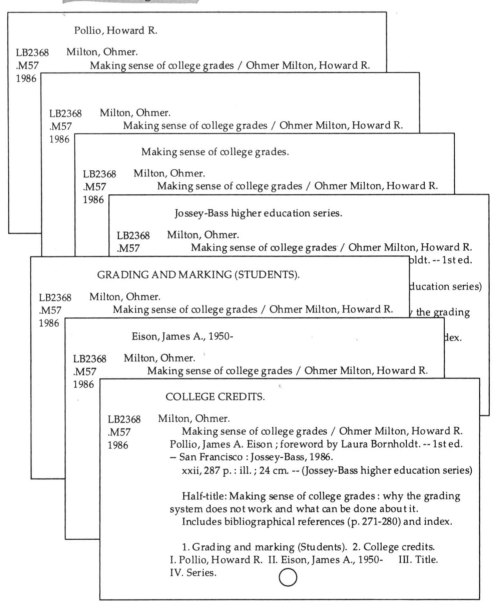

In a two-way divided catalog the subject added entries would be located in a catalog separate from the main entry and non-subject added entries.

ONLINE CATALOGS

Format and Displays. The online catalog provides flexibility that allows varying levels of cataloging information to be provided to users. Although catalog cards can be prepared at different levels of description, once a level is chosen, generally, most libraries will make unit cards for all entries. The online catalog provides a library with the opportunity to prepare a detailed master catalog record but then provide displays of varied detail to catalog users. Using a master record, an online catalog might make two or more different displays available to its users. It is not uncommon for these displays also to provide labels for the data elements and to have circulation information included as part of the display. The following are examples of "partial" and "full" displays for *Making Sense of College Grades* based on the master record prepared at the second level of description.

OCLC/MARC Master Record

020		0875896871
050	0 0	LB2368 ‡b .M57 1986
100	1	Milton, Ohmer.
245	1 0	Making sense of college grades / ‡c Ohmer Milton, Howard R. Pollio, James A. Eison ; foreword by Laura Bornholdt.
246	0 ⁄b	‡i Half title: ‡a Making sense of college grades : ‡b why the grading system does not work and what can be done about it
250		1st ed.
260		San Francisco : ‡b Jossey-Bass, ‡c 1986.
300		xxii, 287 p. : ‡b ill. ; ‡c 24 cm.
440	4	The Jossey-Bass higher education series
504		Includes bibliographical references (p. 271-280) and index.
650	0	Grading and marking (Students)
650	0	College credits.
700	1 ⁄b	Pollio, Howard R.
700	1 ⁄b	Eison, James A., ‡d 1950-

Online Catalog Partial Display

                                            LIBRARY_CATALOG
                AUTHOR: Milton, Ohmer.
                 TITLE: Making sense of college grades

             PUBLISHER: Jossey-Bass, 1986.
              SUBJECTS: Grading and marking (Students)
                         College credits.

LIBRARY HOLDINGS:
    1. LOCATION: Main -- CALL NUMBER: LB2368 .M57 1986
         STATUS: Checked out

No more holdings. Enter 'H' to redisplay all Holdings
information.
Select a line number for detailed information about
that line.

Enter: B   to go Back
         F   to see the FULL title record
         REL   to search for RELated works

                                            Enter ? for HELP.

Online Catalog Full Display

```
                                          LIBRARY_CATALOG
                    AUTHOR:   Milton, Ohmer.
                     TITLE:   Making sense of college grades / Ohmer
                              Milton, Howard R. Pollio, James A. Eison
                              ; foreword by Laura Bornholdt.

                   EDITION:   1st ed.
               PUBLICATION:   San Francisco : Jossey-Bass, 1986.
               DESCRIPTION:   xxii, 287 p. : ill. ; 24 cm.
                    SERIES:   The Jossey-Bass higher education series

                     NOTES:   Half-title: Making sense of college grades
                              : why the grading system does not work
                              and what to do about it.
                     NOTES:   Includes bibliographical references
                              (p. 271-280) and index.

                   SUBJECT:   Grading and marking (Students)
                   SUBJECT:   College credits.

               ADDED ENTRY:   Pollio, Howard R.
               ADDED ENTRY:   Eison, James A., 1950-
        SERIES ADDED ENTRY:   The Jossey-Bass higher education series

        LIBRARY HOLDINGS:
            1.  LOCATION:  Main -- CALL NUMBER: LB2368 .M57 1986
                  STATUS:  Checked out

        No more holdings.  Enter 'H' to redisplay all Holdings
        information.
        Select a line number for detailed information about
        that line.

        Enter:   B           to go Back
                 REL         to search for RELated works

                 You may enter a ? for HELP or enter a new search.
```

Each access point would have an index entry created for it in the online catalog. Whenever a search was conducted for any indexed item the record displayed could be viewed at different levels. While the examples are not illustrative of all online catalogs, indeed some have more display capabilities and some less, they are indicative of the flexibility provided by the online catalog over than of the card catalog for record display.

SHELF LIST

The shelf list is a tool used by libraries to manage their collection inventory. Although still generally in card format even for those libraries that have converted to an online catalog there are a number of libraries that now utilize an online shelf list.

The shelf list, usually a copy of the main entry card, is filed in call number order thus reproducing the order of the documents on the shelf. It contains information about each copy of a document owned. The amount of information recorded is a local library decision. In the examples that follow the copy and acquisition information recorded are: the bar code number, acquisition source, date acquired, and price.

Shelf List

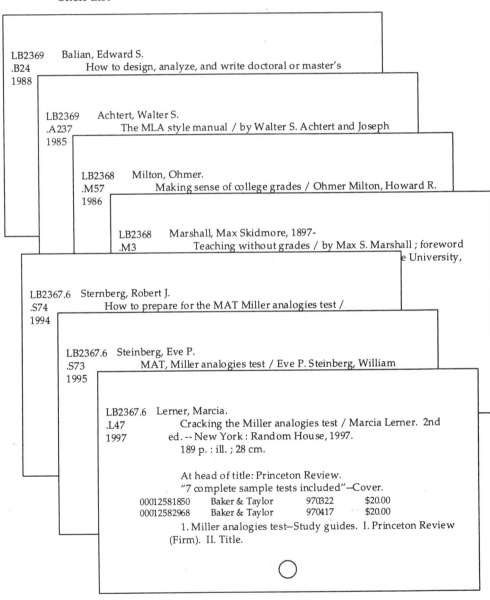

LB2369   Balian, Edward S.
.B24   How to design, analyze, and write doctoral or master's
1988

LB2369   Achtert, Walter S.
.A237   The MLA style manual / by Walter S. Achtert and Joseph
1985

LB2368   Milton, Ohmer.
.M57   Making sense of college grades / Ohmer Milton, Howard R.
1986

LB2368   Marshall, Max Skidmore, 1897-
.M3   Teaching without grades / by Max S. Marshall ; foreword
                                                                        e University,

LB2367.6   Sternberg, Robert J.
.S74   How to prepare for the MAT Miller analogies test /
1994

LB2367.6   Steinberg, Eve P.
.S73   MAT, Miller analogies test / Eve P. Steinberg, William
1995

LB2367.6   Lerner, Marcia.
.L47   Cracking the Miller analogies test / Marcia Lerner. 2nd
1997   ed. -- New York : Random House, 1997.
                189 p. : ill. ; 28 cm.

                At head of title: Princeton Review.
                "7 complete sample tests included"–Cover.
00012581850   Baker & Taylor   970322 $20.00
00012582968   Baker & Taylor   970417 $20.00
                1. Miller analogies test–Study guides. I. Princeton Review
                (Firm). II. Title.

N.B. *In the examples that follow, the access points only indicate the appropriate headings to use as access points. As is done in Chapter 21 of AACR2R, the headings are not in their proper form but rather in the form in which they appeared on the prescribed source of information. The only exception is the addition of forenames when only the surname appeared on the chief source of information. The forms of personal, corporate and uniform title headings are addressed in Chapters 3, 4 and 5 of this text.*

21.1   GENERAL RULE
21.1A   Works of personal authorship

21.4   WORKS FOR WHICH A SINGLE PERSON OR CORPORATE BODY IS RESPONSIBLE
21.4A   Works of single personal authorship

119   **Rule 21.1A2**   Personal authorship

Rule 21.4A1   Work of single personal authorship
[Field 100 -- Main Entry—Personal Name]
[Subfield a -- Personal name]

Rule 21.30J1   Titles
[Field 245 -- Title Statement]
[1st Indicator 1 -- Title added entry]
[2nd Indicator 2 -- Number of nonfiling characters present]

020		0805036539 (alk. paper)
100	_	**Basbanes, Nicholas A.**
245	1 2	A gentle madness : ‡b bibliophiles, bibliomanes, and the eternal passion for books / ‡c Nicholas A. Basbanes.
250		1st ed.
260		New York : ‡b H. Holt, ‡c 1995.
300		xvi, 638 p., [32] p. of plates : ‡b ill. ; ‡c 24 cm.
504		Includes bibliographical references (p. 575-612) and index.

120   **Rule 21.1A2   Personal authorship**

    Rule 21.4A1   Work of single personal authorship—Compiler of a
                 bibliography

020		0810308320
100	_	**Bakewell, K. G. B.**
245	1 0	Management principles and practice : ‡b a guide to information sources / ‡c K.G.B. Bakewell.
260		Detroit, Mich. : ‡b Gale Research Co., ‡c c1977.
300		xix, 519 p. ; ‡c 23 cm.
440	0	Management information guide ; ‡v 32
500		Includes indexes.

121   **Rule 21.1A2   Personal authorship**

    Rule 21.4A1   Work of single personal authorship—Writer of a
                 comic strip

    Rule 21.30G1 Related work
        [Field 730 -- Added Entry—Uniform Title]
          [1st Indicator 0 -- Nonfiling characters]
          [2nd Indicator ƀ -- No information provided. The added entry is
                   not for an analytic]
       [Subfield a -- Uniform title]

020		0836218051 (pbk.)
020		0836218094 (hardback)
100	_	**Watterson, Bill.**
245	1 4	The essential Calvin and Hobbes : ‡b a Calvin and Hobbes treasury / ‡c Bill Watterson.
260		Kansas City : ‡b Andrews and McMeel, ‡c c1988.
300		ca. 250 p. : ‡b ill. (some col.) ; ‡c 28 cm.
730	0 ƀ	**Calvin and Hobbes.**

        *[The Field 730 access point is for the comic strip. The nature and
        use of uniform titles is addressed in Chapter 5 of this text.]*

122   Rule 21.1A2   Personal authorship

Rule 21.4A1   Work of single personal authorship—Person is not
                named in the work

Rule 21.30J1   Titles
     [Field 246 -- Varying Form of Title]
          [1st Indicator 3 -- No note, title added entry]
          [2nd Indicator ƀ -- No information provided]

100 _		Dunne, Finley Peter.
245 1 0		Mr. Dooley in the hearts of his countrymen.
246 3 ƀ		Mister Dooley in the hearts of his countrymen
260		Boston : ‡b Small, Maynard, ‡c 1899.
300		xi, 285 p. ; ‡c 18 cm.
500		Preface signed: F.P.D. [i.e., Finley Peter Dunne].
500		"Third edition (10,000 copies) October, 1899"—T.p. verso.

21.1   GENERAL RULE
21.1B   Entry under corporate body

21.4   WORKS FOR WHICH A SINGLE PERSON OR CORPORATE BODY IS RESPONSIBLE
21.4B   Works emanating from a single corporate body

123   Rule 21.1B2a   Corporate authorship—Administrative work

Rule 21.4B1   Work emanating from a single corporate body
     [Field 110 -- Main Entry—Corporate Name]
          [Subfield a -- Corporate name or jurisdiction name as entry element]

Rule 21.30C1   Writers
     [Field 700 -- Added Entry -- Personal Name]
          [2nd Indicator ƀ -- No information provided. The added entry is
                not for an analytic]
     [Subfield a -- Personal name]

110 _		Inglewood Public Library.
245 1 0		Library of Congress classification adapted for children's books / ‡c [produced by John W. Perkins, Paul N. Clingen, Paul C. Jones].
260		Inglewood, Calif. : ‡b Inglewood Public Library, ‡c c1971.
300		162 p. ; ‡c 28 cm.
500		Cover title.
700 _ ƀ		Perkins, John W.
700 _ ƀ		Clingen, Paul N.
700 _ ƀ		Jones, Paul C.

124   Rule 21.1B2a   Corporate authorship—Administrative work

Rule 21.4B1   Work emanating from a single corporate body

020	0838978770
022	0273-4605
110 _	**American Library Association.**
245 1 0	ALA membership directory, 1996-1997.
246 3 ᵇ	A.L.A. membership directory, 1996-1997
246 3 ᵇ	American Library Association membership directory, 1996-1997
260	Chicago : ‡b American Library Association, ‡c 1996, c1997.
300	668 p. ; ‡c 28 cm.
580	Companion publication: American Library Association. ALA handbook of organization, 1996-1997.

[Cataloged as a single monograph rather than as a serial.]

125   Rule 21.1B2b   Corporate authorship—Legal work

Rule 21.4B1   Work emanating from a single corporate body
[Field 110 -- Main Entry—Corporate name]
[Subfield a -- Corporate name or jurisdiction name as entry element]

Rule 21.30E1   Corporate bodies
[Field 710 -- Added Entry -- Corporate Name]
[2nd Indicator ᵇ -- No information provided. The added entry is
not for an analytic]
[Subfield a -- Corporate name]

---

110 _	**Pennsylvania.**
245 1 4	The library code.
260	Harrisburg : ‡b Pennsylvania State Library, ‡c [1962]
300	iii, 27 p. ; ‡c 23 cm.
500	"To be cited as The library code, the Act of June 14, 1961, P.L. 324."
500	Includes index.
710 _ ᵇ	Pennsylvania State Library.

*[These are laws relating to the establishment, operation and
maintenance of the State Library and public libraries in
Pennsylvania.]*

126   Rule 21.1B2c   Corporate authorship—Collective thought of a corporate body

Rule 21.4B1   Work emanating from a single corporate body

....

020   0910958173
110 _   Committee on Social Issues.
245 1 4   The child and television drama : ‡b the psychosocial impact of cumulative viewing / ‡c formulated by the Committee on Social Issues, Group for the Advancement of Psychiatry.
260   New York : ‡b Mental Health Materials Center, ‡c c1982.
300   xii, 123 p : ‡b ill. ; ‡c 23 cm.
490 1   Publication ; ‡v no. 112
500   "Sixth in a series of GAP publications comprising Volume XI."-- T.p. verso.
504   Includes bibliographical references (p. 120-123).
830   0   Publication (Group for the Advancement of Psychiatry) ; ‡v no. 112.

> *[The Committee provided recommendations and guidelines on the impact of television drama upon children.]*
>
> *[The addition of "(Group for the Advancement of Psychiatry)" to the heading in Field 830 is addressed in Chapter 5 of this text.]*

127   Rule 21.1B2d   Corporate authorship—Collective activity of a conference

Rule 21.4B1   Work emanating from a single corporate body
[Field 111 -- Main Entry—Meeting name]
[Subfield a -- Meeting name or jurisdiction name as entry element]

....

Rule 21.30D1   Editors and Compilers
[Field 700 -- Added Entry -- Personal Name]
[Subfield a -- Personal name]

....

020   0871522128
111 _   Reynolds Conference.
245 1 0   South Carolina journals and journalists : ‡b proceedings of the Reynolds Conference, University of South Carolina, May 17-18, 1974 / ‡c edited by James B. Meriwether.
260   Spartanburg, S.C. : ‡b Published for the Southern Studies Program, University of South Carolina [by] Reprint Co., ‡c 1975.
300   xi, 348 p. ; ‡c 23 cm.
504   Includes bibliographical references and index.
700 _ b   Meriwether, James B.
710 _ b   Southern Studies Program.

128   Rule 21.1B2e   Corporate authorship—Collective activity of a performing group

Rule 21.4B1   Work emanating from a single corporate body

020	0879320273
020	0879320281 (casebound)
110 _	**Firesign Theatre.**
245 1 4	The Firesign Theatre's big book of plays.
246 3 0	Big book of plays
260	San Francisco : ‡b Straight Arrow Books ; ‡a N.Y., [N.Y.] : ‡b Distributed by Quick Fox, ‡c c1972.
300	143 p. : ‡b ill. ; ‡c 26 cm.

> *[The Firesign Theatre is a performing group that has written and performed these works. This work is a transcript version of sound recording presentations of these plays.]*

129   Rule 21.1B3   Work emanating from a corporate body falls outside the categories in Rule 21.1B2

Rule 21.1C1c   Entry under title proper
[Field 245 -- Title Statement]
    [1st Indicator 0 -- No title added entry]
    [2nd Indicator 2 -- Number of nonfiling characters present]

[See also Rule 21.5 and 21.6C2]

245 0 2	**A programmed introduction to PERT** : ‡b program evaluation and review technique / ‡c Federal Electric Corporation.
260	New York : ‡b John Wiley, ‡c c1963.
300	x, 145 p. : ‡b ill. ; ‡c 23 cm.
500	Includes supplementary problems.
710 _ ∅	**Federal Electric Corporation.**

> *[This work gives no evidence of being produced as an administrative work or as a resource of the Corporation.]*

21.4C   Works erroneously or fictitiously attributed to a person or corporate body

130   Rule 21.4C1   Work fictitiously attributed to a person

[An added entry is provided for the person to whom the work is attributed because she is a real person.]

---

100 _	Stein, Gertrude.
245 1 4	The autobiography of Alice B. Toklas.
250	1st ed.
260	New York, N.Y. : ‡b Literary Guild, ‡c c1933.
300	vii, 310 p., [16] leaves of plates : ‡b ill. ; ‡c 23 cm.
500	By Gertrude Stein. Cf. p. 310.
700 _ ♭	Toklas, Alice B.

> *[P. 310 : "About six weeks ago Gertrude Stein said, it does not look to me as if you were ever going to write that autobiography. You know what I am going to do. I am going to write it for you…. And she has and this is it."]*

131   Rule 21.4C1   Work fictitiously attributed to a person
[Field 246 -- Varying Form of Title]
[1st Indicator 3 -- No note, title added entry]
[2nd Indicator 0 -- Portion of title]

020	0671220292
020	0671220306 (pbk.)
100 _	Bailey, Adrian.
245 1 0	Mrs. Bridges' upstairs downstairs cookery book / ‡c edited by Adrian Bailey ; with photographs by John Hedgecoe.
246 3 0	Upstairs downstairs cookery book
260	New York : ‡b Simon and Schuster, ‡c c1974.
300	193 p. : ‡b ill. ; ‡c 22 cm.
500	By Adrian Bailey. Cf. British national bibliography.
500	Purports to be adapted from "Practical household cookery" by Kate Bridges.
500	Includes glossary and index.
700 _ ♭	Hedgecoe, John.

> *[No added entry is provided for the person to whom the work is attributed because she is a not real person. Mrs. Bridges was a fictional character in the television series "Upstairs, Downstairs."]*

21.4D Works by heads of state, other high government officials, popes, and other high ecclesiastical officials

132 Rule 21.4D1 Official communications of a head of state

[An added entry is provided for the person holding the office.]

---

110 _ United States. President.
245 1 4 The economic reports of the President as transmitted to the Congress, January 1949, January 1947, July 1947, January 1948, July 1948, together with the Joint Congressional Committee reports of 1947 & 1948 / ‡c introduction by the Council of Economic Advisers.
260 New York : ‡b Harcourt, Brace, ‡c [1949?]
300 1 v. (various pagings) : ‡b ill. ; ‡c 23 cm.
500 Includes the Annual economic review, January 1949, and the economic situation at midyear 1948, reports to the President by the Council of Economic Advisers.
500 Includes index.
700 _ ‡ Truman, Harry S.
710 _ ‡ Joint Economic Committee.
710 _ ‡ Council of Economic Advisers.

[The addition of "President" to the heading in Field 110 is addressed in Chapter 3 of this text.]

133 Rule 21.4D3 Collection of official communications of a head of state and other works

[An added entry is provided for the office of the head of state.]

---

100 _ Wilson, Woodrow.
245 1 0 President Wilson's state papers and addresses / ‡c introduction by Albert Shaw.
260 New York : ‡b G.H. Doran, ‡c c1918.
300 xiv, 484 p. ; ‡c 22 cm.
500 Includes index.
700 _ ‡ Shaw, Albert.
710 _ ‡ United States. President.

[This work contains both official communications as well as other works of President Woodrow Wilson including proclamations, addresses to various groups, veto messages and speeches.]

134 Rule 21.4D2 Other works by a head of state

100 _	Kennedy, John F.
245 1 0	Profiles in courage / ‡c John F. Kennedy.
250	Memorial ed.
260	New York : ‡b Harper & Row, ‡c [1964?]
300	287 p., [9] p. of plates : ‡b ill. ; ‡c 22 cm.
500	Foreword by Robert F. Kennedy.
504	Includes bibliographical references (p. 269-281) and index.

21.5 WORKS OF UNKNOWN OR UNCERTAIN AUTHORSHIP OR BY UNNAMED GROUPS

135 Rule 21.5C Personal author unknown, but chief source of information has a characterizing word

100 _	Nobody.
245 1 4	The notion-counter : ‡b a farrago of foibles : being notes about nothing / ‡c by Nobody ; illustrated by Somebody.
260	Boston : ‡b Atlantic Monthly Press, ‡c c1922.
300	108 p. : ‡b ill. ; ‡c 16 cm.

        [No added entry is provided for the illustrator because the requirements of Rule 21.30K2 were not met. See Example 146.]

136 Rule 21.5C Personal author unknown, but chief source of information has a characterizing phrase

100	Author of The mountain refuge.
245 1 4	The schoolmistress of Herondale, or, Sketches of life among the hills / ‡c the author of The mountain refuge.
246 3 0	Schoolmistress of Herondale
246 3 0	Sketches of life among the hills
260	London : ‡b Seeley, Jackson, and Halliday, ‡c 1866.
300	390 p. : ‡b ill. ; ‡c 19 cm.

        [OCLC guidelines call for the deletion of initial articles at the beginning of a title in Field 246.]

137   Rule 21.5A   Work emanates from a body that lacks a name

020	0838902626
245 0 4	**The copyright dilemma** : ‡b proceedings of a conference held at Indiana University, April 14-15, 1977 / ‡c edited by Herbert S. White.
260	Chicago : ‡b American Library Association, ‡c 1978.
300	xiii, 199 p. ; ‡c 23 cm.
500	Sponsored by the Indiana University Graduate Library School.
700 _ ₿	White, Herbert S.
710 _ ₿	Indiana University Graduate Library School.

[This conference did not have a name.]

21.6   WORKS OF SHARED RESPONSIBILITY
21.6B   Principal responsibility indicated

138   Rule 21.6B1   Work of shared responsibility with principal responsibility attributed to an individual

[Added entries are provided for the others authors because there are not more than two.]

100 _	**Menninger, Karl.**
245 1 4	The vital balance : ‡b the life process in mental health and illness / ‡c Karl Menninger with Martin Mayman and Paul Pruyser.
260	New York : ‡b Viking, ‡c 1963.
300	531 p. ; ‡c 25 cm.
504	Includes bibliographical references (p. 491-509) and index.
700 _ ₿	**Mayman, Martin.**
700 _ ₿	**Pruyser, Paul.**

21.6C   Principal responsibility not indicated

139   Rule 21.6C1   Work of shared responsibility between three persons, and principal responsibility not attributed to anyone

[Added entries are provided for the other two authors.]

Rule 21.30B1   Collaborators

020	0812906195
100 _	**Eddy, Paul.**
245 1 0	Destination disaster : ‡b from the tri-motor to the DC-10 : the risk of flying / ‡c by Paul Eddy, Elaine Potter and Bruce Page.
260	New York, N.Y. : ‡b Quadrangle, ‡c c1976.
300	xii, 434 p., [32] p. of plates : ‡b ill. ; ‡c 25 cm.
504	Includes bibliographical references and index.
700 _ b	**Potter, Elaine.**
700 _ b	**Page, Bruce.**

140   Rule 21.6C2   Work of shared responsibility among more than three individuals, and principal responsibility not attributed to anyone

[An added entry is made for only the first named author.]

245 0 2	**A dictionary of basic geography** / ‡c Allen A. Schmieder ... [et al.].
260	Boston : ‡b Allyn and Bacon, ‡c c1970.
300	xii, 299 p. : ‡b ill. ; ‡c 22 cm.
504	Includes bibliographical references (p. 226-238) and index.
700 _ b	**Schmieder, Allen A.**

21.6D   Shared pseudonyms

141   Rule 21.6D1   Shared pseudonym

020	0451400054
100 _	**Slade, Michael.**
245 1 0	Headhunter / ‡c by Michael Slade.
260	New York : ‡b New American Library, ‡c [1986], c1984.
300	422 p. : ‡b map ; ‡c 18 cm.
500	"An Onyx book."
504	Includes bibliographical references (p. 421-422).

[Michael Slade is the shared pseudonym of Jay Clarke, John Banks, and Richard Covell.]

21.7   COLLECTIONS OF WORKS PRODUCED UNDER EDITORIAL DIRECTION

21.7B   With collective title

142   Rule 21.7B1   Collection of works by different persons, published with a collective title

[An added entry is provided for the editor because there are no more than three editors named prominently.]

020	0231037953
245 0 4	**The feminist papers** : ‡b from Adams to de Beauvoir / ‡c edited and with introductory essays by Alice S. Rossi.
260	New York : ‡b Columbia University Press, ‡c 1973.
300	xix, 716 p. : ‡b ill. ; ‡c 21 cm.
504	Includes bibliographical references (p. [707]-716).
700 _ ♭	Rossi, Alice S.

143   Rule 21.7B1   Collection of three independent works, published with a collective title

[Name-title added entries are provided for each work because there are no more than three.]

Rule 21.30M1 Analytical entries
[Field 700 → Added Entry—Personal Name]
        [2nd Indicator 2 -- Analytical entry. The item contains the work that is represented by the added entry]
        [Subfield a -- Personal name]
        [Subfield t -- Title of a work]

245 0 0	Three Restoration comedies / ‡c edited by G.G. Falle.
260	Toronto : ‡b Macmillan of Canada ; ‡a New York : ‡b St. Martin's Press, ‡c c1964.
300	342 p. ; ‡c 19 cm.
440 0	College classics in English
504	Includes bibliographical references (p. 341-342).
505 0 ♭	The country wife / by William Wycherley — The way of the world / by William Congreve — The rehearsal / by George Villiers.
700 _ _	Falle, G. G.
700 _ 2	Wycherley, William. ‡t Country wife.
700 _ 2	Congreve, William. ‡t Way of the world.
700 _ 2	Villiers, George. ‡t Rehearsal.

[Although no rule or guidelines specifically call for the deletion of initial articles at the beginning of a title in Field 700, Subfield t, it is useful to do so because there is no way to control for non-filing characters in this field.]

21.7C   Without collective title

> **144   Rule 21.7C1   Collection of works by different persons, published without a collective title**
>
> *[Name-title added entries are provided for the 2nd and 3rd works.]*

....

100 _	**Dibdin, Michael.**
245 1 4	The last Sherlock Holmes story / ‡c by Michael Dibdin. The empty copper sea / by John D. MacDonald. Catch me, kill me / by William H. Hallahan.
260	Roslyn, N.Y. : ‡b Published for the Detective Book Club by Walter J. Black, ‡c [197-]
300	158, 158, 184 p. ; ‡c 20 cm.
700 _ 2	**MacDonald, John D. ‡t Empty copper sea.**
700 _ 2	**Hallahan, William H. ‡t Catch me, kill me.**

WORKS THAT ARE MODIFICATIONS OF OTHER WORKS

Modifications of Texts

21.10   ADAPTATIONS OF TEXTS

> **145   Rule 21.10A   Adaptation of a text**
>
> *[A name-title added entry is provided for the original work.]*

....

020	0446895571
100 _	**Grossbach, Robert.**
245 1 4	The cheap detective / ‡c a novelization by Robert Grossbach ; based on the original screenplay by Neil Simon.
250	Warner Books ed.
260	New York, N.Y. : ‡b Warner Books, ‡c c1978.
300	221 p. ; ‡c 18 cm.
700 _ b	**Simon, Neil. ‡t Cheap detective.**

21.12   REVISIONS OF TEXTS
21.12A   Original author considered responsible

**146   Rule 21.12A1 Work that has been revised and, (1) the
original author is named in the title, and (2) no one
is named in the Area 1 statement of responsibility**

[An added entry is provided for the reviser.]

....

020	064920321 (U.S.)
020	040100014 (British)
100 _	**Esdaile, Arundell.**
245 1 0	Esdaile's manual of bibliography.
246 3 0	Manual of bibliography
250	4th rev. ed. / ‡b revised edition by Roy Stokes.
260	London : ‡b Allen & Unwin ; ‡a New York : ‡b Barnes & Noble, ‡c 1967.
300	x, 336 p., [8] p. of plates : ‡b ill. ; ‡c 22 cm.
504	Includes bibliographical references and index.
700 _ b	**Stokes, Roy.**

21.12B   Original author no longer considered responsible

**147   Rule 21.12B1 Person responsible for the original work is no
longer considered responsible for it**

[A name-title added entry is provided for the original work.]

....

100 _	**Abrams, M. H.**
245 1 2	A glossary of literary terms / ‡c by M.H. Abrams ; based on an earlier book by Dan S. Norton and Peters Rushton.
260	New York : ‡b Holt, Rinehart and Winston, ‡c c1957.
300	102 p. ; ‡c 23 cm.
700 _ b	**Norton, Dan S. ‡t Glossary of literary terms.**

21.11   ILLUSTRATED TEXTS

148   Rule 21.11A1 A text for which an artist has provided illustrations

···

Rule 21.30K2 Illustrators

···

100 _	**Loos, Anita.**
245 1 0	"Gentlemen prefer blondes" : ‡b the illuminating diary of a professional lady / ‡c by Anita Loos ; intimately illustrated by Ralph Barton.
260	New York : ‡b Boni & Liveright, ‡c 1925.
300	217 p. : ‡b ill. ; ‡c 20 cm.
700 _ ♭	**Barton, Ralph.**

[This work is primarily textual material.]

21.14   TRANSLATIONS

149   Rule 21.14A   Translation

···

Rule 21.30K1 Translators

···

100 _	**Milnei, A. A.**
245 1 0	Winnie ille Pu / ‡c A.A. Milnei ; liber celeberrimus omnibus fere pueris puellisque notus nunc primum de angelico sermone in Latinum conversus auctore Alexandro Lenardo.
260	Novi Eboraci [New York] : ‡b Sumptibus Duttonis, ‡c 1960.
300	121 p. : ‡b ill., map ; ‡c 19 cm.
500	Translation of: Winnie-the-Pooh.
700 _ ♭	**Lenardo, Alexandro.**

21.15   TEXTS PUBLISHED WITH BIOGRAPHICAL/CRITICAL MATERIAL

150   Rule 21.15A   Work by a writer, with biographical or critical
                       material by another person and the work is
                       presented as a biographical or critical work

---

100 _	Mahler, Alma.
245 1 0	Gustav Mahler : ‡b memories and letters / ‡c by Alma Mahler.
250	Enl. ed. / ‡b revised and edited and with an introduction by Donald Mitchell ; translated by Basil Creighton.
260	New York : ‡b Viking, ‡c 1969.
300	xl, 369 p., [16] p. of plates : ‡b ill., facsims., ports. ; ‡c 24 cm.
500	Translated from Gustav Mahler : Erinnerungen und Briefe.
504	Includes bibliographical references (p. [343]-353) and index.
700 _ ⌿	Mahler, Gustav.
700 _ ⌿	Mitchell, Donald.

151   Rule 21.15B   Biographical or critical work in which the
                       biographer or critic is presented as an editor,
                       compiler, etc.

[An added entry is provided for the biographer/critic.]

020	0836951107
100 _	Beethoven, Ludwig van.
245 1 0	Beethoven's letters : ‡b a critical edition / ‡c with explanatory notes by Alf C. Kalischer ; translated with preface by J.S. Shedlock.
260	Freeport, N.Y. : ‡b Books for Libraries Press, ‡c 1969.
300	2 v. : ‡b ill., facsims., music, ports. ; ‡c 23 cm.
440 0	Select bibliographies reprint series
500	Originally published: 1909.
700 _ ⌿	Kalischer, Alf C.

MIXED RESPONSIBILITY IN NEW WORKS

21.24 COLLABORATION BETWEEN ARTIST AND WRITER

152 Rule 21.24A Collaborative work between artist and writer

[An added entry is provided for the person not named first or given prominence on the chief source of information.]

020	08071210X (cloth : alk. paper)
100 _	Meek, A. J.
245 1 4	The gardens of Louisiana : ‡b places of work and wonder / ‡c photographs by A.J. Meek ; text by Suzanne Turner.
260	Baton Rouge : ‡b Louisiana State University Press, ‡c c1997.
300	xii, 237 : ‡b ill. (some col.), col. map ; ‡c 29 cm.
504	Includes bibliographical references (p. 231-232) and index.
700 _ ʬ	Turner, Suzanne.

21.25 REPORTS OF INTERVIEWS OR EXCHANGES

153 Rule 21.25A Report is essentially confined to the words of the person(s) interviewed

020	0878053859 (alk. paper)
020	0878053867 (pbk : alk. paper)
100 _	Foote, Shelby.
245 1 0	Conversations with Shelby Foote / ‡c edited by William C. Carter.
260	Jackson : ‡b University Press of Mississippi, ‡c c1989.
300	xviii, 276 p. : ‡b port. ; ‡c 24 cm.
440 0	Literary conversations series
500	Includes index.
700 _ ʬ	Carter, William C.

[This work consists of interviews conducted by a number of reporters, thus no added entry is provided for the reporters.]

154   Rule 21.25B   Report to a considerable extent in the words of the
                     reporter

020   0394408551
100 _   **Bragg, Melvyn.**
245 1 0   Speak for England : ‡b an oral history of England, 1900-1975,
           based on interviews with the inhabitants of Wigton,
           Cumberland / ‡c Melvyn Bragg.
250   1st American ed.
260   New York : ‡b Knopf : ‡b Distributed by Random House, ‡c
           1977, c1976.
300   498 p., [32] p. of plates : ‡b ill., maps ; ‡c 25 cm.

> *[No added entries are provided for the persons interviewed because*
> *they are not named on the chief source of information. The*
> *interviewees number several score.]*

RELATED WORKS

21.28   RELATED WORKS

155   Rule 21.28B1   Related works

> *[A name-title added entry is provided for the work to which this work is*
> *related.]*

Rule 21.30F1   Other related persons of bodies [Publishers]

020   0813902878
100 _   **Bristol, Roger P.**
245 1 0   Supplement to Charles Evans' American bibliography / ‡c by
           Roger P. Bristol.
260   Charlottesville : ‡b Published for the Bibliographical Society of
           America and the Bibliographical Society of the University of
           Virginia [by the] University Press of Virginia, ‡c 1970.
300   xix, 636 p. ; ‡c 29 cm.
500   A chronological list, 1646-1800, of items "not-in-Evans."
504   Includes bibliographical references (p. [xiii]-xvi).
700 _ ‖   **Evans, Charles. ‡t American bibliography.**
710 _ ‖   **Bibliographical Society of America.**
710 _ ‖   **Bibliographical Society of the University of Virginia.**

ADDED ENTRIES

21.30   SPECIFIC RULES
21.30J   Titles

156   Rule 21.30J1   Title added entries

[Although nothing in this rule specifically calls for the provision of the second added entry in this and the next example, the Library of Congress uses it to provide for potential retrieval problems based on filing rules used.]

020	0822940361
100 _	Horne, Bernard S.
245 1 4	The compleat angler, 1653-1967 : ‡b a new bibliography / ‡c by Bernard S. Horne.
246 3 ƀ	**Complete angler, 1653-1967**
260	[Pittsburgh, Pa.] : ‡b Pittsburgh Bibliophiles : ‡b Distributed by the University of Pittsburgh Press, ‡c 1970.
300	xx, 350 p. : ‡b ill., facsims., col. port. ; ‡c 26 cm.
500	"Edition of 500 copies"—Colophon.
500	Includes index.
500	Copy no. 155.

[OCLC guidelines call for the deletion of initial articles at the beginning of a title in Field 246.]

157   Rule 21.30J1   Title added entries

020	0027334503
100 _	Ellis, L. Ethan.
245 1 0	40 million schoolbooks can't be wrong : ‡b myths in American history / ‡c by L. Ethan Ellis.
246 3 ƀ	**Forty million schoolbooks can't be wrong**
260	New York : ‡b Macmillan, ‡c c1975.
300	x, 100 p. : ‡b ill. ; ‡c 24 cm.
504	Includes bibliographical references (p. 95) and index.

158   Rule 21.30J1   Title added entries

020	051752385X (pbk.)
020	0517523841
100 _	Hogarth, Paul.
245 1 0	Paul Hogarth's walking tours of old Philadelphia : ‡b through Independence Square, Society Hill, Southwark, and Washington Square.
246 3 0	**Walking tours of old Philadelphia**
260	Barre, Mass. : ‡b Barre Pub. ; ‡a New York : ‡b Distributed by Crown, ‡c c1976.
500	xiii, 154 p. : ‡b ill. (some col.) ; ‡c 22 cm.
504	Includes bibliographical references (p. 149) and index.

21.30L   Series

159   Rule 21.30L1   Series added entry—Title access
[Field 440 -- Series Statement/Added Entry]
[2nd Indicator 4 -- Number of nonfiling characters present]

020	0674924355
020	0674924363 (pbk.)
100 _	Fairbank, John King.
245 1 4	The United States and China / ‡c John King Fairbank.
250	4th ed.
260	Cambridge, Mass. : ‡b Harvard University Press, ‡c 1979.
300	xxiv, 606 p. : ‡b ill., maps ; ‡c 22 cm.
440 4	**The American foreign policy library**
504	Includes bibliographical references (p. [481]-580) and indexes.

160   Rule 21.30L1   Series added entry—Name-title access

[Field 490 -- Series Statement]
  [1st Indicator 1 -- Series traced differently]
  [Subfield a -- Series statement]
  [Subfield t -- Volume number/sequential designation]
[Field 800 -- Series Added Entry —Personal Name]
  [Subfield a -- Personal name]
  [Subfield t -- Title of a work]

020	0937986178 (trade ed.)
020	093798616X (deluxe ed.)
100 _	King, Stephen.
245 1 4	The waste lands / ‡c Stephen King ; illustrated by Ned Dameron.
250	1st ed.
260	Hampton Falls, N.H. : ‡b Donald M. Grant, ‡c c1991.
300	512 p. : ‡b col. ill. ; ‡c 24 cm.
490 1	The dark tower ; ‡v 3
800 _	King, Stephen. ‡t Dark tower ; ‡v 3.

[Although no rule or guidelines specifically call for the deletion of initial articles at the beginning of a title in Field 800, Subfield t, it is useful to do so because there is no way to control for non-filing characters in this field.]

161   Rule 21.30L1   [No] Series added entry

[Field 490 -- Series Statement]
  [1st Indicator 0 -- Series not traced]

020	0226687872
100 _	Allen, Sue.
245 1 0	Victorian bookbindings : ‡b a pictorial survey / ‡c Sue Allen.
250	Rev. ed.
260	Chicago : ‡b University of Chicago Press, ‡c c1976.
300	v, 53 p. ; ‡c 21 cm. + ‡e 3 microfiches (col. ill.)
490 0	University of Chicago Press text/fiche
500	Reduction ratio varies.
500	Microfiches in pocket.
500	"List of books illustrated:" p. 39-53.

[No series added entry is provided because the series items share only a common physical characteristic, i.e., format.]

CHOICE OF ACCESS POINTS EXERCISE

For each of the catalog examples (numbered 1-118) in Chapter 1 (Rules for Description), create new OCLC/MARC fields, or add indicators to existing fields, where appropriate to indicate the main and added entries that should be made for each record. Also indicate those series for which you do not wish to have an access point, i.e., 490 0. It may be helpful to consult the title pages and title page versos for each of these catalog records for determining whether a person or body is prominently named, etc. You should use the personal names as they appear on the catalog records rather than try to complete the name in a fuller form but do place surname first. Do not add any indicators that do not have a bearing on the use of an access point. For example, do not add Indicator 1 or 2 for Field 100 or Field 700 Below is an illustration of what your answer might look like for the Edwin Drood example. The elements added are in bold. Answers to this exercise appear in Appendix B. Those answers include only access point elements.

020		0192545167
100 _		**Dickens, Charles.**
245	**1 4**	The mystery of Edwin Drood / ‡c by Charles Dickens ; with twelve illustrations by Luke Fildes and two by Charles Collins ; and an introduction by S.C. Roberts.
260		Oxford ; ‡a New York : ‡b Oxford University Press, ‡c 1956.
300		xi, 278 p. : ‡b ill. ; ‡c 19 cm.
440	4	The Oxford illustrated Dickens
500		Prior to 1966 the series had the title: The illustrated Dickens.
700 _ _		**Fildes, Luke.**
700 _ _		**Collins, Charles.**

CHAPTER THREE

Headings for Persons and References

Suggested Lecture Outline

Additions to Distinguish Identical Names

Readings: *Anglo-American Cataloguing Rules.* 2nd ed., 1998 revision
                    Chapter 22, Headings for Persons, p. 379-419;
                    Chapter 26, References, p. 539-549.

NAME AUTHORITY RECORDS

The form of name used for a chosen access point in a catalog may differ from the way that name appears in some of an author's works. Similarly, an author may write using different names. Historically, libraries have provided instructions in their card catalogs directing users from the form of a name not used to the form used and also from one name to another.

Entries in a name authority file record the established form of a name used in the catalog, whether as a main or added entry. They also record references made from unauthorized or unused forms of the name ("see from" references) as well as references from other authorized names for the person or corporate body used in the catalog ("see also from" references).

Card Format. The styles used on name authority records in card format and on reference cards for the public card catalog are a local option. Similarly, the amount of information recorded on the name authority record also may vary from library to library. Some libraries provide extensive information about the works being cataloged when name decisions were made, the form in which the name appeared in that work, as well as other sources of information consulted. To conserve the limited space on the catalog card the name authority records in card format that follow contain only the minimal amount of information sufficient to accomplish the objectives of name authority.

In the following name authority file the authority record reveals that the authorized form of name used is the catalog is "Cross, Amanda, 1926-" and that a "see from" reference has been made from "Heilbrun, Carolyn G., 1926-." The latter is the author's real name and a name under which she has written works, but a name that has not been used as an access point in the library's catalog, i.e., the library owns no books written under the name "Carolyn G. Heilbrun." To assist librarians using the name authority file references that appear in the public catalog are also used in the name authority file to direct the librarian from a name or form of name not used as an access point to the name or form of name that has been used.

Name Authority File

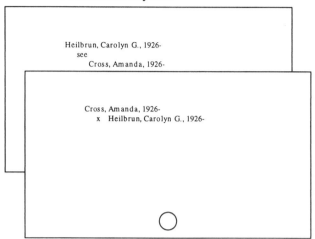

The card catalog below reflects the two works the library has by Amanda Cross as well as the name reference from Heilbrun that the name authority record indicated was made.

Public Catalog

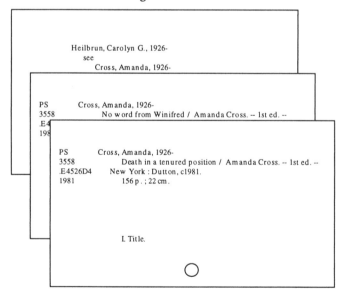

OCLC/MARC Format. As was the case with bibliographic records, there is a MARC format for recording name authority information. Also, as with bibliographic records, OCLC and other bibliographic utilities and vendors display this information in a more readable way than it is presented on the MARC records issued by the Library of Congress. OCLC provides for two different displays of name authority records -- a tagged format very similar to that of the bibliographic record and a mnemonic format that replaces some of the coding with labels. In the following example a modified version of the LC NAF record available on OCLC for Amanda Cross is presented using the mnemonic display. This record has been edited slightly from that created by LC to reflect the local library's holdings mentioned previously.

OCLC/MARC Authority Record

ARN: 601723   REC STAT: REVISED   ENTERED: 19810615

NAME/SUBJECT   ESTABLISHED HEADING   EVALUATED
LC

010	n 81056248 ‡z sh 88000194
040	DLC ‡c DLC ‡d DLC ‡d NOA
005	19970722051103.7
053	PS3558.E4526
100 1	Cross, Amanda, ‡d 1926- [AACR2]
400 1	Heilbrun, Carolyn G., ‡d 1926-
670	Her Poetic justice, 1981, c1970: ‡b t.p. (Amanda Cross) verso t.p. (copr.: Carolyn Heilbrun)
670	Cont. auth., ‡b v. 45 (under Heilbrun, Carolyn G(old): pseud. Amanda Cross; b. 1/13/26)

The definitions for the fields used in this records are:

ARN	[OCLC] Authority Record Number
010	Library of Congress Control Number
040	Cataloging Source
005	Date and Time of Last Transaction
053	LC Classification Number
100	Heading—Personal Name
400	*See from* tracing—Personal Name
500	*See also from tracing*—Personal Name
670	Source data found

Many, but not all, online catalogs provide some form of name reference structure. This may be in the form of electronic links from one name to another -- references that are essentially invisible to the user -- or it may be no more than an electronic version of the "see from" instructions to the catalog user similar to those used in a card catalog. This online catalog is of the latter type where searches under Heilbrun and Cross would result in the following two displays respectively:

Online Catalog "See from" Reference

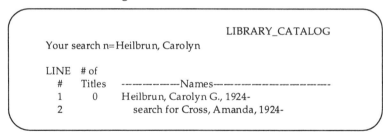

Online Catalog Display

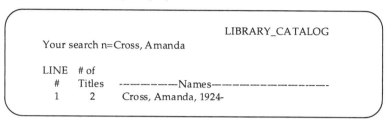

Because this library has books only under the name Cross and none where Heilbrun is used as an access point no "see from" references are needed -- whether a card catalog or an online catalog is used.

There are situations, however where a library has works by an author written under different names. Consider this situation. A library has books by an author with the name "Edward Gorman" and also books written by the same person using the name Daniel Ransom. Additionally, this author has used over time several variations of the name "Edward Gorman." The following name authority records in card format address this situation:

Name Authority File

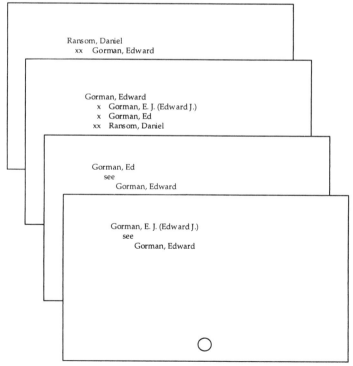

The cards and references in the public catalog that reflect this situation are:

Public Catalog

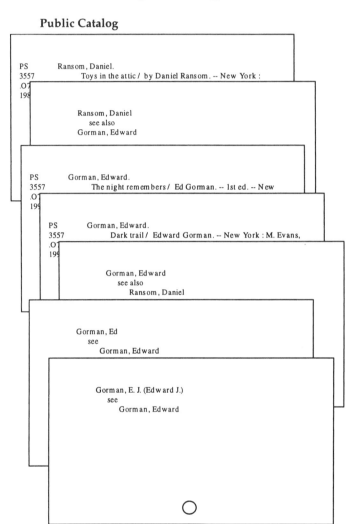

In an online name authority environment, as with cards, separate name authority records would be created for Gorman and Ransom. However, rather than separate references ("see from" and "see also from") existing in the automated authority file, the 4xx and 5xx fields on the authority record are indexed so that a search on the names in those fields will retrieve the authority record. Again in these examples, the OCLC/MARC name authority records have been edited to conform to the local library's holdings.

OCLC/MARC Name Authority Records

ARN: 1255081   REC STAT: REVISED   ENTERED: 19850103

NAME/SUBJECT   ESTABLISHED HEADING   EVALUATED
LC

010	n 84162200
040	DLC ‡c DLC ‡d DLC ‡d OCl
005	19950426054741.4
053	PS3557.O759
100 1	Gorman, Edward [AACR2]
400 1	Gorman, Ed
400 1	Gorman, E. J. ‡q (Edward J.)
500 1	Ransom, Daniel
670	Roughcut, 1985: ‡b CIP t.p. (Edward Gorman) pubr. info. (works in the advertising business; lives in Cedar Rapids, Iowa; first book)
670	Murder on the aisle, c1987: ‡b t.p. (Edward Gorman) jacket (Ed Gorman)
670	The Second Black Lizard anthology ... 1988: ‡b CIP t.p. (Ed Gorman) data sheet (b. 11/29/41)
670	The Marilyn tapes, 1995: ‡b CIP t.p. (E.J. Gorman) pub. info. (lives in Cedar Rapids, Iowa)
670	The serpent's kiss, c1992: ‡b t.p. (Daniel Ransom) copyr. (Ed Gorman)

ARN: 3822557   REC STAT: REVISED   ENTERED: 19950425

NAME/SUBJECT   ESTABLISHED HEADING   EVALUATED
LC

010	no 95020518
040	OCl ‡c OCl
005	19950426054746.2
053	PS3557.O759
100 1	Ransom, Daniel [AACR2]
500 1	Gorman, Edward
670	The serpent's kiss, c1992: ‡b t.p. (Daniel Ransom) copyr. (Ed Gorman)

The online catalog displays for the holdings of this author would be:

Online Catalog Displays

```
                                                    LIBRARY_CATALOG
          Your search n=Gorman, E

          LINE  # of
           #    Titles    ---------Names-----------------
           1     0        Gorman, E. J. (Edward J.)
           2                  Search for Gorman, Edward
           3     0        Gorman, Ed
           4                  Search for Gorman, Edward
           5     2        Gorman, Edward
           6                  for related titles by the author also search
                              for Ransom, Daniel
```

```
                                                    LIBRARY_CATALOG
          Your search n=Ransom, Daniel

          LINE  # of
           #    Titles    ---------Names-----------------
           1     1        Ransom, Daniel
           2                  for related titles by the author also search
                              for Gorman, Edward
```

Regardless of the form that the reference structure takes in the online catalog, the information it uses is derived from a MARC name authority record. The name authority file of the Library of Congress is generally the primary starting point in developing a machine-readable authority file for a library, although libraries may add additional references to that file. It is not uncommon to have some or all of the name authority work done for the library by a service provider or vendor.

N.B. In the examples that follow, an abridged copy of the Library of Congress authority record, available using OCLC, is provided below the catalog record. These name authority records, in the tagged format, reproduce only the variable fields numbered 1xx, 4xx and 5xx. The references indicated are not exhaustive, but rather, are those references likely to have been used in a typical catalog. In some instances the nature of the reference may have been changed from a "see also from" reference to a "see from" reference The authorized form of name is the AACR2R form. All authorized names and references are from the Library of Congress unless indicated as "[non-LC]."

Fields x00, x10, x11, and x51 in name authority record examples in this chapter have the second indicator value blank. This reflects the decision by the Library of Congress to make the second indicator value (Number of Nonfiling Characters) obsolete. Although this practice has been implemented, the value "0" will continue to appear on many LC name authority records, including the source records from which these examples were derived, because LC has no plans to update existing records to conform to the new practice.

Additionally, the Library of Congress plans to discontinue the use of the 1st indicator value "2" for "Multiple Surname" in late 1999. This will also change the wording for the indicator value "1" that has been "Single Surname." When implemented both types of surnames will be coded as "1" with the wording changed to "Surname." This change will have an impact on OCLC/MARC fields 100, 700, and 800 for main and non-subject added entries and name authority records. It also will effect Field 600 for personal name subject headings. This revised use of the 1st indicator has been implemented in all examples in this chapter, its associated appendix and Chapter 8 and its appendix.

Name authority records have been provided <u>only</u> for the personal name(s) that illustrate the rule being presented. Although name authority records would be made for other personal name access points, they are not presented here for reasons of space. Similarly, no name authority information for corporate name or uniform titles is provided in this chapter. They are addressed in Chapters 4 and 5 respectively of this text.

In this chapter the indication of the meanings of MARC fields, indicators and subfields are to the bibliographic record <u>not</u> the name authority record.

CHOICE OF NAME

22.1   GENERAL RULE

162   Rule 22.1A/22.1B   Name by which a person is commonly known
[Field 100 -- Main Entry—Personal Name]

[1st Indicator 1 -- Surname[*]]
[Subfield a -- Personal name]

[The use of dates in Subfield d is addressed by Example 194.]

020	0395377226
100 1	**Carter, Jimmy,** ‡d 1924-
245 1 4	The blood of Abraham / ‡c Jimmy Carter.
260	Boston : ‡b Houghton Mifflin, ‡c 1985.
300	xx, 257 p., [6] p. of plates : ‡b maps ; ‡c 24 cm.
500	Includes index.

100	1	Carter, Jimmy, ‡d 1924-
400	1	Carter, James Earl, ‡d 1924-
510	1	Georgia. ‡b Governor (1971-1975 : Carter)
510	1	United States. ‡b President (1977-1981 : Carter)

[The use of the "510" references assumes the library already has entries under those names in the catalog.]

---

[*] See the N.B. comment at the beginning of this chapter for the change in OCLC/MARC coding practice for the first indicator which changes the wording for value "1" from "Single surname" to "Surname."

163   Rule 22.1A/22.1B   Name by which a person is commonly
known

---

020   038524942X
100 1   **Neuharth, Allen.**
245 1 0   Confessions of an S.O.B. / ‡c Al Neuharth.
250   1st ed.
260   New York : ‡b Doubleday, ‡c 1989.
300   372 p. ; ‡c 24 cm.
500   Includes index.

100 1	Neuharth, Allen
400 1	Neuharth, Al

[LC has determined that the name commonly used is Allen Neuharth.]

22.1D   Diacritical marks and hyphens

164   Rule 22.1D1   Diacritical marks

---

100 1   **König, Paul.**
245 1 0   Voyage of the Deutschland : ‡b the first merchant submarine /
‡c by Paul König.
260   New York : ‡b Hearst's International Library Co., ‡c 1916.
300   xii, 247 p., [29] p. of plates : ‡b ill. ; ‡c 20 cm.

[The author's name on cover and spine: Paul Koenig.]

100 1	König, Paul [non-LC]
400 1	Koenig, Paul [non-LC]

165   Rule 22.1D2   Hyphens*

---

100 1   **Lane-Claypon, Janet E.**
245 1 4   The child welfare movement / ‡c by Janet E. Lane-Claypon.
260   London : ‡b G. Bell, ‡c 1920.
300   xi, 341 p. : ‡b maps ; ‡c 19 cm.
504   Includes bibliographical references and index.

100 1	Lane-Claypon, Janet E.
400 1	Claypon, Janet E. Lane-

22.2   CHOICE AMONG DIFFERENT NAMES
22.2B   Pseudonyms

166   Rule 22.2B1   One pseudonym

---

020   0394530152
100 1   **Le Carré, John**, ‡d 1931-
245 1 0   Little drummer girl / ‡c John Le Carré.
250   1st ed.
260   New York : ‡b Knopf, ‡c 1983.
300   429 p. ; ‡c 24 cm.

100 1	Le Carré, John, ‡d 1931-
400 1	Cornwell, David John Moore, ‡d 1931-
400 1	LeCarré, John, ‡d 1931-
400 1	Carré, John Le, ‡d 1931-

[The author's real name is David John Moore Cornwell.]

---

* See the N.B. comment at the beginning of this chapter for the change in OCLC/MARC coding practice for the first indicator when the name is a multiple surname. This change also changed the wording for the first indicator, value "1" from Single surname" to "Surname."

167   Rule 22.2B2   **Separate bibliographic entities**

Rule 22.2B3   **Contemporary author**

020   0316776467
100 1   **Scoppettone, Sandra.**
245 1 0   Everything you have is mine / ‡c Sandra Scoppettone.
250   1st ed.
260   Boston : ‡b Little, Brown, ‡c c1991.
300   261 p. ; ‡c 25 cm.

| 100 1 | Scoppettone, Sandra |
| 500 1 | Early, Jack |

[Sandra Scoppettone has published 8 novels under her own name and 3 under the pseud. Jack Early.]

[The use of the "500" reference assumes the catalog has entries under Jack Early.]

168   Rule 22.2B2   **Separate bibliographic entities**

Rule 22.2B3   **Contemporary author**

020   053109796X
100 1   **Early, Jack.**
245 1 0   Razzamatazz : ‡b a novel / ‡c by Jack Early.
260   New York : ‡b F. Watts, ‡c 1985.
300   331 p. ; ‡c 24 cm.

| 100 1 | Early, Jack |
| 500 1 | Scoppettone, Sandra |

22.3 CHOICE AMONG DIFFERENT FORMS OF THE SAME NAME
22.3A Fullness

169 Rule 22.3A1 **Variation in fullness of name -- Use of the form commonly found**

```
100  1    Shaw, Bernard, ‡d 1856-1950.
245  1 0  Everybody's political what's what? / ‡c by Bernard Shaw.
260       New York : ‡b Dodd, Mead, ‡c 1944.
300       viii, 380 p. : ‡b port. ; ‡c 21 cm.
500       Includes index.
```

100 1	Shaw, Bernard, ‡d 1856-1950
400 1	Shaw, George Bernard, ‡d 1856-1950 [OLD CATALOG HEADING]
400 1	Shaw, G. B. ‡q (George Bernard), ‡d 1856-1950

[Full name: George Bernard Shaw]

ENTRY ELEMENT

22.5 ENTRY UNDER SURNAME
22.5C Compound surnames

170 Rule 22.5C2 **Preferred or established form known**

```
100  1    Lloyd George, David, ‡d 1863-1945.
245  1 0  Coal and power : ‡b the report of an enquiry presided over by
          the Right Hon. D. Lloyd George, O.M., M.P.
260       London : ‡b Hodder and Stoughton, ‡c [1924]
300       xiv, 139 p., [16] p. of plates : ‡b ill. ; ‡c 18 cm.
```

100 1	Lloyd George, David, ‡d 1863-1945
400 2	Lloyd George, David Lloyd George, ‡c 1st Earl, ‡d 1863-1945 OLD CATALOG HEADING]
400 1	George, David Lloyd, ‡d 1863-1945

171   Rule 22.5C3   Hyphenated surnames

....

[Field 700 -- Added Entry—Personal Name]
[1st Indicator 1 -- Surname]
[Subfield a -- Personal name]

....

020   0374190224
100 1   **Panter-Downes, Mollie,** ‡d 1906-
245 1 0   London war notes, 1939-1945 / ‡c Mollie Panter-Downes ;
             edited by William Shawn.
260   New York : ‡b Farrar, Strauss and Giroux, ‡c c1971.
300   378 p., [1] leaf of plates : ‡b ill. ; ‡c 25 cm.
500   "All of the material in this book appeared originally in the New
             Yorker"—T.p. verso.
700 1 ⌀   Shawn, William.

100	1	Panter-Downes, Mollie, ‡d 1906-
400	1	Downes, Mollie, Panter-, ‡d 1906- [non-LC]

172   Rule 22.5C5   Other compound surnames. Married women whose
surname consists of her surname before marriage
and her husband's surname

....

100 1   **Rinehart, Mary Roberts,** ‡d 1876-1958.
245 1 4   The swimming pool / ‡c Mary Roberts Rinehart.
260   New York : ‡b Rinehart, ‡c c1952.
300   312 p. ; ‡c 22 cm.

100	1	Rinehart, Mary Roberts, ‡d 1876-1958

*[No reference is provided for Mary Roberts. She did not write
under that name.]*

173   Rule 22.5C6   Nature of surname uncertain

020	0891630287
100 1	**Post, Melville Davisson, ‡d 1871-1930.**
245 1 4	The complete Uncle Abner / ‡c Melville Davisson Post ; with introduction and annotated bibliography by Allen J. Hubin ; illustrations by Darrel Millsap.
260	Del Mar, CA : ‡b Publication of University Extension, University of California, San Diego in cooperation with Publisher's Inc., ‡c c1977.
300	xvi, 423 p. : ‡b ill. ; ‡c 21 cm.
440 4	The mystery library ; ‡v 4
504	Includes bibliographical references (p. 399-410).

> 100 1   Post, Melville Davisson, ‡d 1871-1930
>
> *[No reference is required for Davisson Post — it is not treated as a compound surname in reference sources]*

174   Rule 22.5C8   Omission of words indicating relationship following surnames

[The addition of parenthetical qualifiers (Subfield q) is addressed by Example 195.]

100 1	**Schlesinger, Arthur M. ‡q (Arthur Meier), ‡d 1917-**
245 1 2	A thousand days : ‡b John F. Kennedy in the White House / ‡c Arthur M. Schlesinger, Jr.
260	Boston : ‡b Houghton Mifflin, ‡c 1965.
300	xiv, 1087 p. ; ‡c 22 cm.
504	Includes bibliographical references and index.

> 100 1   Schlesinger, Arthur M. ‡q (Arthur Meier), ‡d 1917- [non-LC]
> 400 1   Schlesinger, Arthur, ‡d 1917-
> 400 1   Schlesinger, Arthur Meier, ‡d 1917- [COMPATIBLE]
>
> *[The "100" heading conforms to AACR2R. The LC NAF uses this heading as a "400" and instead uses the "COMPATIBLE" heading below as the authorized form of name.]*

22.5D   Surnames with separately written prefixes

175   Rule 22.5D1   Articles and prepositions -- English

....

100 1   **De La Roche, Mazo,** ‡d 1879-1961.
245 1 4 The building of Jalna / ‡c by Mazo De La Roche.
250   Whiteoak ed.
260   Boston : ‡b Little, Brown, ‡c 1944.
300   366 p. ; ‡c 19 cm.
500   "An Atlantic Monthly Press book."

100	1	De la Roche, Mazo, ‡d 1879-1961
400	1	La Roche, Mazo de, ‡d 1879-1961
400	1	Roche, Mazo de la, ‡d 1879-1961

[This author wrote in English.]

176   Rule 22.5D1   Articles and prepositions -- English

....

100 1   **Von Laue, Theodore H.** ‡q (Theodore Hermann)
245 1 4 The global city : ‡b freedom, power, and necessity in the age of
           world revolutions / ‡c Theodore H. Von Laue.
250   1st ed.
260   Philadelphia : ‡b Lippincott, ‡c c1969.
300   xv, 302 p. ; ‡c 22 cm.
504   Includes bibliographical references and index.

100	1	Von Laue, Theodore H. ‡q (Theodore Hermann)
400	1	Von Laue, Theodore Hermann [OLD CATALOG HEADING]
400	1	Laue, Theodore H. von ‡q (Theodore Hermann)

[This author writes in English.]

177   Rule 22.5D1   **Articles and prepositions -- German**

020	0312004222
100 1	**Beyme, Klaus von.**
245 1 0	America as a model : ‡b the impact of American democracy in the world / ‡c Klaus von Beyme.
260	New York : ‡b St. Martin's Press, ‡c 1987.
300	137 p. ; ‡c 23 cm.
504	Includes bibliographical references and index.

100 1	Beyme, Klaus von
400 1	Von Beyme, Klaus

[Although this particular work is in English, most of the author's works are in German.]

178   Rule 22.5D1   **Articles and prepositions -- English**

020	0385033273 (prebound)
020	0385033176 (trade)
100 1	**De Angeli, Marguerite**, ‡d 1889-
245 1 4	The lion in the box / ‡c Marguerite de Angeli.
260	Garden City, N.Y. : ‡b Doubleday, ‡c c1975.
300	x, 63 p. : ‡b ill. ; ‡c 24 cm.
520 ƀ	Retells the events of a special Christmas for a poor family in New York City at the turn of the century.

100 1	De Angeli, Marguerite, ‡d 1889-
400 1	Angeli, Marguerite De, ‡d 1889-
400 1	De Angeli, Marguerite Lofft, ‡d 1889- [OLD CATALOG HEADING]

[This author wrote in English.]

179   Rule 22.5D1   Articles and prepositions -- French

....

020	0671211188
100 1	**Gaulle, Charles de, ‡d 1890-1970.**
245 1 0	Memoirs of hope : ‡b renewal and endeavor / ‡c Charles de Gaulle ; translated by Terence Kilmartin.
260	New York : ‡b Simon and Schuster, ‡c c1971.
300	392 p., [1] leaf of plates : ‡b ill. ; ‡c 23 cm.
500	First published in France under the title: Mémoires d'espoir.
500	Includes index.

100	1	Gaulle, Charles de, ‡d 1890-1970
400	1	De Gaulle, Charles, ‡d 1890-1970
400	1	Gaulle, Charles de, ‡c Pres. France, ‡d 1890-1970 [OLD CATALOG HEADING]
510	1	France. ‡b President (1959-1969 : De Gaulle)

[Although this particular work is in English, de Gaulle's works were written in French.]

[The use of the "510" reference assumes the library already has an entry under that name in the catalog.]

180   Rule 22.5D1   Articles and prepositions -- French (contraction of an article and a preposition)

....

100 1	**Des Granges, Charles Marc, ‡d 1861-**
245 1 0	Histoire de la civilisation française des origines à nos jours / ‡c par Ch.-M des Granges et Oliver Towles.
260	New York : ‡b Prentice-Hall, ‡c c1933.
300	xxi, 473 p., [1] leaf of plates : ‡b ill., maps ; ‡c 21 cm.
700 1 ᛒ	Towles, Oliver.

100	1	Des Granges, Charles Marc, ‡d 1861- [COMPATIBLE]
400	1	Granges, Charles Marc Des, ‡d 1861-

[This author wrote in French.]

22.6   ENTRY UNDER TITLE OF NOBILITY
22.6A   General rule

181   Rule 22.6A1   Title of nobility

[Field 100 -- Main Entry—Personal Name]
[Subfield c -- Titles and other words associated with a name.]

020		0836980883
100	**1**	**Mersey, Charles Clive Bigham, ‡c Viscount, ‡d 1872-1956.**
245	1 4	The viceroys and governors-general of India, 1757-1947 / ‡c by Viscount Mersey (Clive Bigham Mersey).
260		Freeport, N.Y. : ‡b Books for Libraries Press, ‡c 1971.
300		xi, 179 p., [34] leaves of plates : ‡b ill., map, ports. ; ‡c 23 cm.
440	0	Bibliography index reprint series
500		Originally published: London : J. Murray, 1949.
500		Includes index.

100	1	Mersey, Charles Clive Bigham, ‡c Viscount, ‡d 1872-1956
400	1	Mersey, Clive Bigham, ‡c 2d Viscount, ‡d 1872-1956 [OLD CATALOG HEADING]
400	1	Bigham, Clive, ‡d 1872-1956
400	1	Bigham, Charles Clive, ‡c Viscount Mersey, ‡d 1872-1956

22.6B   Special rules

182 **Rule 22.6B3   Disclaimer of a title**

Rule 22.2C   Change of name -- Latest name

....

100 1   Webb, Sidney, ‡d 1859-1947.
245 1 4   The decay of capitalist civilization / ‡c by Sidney and Beatrice
           Webb.
260   New York : ‡b Harcourt, Brace, ‡c c1923.
300   xvii, 242 p. ; ‡c 20 cm.
504   Includes bibliographical references and index.
700 1 ⃞ Webb, Beatrice, ‡d 1858-1943.

100	1	Webb, Sidney, ‡d 1859-1947
400	1	Passfield, Sidney James Webb, ‡c Baron, ‡d 1859-1947 [OLD CATALOG HEADING]

[He renounced the title Baron Passfield.]

100	1	Webb, Beatrice, ‡d 1858-1943 [non-LC]
400	1	Webb, Beatrice Potter, ‡d 1858-1943 [COMPATIBLE]
400	1	Passfield, Beatrice Potter Webb, ‡c Baroness, ‡d 1858-1943
400	1	Webb, Sidney, ‡c Mrs., ‡d 1858-1943
400	1	Potter, Beatrice, ‡d 1858-1943
400	1	Potter, Martha Beatrice, ‡d 1858-1943

[She renounced the title Baroness Passfield.]

[The "100" heading conforms to AACR2R. The LC NAF uses this heading as a "400" and instead uses the "COMPATIBLE" heading as the authorized form of name.]

22.8 ENTRY UNDER GIVEN NAME, ETC.

22.8A General rule

183 Rule 22.8A1 Name that does not include a surname

[Field 100 -- Main Entry—Personal Name]
[1st Indicator 0 -- Forename]

100 0		**Leonardo, ‡c da Vinci, ‡d** 1452-1519.
245 1 4		The notebooks of Leonardo da Vinci / ‡c arranged, rendered into English and introduced by Edward MacCurdy.
260		New York : ‡b G. Braziller, ‡c 1954.
300		1247 p., [8] leaves of plates : ‡b ill. ; ‡c 22 cm.
500		Originally published: Reynal & Hitchcock, 1939.
504		Includes bibliographical references (p. 1163-1173) and indexes.
700 1 ȸ		McCurdy, Edward, ‡d b. 1871.

100 0	Leonardo, ‡c da Vinci, ‡d 1452-1519
400 1	Vinci, Leonardo da, ‡d 1452-1519
400 0	Leonardo da Vinci, ‡d 1452-1519 [OLD CATALOG HEADING]
400 1	Da Vinci, Leonardo, ‡d 1452-1519

22.10 ENTRY UNDER INITIALS, LETTERS, OR NUMERALS

184 Rule 22.10A Name consists of an initial

100 0	**M.**
245 1 4	The sensuous man : ‡b the first how-to book for the man who wants to be a great lover / ‡c by M.
260	New York, N.Y. : ‡b Lyle Stuart, ‡c c1971.
300	253 p. ; ‡c 21 cm.

100 0	M. [non-LC]

22.11   ENTRY UNDER PHRASE

185   Rule 22.11A   Name is a phrase or appellation

```
020      0870001892
100  0   Professor X.
245  1 0 This beats working for a living : ‡b the dark secrets of a college
         professor / ‡c by Professor X.
260      New Rochelle, N.Y. : ‡b Arlington House, ‡c c1973.
300      160 p. ; ‡c 22 cm.
```

```
100  0    Professor X.
400  0    X, ‡c professor
```

186   Rule 22.11D   Phrase naming another work

```
020      0809129728 (pbk.)
020      0809104040
100  0   Author of The cloud of unknowing.
245  1 4 The pursuit of wisdom and other works / ‡c by the author of
         The cloud of unknowing ; translated, edited, and annotated by
         James A. Walsh ; preface by George A. Maloney.
260      New York : ‡b Paulist Press, ‡c c1988.
300      ix, 325 p. ; ‡c 23 cm.
440    0 Classics of western spirituality
500      Writings of a 14th century mystic.
504      Includes bibliographical references (p. 314-319) and index.
700  1 ƀ Walsh, James, ‡d 1920-
```

```
100  0    Author of The cloud of unknowing
400  2    Cloud of unknowing, Author of The
```

187   Rule 22.11D   Person is commonly identified by a real name or another name, but was identified on the chief source of information by a phrase including the title of another work

100 1   Burney, Fanny, ‡d 1752-1840
245 1 0   Camilla, or, A picture of youth / ‡c by the authoress of Evelina and Cecilia.
246 3 0   Camilla
246 3 0   Picture of youth
260   Philadelphia : ‡b Printed by Ormrod & Conrad, ‡c 1797.
300   5 v. in 3 ; ‡c 18 cm.
500   By Fanny Burney.

100 1	Burney, Fanny, ‡d 1752-1840.	
400 0	Authoress of Evelina and Cecilia [non-LC]	
400 0	Evelina and Cecilia, Authoress of [non-LC]	
400 1	Burney, Frances, ‡d 1752-1840	
400 1	Arblay, Frances Burney d', ‡d 1752-1840 [OLD CATALOG HEADING]	
400 1	Arblay, ‡c Madame d', ‡d 1752-1840	
400 1	D'Arblay, ‡c Madame, ‡d 1752-1840	
400 1	D'Arblay, Frances Burney, ‡d 1752-1840	

General

22.12   TITLES OF NOBILITY AND TERMS OF HONOUR
22.12B   British terms of honour

188   Rule 22.12B1   British terms of honor

020	0198124449
100 1	**Montagu, Mary Wortley, ‡c Lady, ‡d 1689-1762.**
245 1 0	Essays and poems ; and, Simplicity : ‡b a comedy / ‡c Lady Mary Wortley Montagu ; edited by Robert Halsband and Isobel Grundy.
246 3 0	Essays and poems
246 3 0	Simplicity
260	Oxford : ‡b Clarendon Press, ‡c 1977.
300	viii, 412 p., [7] p. of plates : ‡b ill. ; ‡c 23 cm.
504	Includes bibliographical references and indexes.
700 1 ⠀	Halsband, Robert, ‡d 1914-
700 1 ⠀	Grundy, Isobel.

100	1	Montagu, Mary Wortley, ‡c Lady, ‡d 1689-1762
400	1	Montagu, Mary Pierrepont Wortley, ‡c Lady, ‡d 1689-1762 [OLD CATALOG HEADING]

> *[AACR2R calls for the title "Lady" to be placed as follows: Montagu, Lady Mary Wortley, 1689-1762. The MARC format requires a change in the location to: Montagu, Mary Wortley, Lady, 1689-1762. LC has coded that latter heading as "AACR2." and it is used in this example.]*

189   Rule 22.12B1   British term of honor does not commonly appear with the name in the person's works or in reference sources

100 1	**Fraser, Antonia, ‡d 1932-**
245 1 0	Mary, Queen of Scots / ‡c by Antonia Fraser.
250	1st American ed.
260	New York : ‡b Delacorte Press, ‡c c1969.
300	xv, 613 p., [24] p. of plates : ‡b ill., geneal. tables ; ‡c 25 cm.
504	Includes bibliographical references (p. [585]-594) and index.

100	1	Fraser, Antonia, ‡d 1932-
400	1	Fraser, Antonia Pakenham, ‡c Lady, ‡d 1932- [OLD CATALOG HEADING]

> *[Born: Lady Antonia Pakenham Fraser]*

22.14   SPIRITS

190   Rule 22.14A   Spirits

[See also Rule 21.26.]

....

020	0130185159
020	0130185647 (pbk.)
100 1	**James, William, ‡d 1842-1910 ‡c (Spirit)**
245 1 4	The afterdeath journal of an American philosopher : ‡b the world view of William James / ‡c Jane Roberts.
260	Englewood Cliffs, N.J. : ‡b Prentice-Hall, ‡c c1978.
300	241 p. ; ‡c 24 cm.
500	Includes index.
700 1 ⌀	Roberts, Jane, ‡d 1929-

> | 100 1 | James, William, ‡d 1842-1910 ‡c (Spirit) [non-LC] |
> |---|---|
>
> *This authority record is based on the LC name authority record for him as a person.*

22.15   ADDITIONS TO NAMES ENTERED UNDER SURNAME

191   Rule 22.15A   Surname and a word or phrase associated with the name

....

020	0394929209 (lib. bdg.)
020	0394829204
100 1	**Seuss, ‡c Dr.**
245 1 0	There's a wocket in my pocket! / ‡c by Dr. Seuss.
260	New York : ‡b Beginner Books, ‡c c1974.
300	[34] p. : ‡b col. ill. ; ‡c 24 cm.
440 2	A bright & early book
520 ⌀	A household of unusual creatures help beginning readers recognize common household words.

> | 100 1 | Seuss, ‡c Dr. |
> |---|---|
> | 400 1 | Seuss, ‡c Doctor [non-LC] |
> | 400 0 | Dr. Seuss [non-LC] |
> | 400 0 | Doctor Seuss [non-LC] |
> | 500 1 | Geisel, Theodor Seuss, ‡d 1904- |
>
> *[His real name is Theodor Seuss Geisel]*
>
> *[The use of the "500" reference assumes the catalog has entries under Theodor Seuss Geisel.]*

22.15B   Terms of address of married women

192   Rule 22.15B1   Term of address of married women

```
020      0192817523 (pbk.)
100 1    Ward, Humphry, ‡c Mrs., ‡d 1851-1920.
245 1 0  Robert Elsmere / ‡c Mrs. Humphry Ward ; edited with an
         introduction by Rosemary Ashton.
260      Oxford ; ‡a New York : ‡b Oxford University Press, ‡c 1987.
300      xxiv, 585 p. ; ‡c 19 cm.
440   4  The world's classics
504      Includes bibliographical references (p. [xix]).
700 1 ⶰ  Ashton, Rosemary, ‡d 1947-
```

```
100 1    Ward, Humphry, ‡c Mrs., ‡d 1851-1920
         [COMPATIBLE]
400 1    Ward, Mary Augusta Arnold, ‡d 1851-1920 [OLD
         CATALOG HEADING]
400 1    Arnold, Mary Augusta, ‡d 1851-1920
```

[AACR2R calls for "Mrs." to be placed as follows: Ward, Mrs. Humphry, 1851-1920. The MARC format requires a change in its location to: Ward, Humphry, Mrs., 1851-1920. In this example the "Compatible" headings has been used.]

22.16   ADDITIONS TO NAMES ENTERED UNDER GIVEN NAME, ETC.
22.16A   Royalty

193 Rule 22.16A1 Person with the highest royal status within a state or people

020		0306701553
100 0		**George ‡b III, ‡c King of Great Britain, ‡d 1738-1820.**
245 1 4		The correspondence of King George the Third with Lord North, 1768 to 1783 / ‡c edited with an introduction and notes by W. Bodham Donne.
246 1 7		George the Third's Letters to Lord North
260		New York : ‡b Da Capo Press, ‡c 1971.
300		2 v. (lcii, 307, 452) ; ‡c 24 cm.
440	4	The Era of the American Revolution
500		"A Da Capo Press reprint edition"—T.p. verso.
500		Reprint. Originally published: London : J. Murray, 1867.
504		Includes bibliographical references.
700 1 ⱈ		North, Frederick, ‡c Lord, ‡d 1732-1792.
700 1 ⱈ		Donne, William Bodham, ‡d 1807-1882.

100 0	George ‡b III, ‡c King of Great Britain, ‡d 1738-1820
410 1	Great Britain. ‡b Sovereigns, etc., 1760-1820 (George III) [OLD CATALOG HEADING]
510 1	Great Britain. ‡b Sovereign (1760-1820 : George III)

[The use of the "510" reference assumes the library already has an entry under that name in the catalog.]

Additions to Distinguish Identical Names

22.17   DATES

194   Rule 22.17A   Addition of a person's dates
[Field 100 -- Main Entry—Personal Name]
[Subfield d -- Dates associated with a name.]

[Field 700 -- Added Entry—Personal Name]
[Subfield d -- Dates associated with a name.]

020	0933852703
020	093385269X (invalid)
100 1	Mack, William P., ‡**d 1915-**
245 1 0	South to Java : ‡b a novel / ‡c by William P. Mack and William P. Mack, Jr.
260	Baltimore, Md. : ‡b Nautical & Aviation Pub. Co. of America, ‡c c1987.
300	460 p. ; ‡c 24 cm.
700 1 ƀ	Mack, William P., ‡**d 1943-**

```
100  1      Mack, William P., ‡d 1915-
```

```
100  1      Mack, William P., ‡d 1943-
```

22.17   DATES

Date more specific than the year alone

    100 1   Johnson, Cecil

    100 1   Johnson, Cecil, ‡d 1900 Jan. 19-

    100 1   Johnson, Cecil, ‡d 1900 Mar. 2-

    100 1   Johnson, Cecil, ‡d 1924-

One date uncertain

    100 1   Hill, John, ‡d 1714?-1775.

    100 1   Fuller, William, ‡d 1670-1717?

    100 1   Sanford, John F. A., ‡d 1806 or 7-1857.

    100 1   Read, George, ‡d 1816-1851 or 2.

Only one date known and likely to be known

    100 1   Simpson, Joseph W. ‡q (Joseph William), ‡d b. 1878.

    100 1   Middleton, Thomas, ‡d d. 1627.

    100 1   Campbell, William, ‡d b. 1677 or 8.

"ca."

    100 1   Ford, John, ‡d 1586-ca. 1640.

    100 1   O'Heffernan, Liam, ‡d ca. 1715-1802 or 3.

    100 1   Hall, Ellias, ‡d ca. 1780-ca. 1861.

    100 1   Hill, Jamie, ‡d b. ca. 1813.

No date certain

    100 1   Anderson, Edward, ‡d 18th cent.

"fl."

    100 1   Jones, Thomas, ‡d fl. 1756.

    100 1   Nelson, Henry, ‡d fl. 1725-1734.

22.18 FULLER FORMS

195   Rule 22.18A   **Fuller form of a person's name is known and the heading does not include all of the fuller form**

[Field 100 -- Main Entry—Personal Name]
[Subfield q -- Fuller form of name.]

---

100 1   **Lewis, C. S. ‡q (Clive Staples), ‡d 1898-1963.**
245 1 0   That hideous strength : ‡b a modern fairy-tale for grown-ups / ‡c by C.S. Lewis.
260   New York : ‡b Macmillan, ‡c 1946.
300   viii, 459 p. ; ‡c 21 cm.

> 100 1   Lewis, C. S. ‡q (Clive Staples), ‡d 1898-1963
> 400 1   Lewis, Clive Staples, ‡d 1898-1963 [OLD CATALOG HEADING]
> 400 1   Lewis, Jack, ‡d 1898-1963
> 400 1   Hamilton, Clive, ‡d 1898-1963
> 400 1   Clerk, N. W., ‡d 1898-1963

> *[The last three "400" references would be made only if it is a library's policy to make references from other names used by a person even if those names are not represented in the catalog.]*

---

196   Rule 22.18A   **Fuller form of a person's name is known and the heading does not include all of the fuller form**

---

020   0385152329
100 1   **Buckley, William F. ‡q (William Frank), ‡d 1925-**
245 1 0   Marco Polo, if you can / ‡c William F. Buckley, Jr.
250   1st ed.
260   Garden City, N.Y. : ‡b Doubleday, ‡c 1982.
300   233 p. ; ‡c 21 cm.

> 100 1   Buckley, William F. ‡q (William Frank), ‡d 1925-
> 400 1   Buckley, William Frank, ‡d 1925- [OLD CATALOG HEADING]

22.19   **DISTINGUISHING TERMS**
22.19B   **Names in which the entry element is a surname**

       100 1   Smith, William, ‡c army officer.

       100 1   Smith, William, ‡c barrister at law.

       100 1   Smith, William, ‡c blues musician.

       100 1   Smith, William, ‡c freemason.

       100 1   Smith, William, ‡c Gent.

       100 1   Smith, William, ‡c M.D.

       100 1   Smith, William, ‡c managing director.

       100 1   Smith, William, ‡c mariner.

       100 1   Smith, William, ‡c merchant in Paisley.

       100 1   Smith, William, ‡c of Besthorp in Nottinghamshire.

       100 1   Smith, William, ‡c of Park Street, Westminster.

       100 1   Smith, William, ‡c postmaster in Edinburgh.

       100 1   Smith, William, ‡c proctor in the High Court of Admiralty.

       100 1   Smith, William, ‡c soldier.

       100 1   Smith, William, ‡c Vice Admiral.

       100 1   Smith, William, ‡c volunteer.

FORM OF HEADINGS AND REFERENCES EXERCISE
Part A -- Persons

     As you may recall, the access points for the examples in Chapter 2 were not written in their correct form. For each of these examples, (numbered 119-161) use the Library of Congress Authority File to identify the correct AACR2 form of name for the access points for <u>names of persons</u> only. Examples 124-126 and 128-129 do not have any personal name access points. For each personal name make "see from" references for references that you believe would be useful in a typical academic library catalog. Assume you have other works by that individual if those works were written under a different name. If the authorized form of heading in the LC NAF is not in AACR2 form you will need to establish the correct heading using AACR2 and reference sources including the OCLC WorldCat. You will also need to establish appropriate references. The answers to this exercise appear in Appendix C - Part A.

CHAPTER FOUR

Headings for Corporate Bodies and References

Suggested Lecture Outline

Rules

24.1 General Rule

24.2 Variant Names. General Rules

24.3 Variant Names. Special Rules

ADDITIONS, OMISSIONS, AND MODIFICATIONS

24.4 Additions

24.5 Omissions

24.7 Conferences, Congresses, Meetings, etc.

24.10 Local Churches, etc.

SUBORDINATE AND RELATED BODIES

24.12 General Rule

24.13 Subordinate and Related Bodies Entered Subordinately

24.14 Direct or Indirect Subheading

GOVERNMENT BODIES AND OFFICIALS

24.17 General Rule

24.18 Government Agencies Entered Subordinately

24.19 Direct or Indirect Subheading

Special Rules

24.20   Government Officials

24.21   Legislative Bodies

24.24   Armed Forces

Readings: *Anglo-American Cataloguing Rules.* 2nd ed., 1998 revision.
              Chapter 24, Corporate Bodies, p. 439-479;
              Chapter 26, References, p. 549-557.

*N.B. The name authority practice used in the chapter for headings for persons has also been
used in this chapter. This includes having the second indicator value blank rather than "0" in
name authority record Fields x00, x10, x11, and x51 in order to correspond with current LC
policy. Similarly, the discontinuation of the use of 1st indicator value "2" for multiple
surnames has also been implemented. This may effect Fields 100, 700, and 800 in some
examples in this chapter. Additionally, in order to conserve space, name authority records
have been provided only for corporate bodies that illustrate the rule being presented. For the
same reason, if the corporate name element being illustrated by a rule is not the lead filing
element, an assumption has been made that all appropriate name authority work for the lead
element has already been done and thus no authority record is presented here for that element.*

24.1   GENERAL RULE

197   **Rule 24.1A   Name by which the corporate body is commonly
                        identified**

[Field 710 -- Added Entry—Corporate Name]
[1st Indicator 2 -- Name in direct order]
[Subfield a -- Corporate name or jurisdiction name as entry element]

245 0 0   Pocket pal : ‡b a graphic arts production handbook.
250   12th ed.
260   New York : ‡b International Paper Co., ‡c 1979.
300   204 p. : ‡b ill. (some col.) ; ‡c 19 cm.
500   Includes glossary.
710 2 ƅ   International Paper Company.

110 2	International Paper Company
410 2	International Paper (Firm)

**198   Rule 24.1A   Name by which the corporate body is commonly
                      identified**

[Field 110 -- Main Entry—Corporate Name]
[1st Indicator 2 -- Name in direct order]
[Subfield a -- Corporate name or jurisdiction name as entry element]

020	0824208595 (lib. bdg. : alk. paper)
245 0 0	Public library catalog : ‡b guide to reference books and adult nonfiction / ‡c edited by Juliette Yaakov.
250	10th ed.
260	New York : ‡b H. W. Wilson, ‡c 1994.
300	vii, 1325 p. ; ‡c 26 cm.
440 0	Standard catalog series
500	Kept up-to-date between editions with annual supplements.
500	Companion volume to H. W. Wilson Company's Fiction catalog.
500	Includes index.
700 1	Yaakov, Juliette.
710 2	**H.W. Wilson Company.**

110 2	H.W. Wilson Company
410 0	Wilson, H. W., firm, publishers [OLD CATALOG HEADING]
410 0	Wilson (H.W.) Company
410 2	Wilson Company

24.5   OMISSIONS
24.5A   Initial articles

199   Rule 24.5A1   Omission of an initial article

---

245 0 4	The MacArthur Fellows Program : ‡b the first decade, 1981-1991.
260	Chicago : ‡b John D. and Catherine T. MacArthur Foundation, ‡c c1993.
300	203 p. ; ‡c 26 cm.
500	"September 1993"--T.p. verso.
710 2 ƀ	**John D. and Catherine T. MacArthur Foundation.**

110 2	John D. and Catherine T. MacArthur Foundation
410 2	MacArthur Foundation

[The name of the foundation is "The John D. and Catherine T. MacArthur Foundation.]

24.1C   Changes of name

200   Rule 24.1C1   Change of corporate body name

....

[Field 710 -- Added Entry—Corporate Name]
[1st Indicator 1 -- Jurisdiction name]

*[The use of the hierarchical name structure used in Field 710 is addressed by
Example 220.]*

....

110 2		**United States Steel Corporation.**
245 1 0		United States Steel Corporation T.N.E.C. papers : ‡b comprising the pamphlets and charts submitted by United States Steel Corporation to the Temporary National Economic Committee.
246 3 0		T.N.E.C. papers
246 3 0		Temporary National Economic Committee papers
260		[New York?] : ‡b The Corp., ‡c 1940.
300		3 v. : ‡b ill. (some col.), maps ; ‡c 29 cm.
505 0		v. 1. Economic and related studies — v. 2. Chart studies — v. 3. The basing point method.
710 1 b̸		United States. ‡b Temporary National Economic Committee.

110	2	United States Steel Corporation
410	2	United States Steel (Firm)
410	2	U.S. Steel (Firm)
410	2	US Steel (Firm)
410	2	USS
410	2	U.S. Steel Corporation
410	2	US Steel Corporation [non-LC]
510	2	U.S.X. Corporation [LATER HEADING]
510	2	United States Steel Company

*[In 1951 several wholly owned subsidiaries merged to form
United States Steel Company, N.J. In 1953 U.S. Steel Company
merged with U.S. Steel Corporation. In 1986 United States Steel
Corporation changed its name to U.S.X. Corporation.]*

*[The use of the "510" references assumes the library already has
entries under each of those names in the catalog.]*

24.2   VARIANT NAMES, GENERAL RULES

201   Rule 24.2D   Variant names-- Brief form

....

```
020        9231018388
020        9231024949 (Suppl. 1)
020        9231024620 (Suppl. 2)
020        9231029428 (Suppl. 3)
245 0 0    Unesco's standard-setting instruments.
246 1 ƀ    ‡i Suppl. has title: ‡a Unesco standard-setting instruments
260        Paris : ‡b Unesco, ‡c 1981.
300        1 v. (loose-leaf) ; ‡c 24 cm.
710 2 ƀ    Unesco.
```

110	2	Unesco
410	2	U.N.E.S.C.O.
410	2	United Nations Educational, Scientific and Cultural Organization [OLD CATALOG HEADING]
410	2	United Nations. ‡b Educational, Scientific and Cultural Organization

24.3   VARIANT NAMES, SPECIAL RULES
24.3B   Language. International bodies

202   Rule 24.3B1   International body

[The organization's name appears in English in some of the its publications.]

020		9266005983
245	0 0	Principles of the Universal Decimal Classification (UDC) and rules for its revision and publication = ‡b Principes de la Classification Décimale Universelle (CDU) et règles pour sa révision et sa publication.
250		5th ed.
260		The Hague : ‡b Federation Internationale de Documentation, ‡c 1981.
300		35 p. ; ‡c 30 cm.
440	0	FID publication ; ‡v 598
500		English, French, and German.
500		"Supersedes the 'Universal Decimal Classification (UDC) revision and publication procedure', FID 429"—Pref.
710	**2 b**	**International Federation for Documentation.**

110	2	International Federation for Documentation
410	2	F.I.D.
410	2	FID
410	2	Fédération internationale de documentation
510	2	International Institute of Documentation [EARLIER HEADING]
510	2	International Federation for Information and Documentation [LATER HEADING]

[The use of the "510" references assumes the library already has entries under each of those names in the catalog.]

ADDITIONS, OMISSIONS, AND MODIFICATIONS

24.4   ADDITIONS
24.4B   Names not conveying the idea of a corporate body

> 203   Rule 24.4B1   Addition of a designation to indicate the body is a
>   corporate body

> [Field 810 -- Series Added Entry—Corporate Name]
>   [1st Indicator 2 -- Name in direct order]
>   [Subfield a -- Corporate name or jurisdiction name as entry element]
>   [Subfield t -- Title of a work]
>   [Subfield v -- Volume number/sequential designation]

110 2	**Keith Hogg (Firm)**	
245 1 0	Bibliographica : ‡b a catalogue of books offered for sale by Keith Hogg.	
260	Tenterden, Kent, England : ‡b K. Hogg, ‡c [197-]	
300	43 p. ; ‡c 21 cm.	
490 1	Catalogue ; ‡v no. 100	
500	Cover title.	
810 2	**Keith Hogg (Firm). ‡t Catalogue ; ‡v no. 100.**	

110 2	Keith Hogg (Firm) [non-LC]
410 1	Hogg (Firm) [non-LC]

110 2	Keith Hogg (Firm). ‡t Catalogue [non-LC]
430 0	Catalogue (Keith Hogg (Firm)) [non-LC]

204   Rule 24.4B1   Addition of a designation to indicate the body is a corporate body

[The use of a uniform title in Field 730 is addressed in Chapter 5 of this text.]

020		0413533808
110	**2**	**Monty Python (Comedy troupe)**
245	1 0	Monty Python's the meaning of life / ‡c written and performed by Graham Chapman ... [et al.].
246	3 0	Meaning of life
260		[London] : ‡b Methuen, ‡c [1983]
300		[128] p. : ‡b col. ill. ; ‡c 28 cm.
440	2	A Methuen paperback
500		From the motion picture of the same title.
700	1 ⸸	Chapman, Graham, ‡d 1941?-
730	4 ⸸	The meaning of life (Motion picture)

110	2	Monty Python (Comedy troupe)
410	2	Monty Python's Flying Circus (Comedy troupe)
400	0	Python (Monty) [non-LC]

24.4C   Two or more bodies with the same or similar names

205   Rule 24.4C2   Addition of a country

[Field 810 -- Series Added Entry—Corporate Name]
[Subfield b -- Subordinate unit]

020	0894680935 (pbk.)
020	0521340160
110 2	**National Gallery of Art (U.S.)**
245 1 0	Early Netherlandish painting / ‡c John Oliver Hand, Martha Wolff.
260	Washington : ‡b National Gallery of Art, ‡c c1986.
300	xv, 271 p. : ‡b ill. (some col.) ; ‡c 29 cm.
490 1	The Collections of the National Gallery of Art : systematic catalogue
504	Includes bibliographical references and index.
700 1 ⱕ	Hand, John Oliver, ‡d 1941-
700 1 ⱕ	Wolff, Martha.
810 2	**National Gallery of Art (U.S.). ‡t Collections of the National Gallery of Art.**

110 2	National Gallery of Art (U.S.)	
410 2	National Art Gallery (U.S.)	
410 1	Washington (D.C.). ‡b National Gallery of Art	
410 2	Smithsonian Institution. ‡b National Gallery of Art	
410 1	United States. ‡b National Gallery of Art [OLD CATALOG HEADING]	

110 2	National Gallery of Art (U.S.). ‡t Collections of the National Gallery of Art	
430 0	Collections of the National Gallery of Art	

206 Rule 24.4C2 Addition of a state

020	0821405500
100 1	Becker, Carl M.
245 1 4	The village : ‡b a history of Germantown, Ohio, 1804-1976 / ‡c Carl M. Becker.
260	Germantown, Ohio : ‡b Historical Society of Germantown ; ‡a [Athens] : ‡b Ohio University Press [distributor], ‡c c1981.
300	xvi, 214 p. : ‡b ill. ; ‡c 24 cm.
504	Includes bibliographical references (p. [203]-207) and index.
710 2 ƀ	**Historical Society of Germantown (Ohio)**

110 2	Historical Society of Germantown (Ohio)
410 2	Germantown Historical Society (Ohio)

207 Rule 24.4C3 Addition of a local place name

020	0810916371
245 0 0	Sets, series & ensembles in African art / ‡c George Nelson Preston ; introduction, Susan Vogel ; catalogue, Polly Nooter.
246 3 ƀ	Sets, series and ensembles in African art
260	New York : ‡b Center for African Art, ‡c c1985.
300	96 p. : ‡b ill. (some col.) ; ‡c 31 cm.
500	"Published in conjunction with the exhibition, Sets, series & ensembles organized by the Center for African Art, July 17, 1985-October 27, 1985"—T.p. verso.
504	Includes bibliographical references (p. 94-95) and index.
700 1 ƀ	Preston, George Nelson.
710 2 ƀ	**Center for African Art (New York, N.Y.)**

110 2	Center for African Art (New York, N.Y.)
510 2	Museum for African Art (New York, N.Y.) [LATER HEADING]

[The use of the "510" reference assumes the library already has an entry under that name in the catalog.]

24.5C   **Terms indicating incorporation and certain other terms**

208   **Rule 24.5C1   Term indicating incorporation**

110 2   **Lathrop C. Harper, Inc.**
245 1 0   Uncommon and early books.
260   New York : ‡b Lathrop C. Harper, ‡c 1977.
300   121 p. : ‡b ill. ; ‡c 23 cm.
490 1   Catalogue / Lathrop C. Harper ; ‡v 229
500   "Winter — 1977".
500   Includes index.
810 2   **Lathrop C. Harper, Inc.** ‡t Catalogue ; ‡v 229

110 2	Lathrop C. Harper, Inc.
410 0	Harper (Lathrop C.) inc., New York [OLD CATALOG HEADING]
410 2	Lathrop C. Harper (Firm)
410 2	Harper, Inc.

110 2	Lathrop C. Harper, Inc. ‡t Catalogue [non-LC]
430 0	Catalogue (Lathrop C. Harper, Inc.) [non-LC]

24.7   CONFERENCES, CONGRESSES, MEETINGS, ETC.
24.7B   Additions

209   Rule 24.7A1   Omission of a conference number from its name
[Field 111 -- Main Entry—Meeting Name]
[1st Indicator 2 -- Name in direct order]
[Subfield a -- Meeting name or jurisdiction name as entry element]

Rule 24.7B2   Addition of number
[Subfield n -- Number of part/section/meeting]

Rule 24.7B3   Addition of date
[Subfield d -- Date of meeting]

Rule 24.7B4   Addition of location
[Subfield c -- Location of meeting]

....

111 2	**Conference on Satellite Meteorology and Oceanography ‡n (3rd : ‡d 1988 : ‡c Anaheim, Calif.)**
245 1 0	Third conference on satellite meteorology and oceanography, Feb. 1-5, 1988, Anaheim, Calif. / ‡c sponsored by American Meteorological Society.
246 3 ⶆ	3rd conference on satellite meteorology and oceanography
260	Boston, Mass. : ‡b The Society, ‡c c1987.
300	xv, 432, [64] p. : ‡b ill., maps ; ‡c 28 cm.
500	"Preprints"—Cover.
504	Includes bibliographical references and index.
500	"D (VT) 500 1/88"—P. 4 of cover.
710 2 ⶆ	American Meteorological Society.

> 111 2   Conference on Satellite Meteorology and
>   Oceanography [non-LC]

24.10   LOCAL CHURCHES, ETC.

210   Rule 24.10B   Addition to a local church name

....

245 0 0	Holy Name Church centennial anniversary, 1845-1945.
260	Sheboygan, Wis. : ‡b [The Church, ‡c 1955]
300	[45] p. : ‡b ill., ports. ; ‡c 28 cm.
710 2 ⶆ	**Holy Name Church (Sheboygan, Wis.)**

> 110 2   Holy Name Church (Sheboygan, Wis.)
> 410 2   Holy Name of Jesus Parish (Sheboygan, Wis.)

SUBORDINATE AND RELATED BODIES

24.12   GENERAL RULE

211   Rule 24.12A   **Non-government subordinate body under its own name**

....

020	0900177012
110 2	**Bodleian Library.**
245 1 0	Bodleian Library visitors' guide.
250	Rev. ed.
260	Oxford : ‡b The Library, ‡c 1969.
300	18 p. : ‡b ill. ; ‡c 22 cm.

110 2	Bodleian Library
410 1	Oxford. ‡b University. ‡b Bodleian Library [OLD CATALOG HEADING]
410 2	University of Oxford. ‡b Bodleian Library

24.13   SUBORDINATE AND RELATED BODIES ENTERED SUBORDINATELY

212   Rule 24.13A   Type 1   Term in the name implies the body is part of another

[Field 110 -- Main Entry—Corporate Name]
[Subfield b -- Subordinate unit]

110 2	**B. H. Blackwell Ltd. ‡b Antiquarian Department.**
245 1 2	A centenary catalogue of antiquarian and rare modern books.
246 1 4	Blackwell's centenary antiquarian catalogue
260	Oxford, England : ‡b Blackwell's Antiquarian Dept., ‡c [1979?]
300	vii, 135 p., [1] leaf of plates : ‡b ill., facsims. ; ‡c 25 cm.
490 1	Blackwell's catalogue ; ‡v A-1
504	Includes bibliographical references.
810 2	**B. H. Blackwell Ltd. ‡b Antiquarian Department. ‡t Catalogue ; ‡v A-1**

110 2	B. H. Blackwell Ltd. ‡b Antiquarian Department [non-LC]
410 2	Blackwell's Antiquarian Department [non-LC]

110 2	B. H. Blackwell Ltd. ‡b Antiquarian Department. ‡t Catalogue [non-LC]
430 0	Blackwell's catalogue [non-LC]
430 0	Catalogue (B. H. Blackwell Ltd. Antiquarian Department) [non-LC]

[No references are shown for "B. H. Blackwell Ltd." It is assumed those references were created previously for other works in the catalog with that heading.]

213 Rule 24.13A Type 2 Term in the name implies administrative subordination

Field 710 -- Added Entry—Corporate Name]
[Subfield b -- Subordinate unit]

020   083897628X
**110 2   American Library Association. ‡b Committee on
            Accreditation.**
245 1 0   Standards for accreditation of master's programs in library &
           information studies.
260   Chicago : ‡b Office for Accreditation, American Library
           Association, ‡c c1992.
300   29 p. ; ‡c 22 cm.
500   Developed by the ALA Committee on Accreditation.
500   "Adopted by the Council of the American Library Association,
           January 28, 1992; effective January 1, 1993."
500   Supersedes: Standards for accreditation, 1972.
504   Includes bibliographical references and index.
710 2 ⌀   American Library Association. ‡b Office for Accreditation.

> 110 2   American Library Association. ‡b Committee on
>   Accreditation

> *[No references are shown for "American Library Association." It
> is assumed those references were created previously for other
> works in the catalog with that heading.]*

214   Rule 24.13A   Type 5   Name of a school

020	0669149276 (alk. paper)
245 0 0	Cooperative strategies in international business / ‡c Farok J. Contractor, Peter Lorange, [editors].
260	Lexington, Mass. : ‡b Lexington Books, ‡c c1988.
300	xxix, 513 p. : ‡b ill. ; ‡c 24 cm.
500	Based on papers presented in Oct. 1986 at a colloquium organized by the Graduate School of Management, Rutgers University and the Wharton School, University of Pennsylvania.
504	Includes bibliographies and index.
700 1 ᵇ	Contractor, Farok J.
700 1 ᵇ	Lorange, Peter.
710 2 ᵇ	**Rutgers University. ‡b Graduate School of Management.**
710 2 ᵇ	Wharton School.

110	2	Rutgers University. ‡b Graduate School of Management
410	2	Rutgers Graduate School of Management
410	2	Rutgers University. ‡b Graduate School of Business Administration [EARLIER HEADING]

[The use of the second "410" reference assumes the library already has no entry under that earlier name in the catalog.]

[No references are shown for "Rutgers University." It is assumed those references were created previously for other works in the catalog with that heading.]

24.14   DIRECT OR INDIRECT SUBHEADING

215   Rule 24.14A   Direct subheading

020	083893255X
110 2	**American Library Association. ‡b Filing Committee.**
245 1 0	ALA filing rules / ‡c Filing Committee, Resources and Technical Services Division, American Library Association.
260	Chicago : ‡b ALA, ‡c 1980.
300	ix, 50 p. ; ‡c 23 cm.
500	Includes index.

110	2	American Library Association. ‡b Filing Committee
410	2	American Library Association. ‡b Resources and Technical Services Division. ‡b Filing Committee

[No references are shown for "American Library Association" or the "Resources and Technical Services Division." It is assumed those references were created previously for other works in the catalog with those headings.]

216   Rule 24.14A   Indirect subheading

[Intervening element is necessary.]

---

245 0 0   Steel data sources / ‡c prepared by Subcommittee of Libraries and Information Centers of the Committee on Commercial Research.
260   Washington, DC : ‡b American Iron and Steel Institute, ‡c 1980.
300   1 v. in various pagings ; ‡c 28 cm.
500   Cover title.
500   Editors: Joanne S. Klein ... [et al.] ; compilers: Barbara M. Banek ... [et al.].
700 1 ⌐   Klein, Joanne S.
700 1 ⌐   Banek, Barbara M.
710 2 ⌐   American Iron and Steel Institute. ‡b Committee on Commercial Research. ‡b Subcommittee of Libraries and Information Centers.

> 110 2   American Iron and Steel Institute. ‡b Committee on Commercial Research. ‡b Subcommittee of Libraries and Information Centers
> 410 2   American Iron and Steel Institute. ‡b Subcommittee of Libraries and Information Centers [non-LC]
> 410 2   AISI Subcommittee of Libraries and Information Centers [non-LC]

> *On p. [1] the Subcommittee is referred to as the "AISI Subcommittee of Libraries and Information Centers."*
>
> *[No references are shown for "American Iron and Steel Institute" or the "Committee on Commercial Research." It is assumed those references were created previously for other works in the catalog with those headings.]*

GOVERNMENT BODIES AND OFFICIALS

24.17   GENERAL RULE

217   Rule 24.17A   Government body entered directly

....

110 2   **Library of Congress.**

245 1 4   The Rosenwald Collection : ‡b a catalogue of illustrated books and manuscripts, of books from celebrated presses, and of bindings and maps, 1150-1950 : the gift of Lessing J. Rosenwald to the Library of Congress.

260   Washington : ‡b [U.S. G.P.O.], ‡c 1954.

300   vi, 292 p. : ‡b ill. ; ‡c 27 cm.

500   Collection cataloged by Marion Schild ; edited and arranged by Frederick R. Goff.

700 1 ∅   Rosenwald, Lessing J. ‡q (Lessing Julius), ‡d 1891-1979.

700 1 ∅   Schild, Marion, ‡d 1907-

700 1 ∅   Goff, Frederick R. ‡q (Frederick Richmond), ‡d 1916-

110	2	Library of Congress
410	1	United States. ‡b Library of Congress [OLD CATALOG HEADING]
410	2	LC
410	2	L.C. [non-LC]

218   Rule 24.17A   Government body entered directly

....

020   1560981539 (alk. paper)
110 2   National Air and Space Museum.
245 1 0   Aircraft of the National Air and Space Museum / ‡c
           Smithsonian Institution ; compiled by Claudia M. Oakes and
           Kathleen L. Brooks-Pazmany ; and edited by F. Robert van der
           Linden.
250   4th ed.
260   Washington, D.C. : ‡b Published for the National Air and Space
           Museum by the Smithsonian Institution Press, ‡c 1991.
300   ca. 200 p. : ‡b ill. ; ‡c 28 cm.
700 1 ⱡ   Oakes, Claudia M.
700 1 ⱡ   Brooks-Pazmany, Kathleen L.
700 1 ⱡ   Van der Linden, F. Robert.
710 2 ⱡ   Smithsonian Institution.

110 2	National Air and Space Museum
410 2	Smithsonian Institution. ‡b National Air and Space Museum
410 1	United States. ‡b National Air and Space Museum
410 2	Smithsonian Air and Space Museum
410 2	Air and Space Museum (U.S.)
410 1	Washington (D.C.). ‡b National Air and Space Museum
510 2	National Air Museum (U.S.) [EARLIER HEADING]

[The use of the "510" reference assumes the library already has an entry under that name in the catalog.]

24.18   GOVERNMENT AGENCIES ENTERED SUBORDINATELY

**219   Rule 24.18A   Type 1   Term in the agency name implies the body
is part of another**

245 0 0   Wise home buying / ‡c U.S. Department of Housing and Urban
Development.

260   Washington, D.C. : ‡b The Dept., ‡c [1974]

300   36 p. : ‡b ill. ; ‡c 21 cm.

500   Cover title.

500   "August, 1974"—P. [4] of cover.

500   HUD-267-F(4).

710 1 ƀ   **United States. ‡b Dept. of Housing and Urban Development.**

110	1	United States. ‡b Dept. of Housing and Urban Development
410	2	H.U.D.
410	2	HUD
410	1	United States. ‡b Housing and Urban Development, Dept. of

*[For this and succeeding name authority example no references
are shown for "United States." It is assumed those references
were created previously for other works in the catalog with that
heading.]*

220 Rule 24.18A Type 2 Term in the agency name implies administrative subordination

[Field 110 -- Main Entry—Corporate Name]
[1st Indicator 1 -- Jurisdiction name]
Subfield a -- Corporate name or jurisdiction name as entry element]
[Subfield b -- Subordinate unit]

110 2	United States. ‡b Commission on Civil Rights.	
245 1 4	The decline of black farming in America : ‡b a report of the United States Commission on Civil Rights.	
260	[Washington, D.C.] : ‡b The Commission, ‡c [1982]	
300	vii, 196 p. ; ‡c 28 cm.	
500	"February 1982."	
504	Includes bibliographical references.	

110 1	United States. ‡b Commission on Civil Rights [non-LC]	
410 2	United States Commission on Civil Rights	
410 1	United States. ‡b Civil Rights, Commission on	
410 1	United States. ‡b Commission on Civil Rights [OLD CATALOG HEADING]	
410 2	U.S. Commission on Civil Rights	
410 1	United States. ‡b Congress. ‡b Commission on Civil Rights	
410 2	Commission on Civil Rights (U.S.)	

[The form of heading used corresponds to the example for the Commission on Civil Rights that appears under Rule 24/18A in AACR2R. The Library of Congress, however, uses the first 410 reference as the authorized heading and has coded it as being "AACR2."]

or

221 Rule 24.18A Type 2 Term in the agency name implies administrative subordination

110 1	United States. ‡b Warren Commission.
245 1 0	Report of the President's Commission on the Assassination of President John F. Kennedy.
246 1 ⊘	‡i Commonly known as: ‡a Warren report
260	Washington, D.C. : ‡b U.S. G.P.O., ‡c 1964.
300	xxiv, 888 p. : ‡b ill., facsims., maps, ports. ; ‡c 24 cm.
504	Includes bibliographical references (p. 817-879) and index.

110 1	United States. ‡b Warren Commission
410 2	Warren Commission (U.S.)
410 1	United States. ‡b President's Commission on the Assassination of President Kennedy
410 1	United States. ‡b Commission on the Assassination of President Kennedy
410 2	Warren Commission [OLD CATALOG HEADING]

24.19   DIRECT OR INDIRECT SUBHEADING

222   Rule 24.19A   Direct subheading

....

[Field 810 -- Series Added Entry—Corporate Name]
1st Indicator 1 -- Jurisdiction name]
[Subfield b -- Subordinate unit]

....

110 1		**United States. ‡b Bureau of Alcohol, Tobacco, and Firearms.**
245 1 0		Explosives usage policy / ‡c Department of the Treasury, Bureau of Alcohol, Tobacco and Firearms.
260		[Washington, D.C.] : ‡b The Bureau, ‡c [1985]
300		1 v. (loose-leaf) ; ‡c 28 cm.
490 1		Order ; ‡v ATF 0 3320.4
500		Cover title.
500		"10/18/85."
810 1		**United States. ‡b Bureau of Alcohol, Tobacco, and Firearms. ‡t Order ; ‡v ATF 0 3320.4.**

110	1	United States. ‡b Bureau of Alcohol, Tobacco, and Firearms
410	1	United States. ‡b Bureau of Alcohol, Tobacco & Firearms [OLD CATALOG HEADING]
410	1	United States. ‡b Dept. of the Treasury. ‡b Bureau of Alcohol, Tobacco, and Firearms
410	1	United States. ‡b Alcohol, Tobacco, and Firearms, Bureau of
410	2	ATF
410	2	A.T.F. [non-LC]
410	2	BATF [non-LC]
410	2	B.A.T.F. [non-LC]
510	1	United States. ‡b Alcohol, Tobacco, and Firearms Division [EARLIER HEADING]

[The use of the "510" reference assumes the library already has an entry under that name in the catalog.]

110	1	United States. ‡b Bureau of Alcohol, Tobacco, and Firearms. ‡t Order
430	0	Order (United States. Bureau of Alcohol, Tobacco, and Firearms)

Special Rules

24.20   GOVERNMENT OFFICIALS
24.20B   Heads of state, etc.

223   Rule 24.20B1   Heads of State -- Sovereign

Rule 24.18A   Type 9 Head of state or government

....

110 1		**England and Wales. ‡b Sovereign (1603-1625 : James I)**
245 1 0		Royal proclamations of King James I, 1603-1625 / ‡c edited by James F. Larkin and Paul L. Hughes.
260		Oxford : ‡b Clarendon Press, ‡c 1973.
300		xxxiv, 679 p. ; ‡c 24 cm.
490 1		Stuart royal proclamations ; ‡v v. 1
504		Includes bibliographical references and index.
700 0 ⠶		James ‡b I, ‡c King of England, ‡d 1566-1625.
700 1 ⠶		Larkin, James F. ‡q (James Francis), ‡d 1912-
700 1 ⠶		Hughes, Paul L.
810 1		**England and Wales. ‡b Sovereign. ‡t Stuart royal proclamations ; ‡v v. 1.**

110 1	England and Wales. ‡b Sovereign (1603-1625 : James I)
410 1	Great Britain. ‡b Sovereigns, etc., 1603-1625 (James I) [OLD CATALOG HEADING]

110 1	England and Wales. ‡b Sovereign. ‡t Stuart royal proclamations
410 1	Great Britain. ‡b Sovereign. ‡t Stuart royal proclamations [OLD CATALOG HEADING]
430 0	Stuart royal proclamations

[No references are shown for "England and Wales." It is assumed those references were created previously for other works in the catalog with that heading.]

224 Rule 24.20B1 Heads of State -- President

Rule 24.18A Type 9 Head of state or government

[The legislative body name structure used in the second Field 710 is addressed by Example 227.]

....

110 1		**United States. ‡b President (1963-1969 : Johnson)**
245 1 0		No retreat from tomorrow : ‡b President Lyndon B. Johnson's 1967 messages to the 90th Congress.
260		[United States? : ‡b s.n., ‡c 1968?]
300		241 p. : ‡b ill. (some col.) ; ‡c 29 cm.
700 1 ƀ		Johnson, Lyndon B. ‡q (Lyndon Baines), ‡d 1908-1973.
710 1 ƀ		United States. ‡b Congress ‡n (90th, 1st session : ‡d 1967)

110 1		United States. ‡b President (1963-1969 : Johnson)
410 1		United States. ‡b President, 1963-1969 (Lyndon B. Johnson) [OLD CATALOG HEADING]

[No references are shown for "United States. President." It is assumed those references were created previously for other works in the catalog with that heading.]

24.21 LEGISLATIVE BODIES

225 Rule 24.21B Committee of a legislature

110 1 United States. ‡b Congress. ‡b Senate. ‡b Committee on Foreign Relations.

245 1 4 The Vietnam hearings / ‡c with an introduction by J. William Fulbright.

250   1st Vintage Books ed.

260   New York : ‡b Vintage Books, ‡c 1966.

300   xiv, 294 p. ; ‡c 19 cm.

500   Complete statements and excerpts from the testimony of Dean Rusk, James M. Gavin, George F. Kennan, and Maxwell D. Taylor given during hearings by the Senate Foreign Relations Committee held Jan. 26-Feb. 18, 1966.

500   First published under the title: Supplemental foreign assistance, fiscal year 1966, Vietnam.

---

110 1 United States. ‡b Congress. ‡b Senate. ‡b Committee on Foreign Relations

410 1 United States. ‡b Congress. ‡b Committee on Foreign Relations

410 1 United States. ‡b Congress. ‡b Senate. ‡b Foreign Relations Committee

---

[No references were made for "United States. Congress" and for "United States. Congress. Senate." It is assumed those references were created previously for other works in the catalog with those headings.]

226   Rule 24.21C   Legislative subcommittee of the U.S. Congress

110 1   United States. ‡b Congress. ‡b House. ‡b Committee on Agriculture. ‡b Subcommittee on Livestock and Grains.

245 1 0   Sale of wheat to Russia : ‡b hearings before the Subcommittee on Livestock and Grains of the Committee on Agriculture, House of Representatives, Ninety-second Congress, second session, September 14, 18, and 19, 1972.

260   Washington : ‡b U.S. G.P.O. : ‡b for sale by the Supt. of Docs., ‡c 1972.

300   iv, 293 p. : ‡b ill. ; ‡c 24 cm.

500   "Serial no. 92-KK."

---

110 1   United States. ‡b Congress. ‡b House. ‡b Committee on Agriculture. ‡b Subcommittee on Livestock and Grains

410 1   United States. ‡b Congress. ‡b House. ‡b Committee on Agriculture. ‡b Subcommittee on Livestock and Feed Grains

410 1   United States. ‡b Congress. ‡b House. ‡b Subcommittee on Livestock and Grains

---

[The form of name used "United States. Congress. House" has been designated an "AACR2" heading in the LC NAF. Accordingly, it was used in this example. It should be noted that the abbreviation "of House" for the "House of Representatives" is not listed in Appendix B of AACR2 nor is it used in heading examples in AACR2.]

[No references were made for "United States. Congress" and for "United States. Congress. House." It is assumed those references were created previously for other works in the catalog with those headings.]

227   Rule 24.21D   Successive legislature numbered consecutively

[Field 710 -- Added Entry—Corporate Name]
[Subfield n -- Number of part/section/meeting]
[Subfield d -- Date of meeting or treaty signing]

---

245 0 0   Memorial addresses and other tributes in the Congress of the
          United States on the life and contributions of William Benton /
          ǂc Ninety-third Congress, first session ; [compiled under the
          direction of the Joint Committee on Printing].
246 1 4   William Benton, late senator from Connecticut
260   Washington : ǂb U. S. G.P.O., ǂc 1973.
300   vi, 110 p. : ǂb port. ; ǂc 24 cm.
710 1 ƀ   **United States. ǂb Congress ǂn (93rd, 1st session : ǂd 1973)**
710 1 ƀ   United States. ǂb Congress. ǂb Joint Committee on Printing.

> 110 1   United States. ǂb Congress ǂn (93rd, 1st session : ǂd
>   1973) [non-LC]

> *[No references were made for "United States. Congress." It is
> assumed those references were created previously for other works
> in the catalog with that heading.]*

24.24   ARMED FORCES

228   Rule 24.24A1 Armed force at the national level

020		0833016121
100	0	Thaler, David E.
245	1 0	Perspectives on theater air campaign planning / ‡c David E. Thaler, David A. Shlapak.
260		Santa Monica, CA : ‡b Rand, ‡c 1995.
300		xix, 50 p. : ‡b ill. ; ‡c 23 cm.
500		"Prepared for the United States Air Force."
500		"Project Air Force."
504		Includes bibliographical references.
700	1 ⱷ	Shlapak, David A.
710	**1 ⱷ**	**United States. ‡b Air Force.**
710	2 ⱷ	Project Air Force (U.S.)
710	2 ⱷ	Rand Corporation.

110	1	United States. ‡b Air Force
410	1	United States. ‡b Dept. of the Air Force. ‡b Air Force
410	2	USAF
410	2	U.S.A.F.
410	2	United States Air Force
410	2	Air Force (U.S.)
410	2	US Air Force
510	1	United States. ‡b Army Air Forces
510	1	United States. ‡b Army. ‡b Air Corps

[The use of the "510" reference assumes the library already has an entry under each of those names in the catalog.]

FORM OF HEADINGS AND REFERENCES EXERCISE
Part B -- Corporate Bodies

Similar to what you did for the names of persons in the previous chapter's exercise now identify the correct AACR2 form of name for the access points for the names of <u>corporate bodies</u>. Again, for each name make "see from" references for references that you believe would be useful in a typical academic library catalog. Assume you have no other works by a corporate body under an older name but do have works cataloged under any later form of name. If the authorized form of heading in the LC NAF is not in AACR2 form you will need to establish the correct heading using AACR2 and reference sources including the OCLC WorldCat. You will also need to establish appropriate references. The answers to this exercise appear in Appendix C - Part B.

The examples that have corporate bodies as access points are:

<u>Example</u>	<u>Access Point</u>
123	Inglewood Public Library
124	American Library Association
125	Pennsylvania
	Pennsylvania State Library
126	Committee on Social Issues
127	Reynolds Conference
	Southern Studies Program
128	Firesign Theater
129	Federal Electric Corporation
132	United States. President (Truman)
	Joint Economic Committee
	Council of Economic Advisors
133	United States. President (Wilson)
135	Indiana University Graduate Library School
155	Bibliographical Society of American

CHAPTER FIVE

Uniform Titles and References

Suggested Lecture Outline

Rules

Readings: *Anglo-American Cataloguing Rules.* 2nd ed., 1998 revision
            Chapter 25, Uniform Titles, p. 480-513;
            Chapter 26, References, p. 557-562.

N.B. The name authority practice used in the chapter for headings for persons has also been used in this chapter. This includes having the second indicator value blank rather than "0" in name authority record Fields x00, x10, x11, and x51 in order to correspond with current LC policy. Similarly, the discontinuation of the use of 1st indicator value "2" for multiple surnames has also been implemented. This may effect Fields 100, 700, and 800 in some examples in this chapter. Additionally, in order to conserve space, name authority records have been provided only for uniform titles that illustrate the rule being presented. For the same reason, when the uniform title is not the lead filing element, an assumption has been made that all appropriate name authority work for the lead element has already been done and thus no authority record is presented here for that element.

INDIVIDUAL TITLES

25.3   WORKS CREATED AFTER 1500

229   Rule 25.3A   Uniform title in the original language of the work -- Main entry under a personal heading

[Field 240 -- Uniform Title]
  [1st Indicator 1 -- Printed on cards]
  [2nd Indicator 0 -- Number of nonfiling characters present]
[Subfield a -- Uniform title]

....

Rule 25.2E2   Added entry for the title proper

....

100 1   Defoe, Daniel, ‡d 1661?-1731.
240 1 0   Fortunes and misfortunes of the famous Moll Flanders
245 1 0   Moll Flanders / ‡c Daniel Defoe ; [introduction by G.T. Aitken].
260   London : ‡b Dent ; ‡a New York : ‡b Dutton, ‡c 1930.
300   xvii, 295 p. ; ‡c 18 cm.
440   0 Everyman's library ; ‡v no. 837. Fiction
500   List of Defoe's works: p. xiv-xv.

100 1	Defoe, Daniel, ‡d 1661?-1731. ‡t Fortunes and misfortunes of the famous Moll Flanders
400 1	Defoe, Daniel, ‡d 1661?-1731. ‡t Moll Flanders

230   Rule 25.3A   Uniform title in the original language of the work --
Main entry under title

[Field 130 -- Main Entry—Uniform Title]
[1st Indicator 0 -- Number of nonfiling characters present]
[Subfield a -- Uniform title]

....

Rule 25.2E1   Added entry for the title proper

....

130	0	**Mother Goose.**
245	1 0	In a pumpkin shell : ‡b a Mother Goose ABC / ‡c Joan Walsh Anglund.
260		New York : ‡b Harcourt, Brace & World, ‡c c1960.
300		[32] p. : ‡b ill. ; ‡c 25 cm.
520	⸬	An alphabet book giving a Mother Goose rhyme for each letter, such as Three Blind Mice for the letter "M."
700	1 ⸬	Anglund, Joan Walsh.

130	0	Mother Goose
430	0	Goose, Mother [non-LC]

25.4   WORKS CREATED BEFORE 1501
25.4A   General rule

231   Rule 25.4A1   Uniform title in the language by which the work is
identified in modern sources

....

020		0824010906
130	0	**Beowulf.**
245	1 0	Beowulf : ‡b an edition with manuscript spacing notation and graphotactic analyses / ‡c Robert D. Stevick.
260		New York : ‡b Garland Pub. Co., ‡c 1975.
300		xxxix, 260 p. ; ‡c 22 cm.
504		Includes bibliographical references (p. xxxix) and index.
700	1 ⸬	Stevick, Robert D., ‡d 1928-

130	0	Beowulf

25.5   ADDITIONS
25.5B   Conflict resolution

232   Rule 25.5B1   Addition of a brief phrase

020		0025486608
100	1	Howard, Sidney Coe, ‡d 1891-1939.
245	1 0	GWTW : ‡b the screenplay / ‡c by Sidney Howard ; based on the novel by Margaret Mitchell ; edited by Richard Harwell.
260		New York : ‡b Macmillan, ‡c c1980.
300		416 p. : ‡b ill. ; ‡c 23 cm.
504		Includes bibliographical references (p. 415-416).
700	1 ♭	Harwell, Richard Barksdale.
700	1 1	Mitchell, Margaret, ‡d 1900-1949. ‡t Gone with the wind.
730	**0 ♭**	**Gone with the wind (Motion picture)**

130	0	Gone with the wind (Motion picture)
430	0	GWTW
430	0	G.W.T.W.

233   Rule 25.5B1   Addition of a designation

[Field 830 -- Series Added Entry—Uniform Title]
    [Second Indicator 0 -- Number of nonfiling characters present]
    [Subfield a -- Uniform title]
    [Subfield v -- Volume number/sequential designation]

[This method is used by the Library of Congress to resolve conflicts in series titles.]

020		0900312823
100	1	Holdsworth, Philip.
245	1 0	Excavations at Melbourne Street, Southampton, 1971-76 / ‡c by Philip Holdsworth ; with contributions on the 'Hamwith' brickearths by Myra L Shackley, and on Hamtvn alias Hamwic (Saxon Southampton), the place-name traditions and their significance by Alexander R Rumble ; edited for SARC by David A Hinton.
260		London : ‡b Published for the Southampton Archaeological Research Committee by the Council for British Archaeology, ‡c c1980.
300		viii, 140 p. : ‡b ill., maps ; ‡c 30 cm.
490	1	Report / Southampton Archaeological Research Committee ; ‡v 1
490	1	CBA research report, ‡x 0589-9036 ; ‡v 33
504		Includes bibliographical references (p. 135-137) and index.
700	1 ⊘	Hinton, David Alban.
710	2 ⊘	Southampton Archaeological Research Committee.
830	**0**	**Report (Southampton Archaeological Research Committee) ; ‡v 1.**
830	**0**	**Research report (Council for British Archaeology) ; ‡v no. 33.**

130	0	Report (Southampton Archaeological Research Committee)
410	2	Southampton Archaeological Research Committee. ‡t Report - Southampton Archaeological Research Committee [OLD CATALOG HEADING]
410	2	Southampton Archaeological Research Committee. ‡t Report
430	0	Southampton Archaeological Research Committee report

130	0	Research report (Council for British Archaeology)
410	2	Council for British Archaeology. ‡t Research report
410	2	Council for British Archaeology. ‡t C.B.A. research reports [OLD CATALOG HEADING]
430	0	CBA research report

25.5C   Language

234   Rule 25.5C1   Language of the item differs from that of the original

[Field 240 -- Uniform Title]
[Subfield l -- Language of a work]

```
100 1      Gide, André, ‡d 1869-1951.
240 1 0    Porte étroite. ‡l English
245 1 0    Strait is the gate = ‡b La porte étroite / ‡c translated from the
           French of André Gide by Dorothy Bussy.
260        New York : ‡b Knopf, ‡c 1924.
300        231 p. ; ‡c 21 cm.
700 1      Bussy, Dorothy.
```

```
100 1      Gide, André, ‡d 1869-1951. ‡t Porte étroite
400 1      Gide, André, ‡d 1869-1951. ‡t Strait is the gate
           [non-LC]
```

25.4B   Classical and Byzantine Greek works

235   Rule 25.4B1   Uniform title in English for a work originally written in classical Greek

```
100 0      Homer.
240 1 0    Iliad. ‡l English
245 1 4    The anger of Achilles : ‡b Homer's Iliad / ‡c translated by
           Robert Graves ; illustrations by Ronald Searle.
260        Garden City, N.Y. : ‡b Doubleday, ‡c c1959.
300        383 p. : ‡b ill. ; ‡c 25 cm.
700 1 ∅    Graves, Robert, ‡d 1895-
700 1 ∅    Searle, Ronald, ‡d 1920-
```

```
100 0      Homer. ‡t Iliad. ‡l English
400 1      Homer. ‡t The anger of Achilles [non-LC]
```

COLLECTIVE TITLES

25.9   SELECTIONS

236   Rule 25.9A   Selection of works in various forms by one person

[Field 240 -- Uniform Title]
   [Subfield f -- Date of a work]

---

020   0030077958
100 1   Poe, Edgar Allan, ‡d 1809-1849.
240 1 0   Selections. ‡f 1968
245 1 0   Selected prose, poetry, and Eureka / ‡c Edgar Allan Poe ; edited
           with an introduction by W.H. Auden.
260   New York : ‡b Holt, Rinehart and Winston, ‡c [1968?]
300   xxvi, 590 p. ; ‡c 21 cm.
490 0   Rinehart editions ; ‡v 42
500   Originally published under the title: Selected prose and poetry.

> 100 1   Poe, Edgar Allan, ‡d 1809-1849. ‡t Selections. ‡f 1968
> 400 1   Poe, Edgar Allan, ‡d 1809-1849. ‡t Selected prose,
>   poetry, and Eureka [non-LC]

25.10   WORKS IN A SINGLE FORM

237   Rule 25.10A   Complete works of a person in one form

---

020   0517615312
100 1   Poe, Edgar Allan, ‡d 1809-1849.
240 1 0   Tales
245 1 4   The annotated tales of Edgar Allan Poe / ‡c edited with an
           introduction, notes, and a bibliography by Stephen Peithman.
260   New York : ‡b Avenel : ‡b Distributed by Crown Publishers, ‡c
           1986, c1981.
300   xv, 685 p. : ‡b ill. ; ‡c 29 cm.
504   Includes bibliographical references (p. 685) and index.
700 1 ‡   Peithman, Stephen.

> 100 1   Poe, Edgar Allan, ‡d 1809-1849. ‡t Tales
> 400 1   Poe, Edgar Allan, ‡d 1809-1849. ‡t Annotated Edgar
>   Allan Poe

SPECIAL RULES FOR CERTAIN TYPES OF WORK

Laws, Treaties, Etc.

25.15 LAWS, ETC.
25.15A Modern laws, etc.

238 Rule 25.15A1 Collection of the laws of a jurisdiction

110 1   Wisconsin.
240 1 0   Laws, etc.
245 1 0   West's Wisconsin statutes annotated : ‡b under arrangement of the official Wisconsin statutes.
246 3 0   Wisconsin statutes annotated
260   St. Paul, Minn. : ‡b West Pub. Co., ‡c c1957-
300   v. : ‡b facsim., forms ; ‡c 27 cm.
500   Kept up-to-date by revised volumes, pocket parts, supplementary and special pamphlets, West's Wisconsin legislative service, and interim annotation service.
500   Includes unnumbered general index and constitution volumes.
710 2 ⌀   West Publishing Company.

> 110 1   Wisconsin. ‡t Laws, etc.
> 410 1   Wisconsin. ‡t West's Wisconsin statutes annotated

239 Rule 25.15A1 Compilation of the laws of a jurisdiction on a specific subject that has a citation title

110 1   California.
240 1 0   Unemployment Insurance Code
245 1 0   Unemployment insurance code, 1986 / ‡c compiled by Bion M. Gregory.
260   North Highlands : ‡b State of Calif., Dept. of General Services, Documents and Publications Section, ‡c [1986?]
300   1 v. (various pagings) ; ‡c 23 cm.
504   Includes bibliographical references and index.
700 1 ⌀   Gregory, Bion M.
710 1 ⌀   California. ‡b Documents and Publications Section.

> 110 1   California. ‡t Unemployment Insurance Code

240 Rule 25.15A2 Different laws having the same title -- Addition of the year of promulgation

110 1   Illinois.

240 1 0 Revenue Act (1939)

245 1 4   The revenue act of 1939 : ‡b as enacted and amended by the 61st General Assembly at its regular session, 1939, together with the Revenue article of the Constitution, the Preadjudication act of 1939, the Rules of the Tax Commission and reference notes and tables.

260   Springfield : ‡b Illinois Tax Commission, ‡c [1939]

300   xiii, 238 p. ; ‡c 23 cm.

500   Includes indexes.

710 1 ⌀   Illinois. ‡b Tax Commission.

---

110 1   Illinois. ‡t Revenue Act [non-LC]

Sacred Scriptures

25.18 PARTS OF SACRED SCRIPTURES AND ADDITIONS
25.18A Bible

[Field 130 -- Main Entry—Uniform Title]

241 Rule 25.18A10 Language

[Subfield l -- Language of a work]

Rule 25.18A11 Version

[Subfield s -- Version]

Rule 25.18A13 Year

[Subfield f -- Date of a work]

---

130 0 Bible. ‡l English. ‡s Authorized. ‡f 1948.

245 1 0   Holy Bible : ‡b containing the Old and New Testaments, authorized King James version, with notes especially adapted for young Christians.

250   Pilgrim ed.

260   New York : ‡b Oxford University Press, ‡c 1948.

300   xxi, 1721 p. : ‡b ill., maps ; ‡c 28 cm.

500   Editor-in-chief: E. Schuyler English.

700 1 ⌀   English, E. Schuyler ‡q (Eugene Schuyler), ‡d 1899-

---

130   0   Bible. ‡l English. ‡s Authorized

430   0   Bible. ‡l English. ‡s King James Version

242   Rule 25.18A2   Testaments
[Field 130 -- Main Entry—Uniform Title]
[Subfield p -- Name of section/part of a work]

---

130 0   Bible. ‡p N.T. ‡l English. ‡s NET Bible. ‡f 1961.
245 1 4   The New English Bible. New Testament.
260   [London?] : ‡b Oxford University Press, ‡c 1961.
300   xiii, 446 p. ; ‡c 24 cm.
500   Translated under the supervision of the Joint Committee on the New Translation of the Bible.
710 2 ⌀   Joint Committee on the New Translation of the Bible.

130	0	Bible. ‡p N.T.
430	0	New Testament
430	0	Bible. ‡p New Testament

130	0	Bible. ‡l English. ‡s NET Bible
430	0	Bible. ‡l English. ‡s New English translation
430	0	Bible. ‡l English. ‡s N.E.T. Bible

243   **Rule 25.18A3   Books**

Rule 25.18A8   Two selections
[Field 730 -- Added Entry—Uniform Title]
    [2nd Indicator 2 -- Analytical entry. The item contains the work
                  that is represented by the added entry]
    [Subfield p -- Name of section/part of a work]
    [Subfield l -- Language of a work]
    [Subfield s -- Version]
    [Subfield f -- Date of a work]

[Field 830 -- Series Added Entry—Uniform Title]
    [Subfield l -- Language of a work]
    [Subfield s -- Version]
    [Subfield f -- Date of a work]

130 0   **Bible. ‡p O.T. ‡p Ezra. ‡l English. ‡s Anchor Bible. ‡f 1964.**
245 1 0   Ezra ; Nehemiah / ‡c introduction, translation, and notes by Jacob M. Myers.
250   1st ed.
260   Garden City, N.Y. : ‡b Doubleday, ‡c 1965.
300   lxxxiii, 268 p. : ‡b ill. ; ‡c 25 cm.
490 1   The Anchor Bible ; ‡v 14
504   Includes bibliographical references (p. [lxxviii]-lxxxiii).
700 1 ⱀ   Myers, Jacob M., ‡d 1904-
730 0 2   **Bible. ‡p O.T. ‡p Nehemiah. ‡l English. ‡s Anchor Bible. ‡f 1964.**
830   0   Bible. ‡l English. ‡s Anchor Bible. ‡f 1964 ; ‡v 14.

| 130 | 0 | Bible. ‡p O.T. |
| 430 | 0 | Old Testament |

| 130 | 0 | Bible. ‡l English. ‡s Anchor Bible. ‡f 1964 |
| 430 | 0 | Anchor Bible [OLD CATALOG HEADING] |

130	0	Bible. ‡p O.T. ‡p Ezra
430	0	Ezra (Book of the Old Testament)
430	0	Bible. ‡p Ezra

130	0	Bible. ‡p O.T. ‡p Nehemiah
430	0	Nehemiah (Book of the Old Testament)
430	0	Bible. ‡p Nehemiah

FORM OF HEADINGS AND REFERENCES EXERCISE
Part C -- Uniform Titles

For the last part of this exercise use the Library of Congress Authority File to identify the correct AACR2 form of name for the any access points that would be covered by the rules for <u>uniform titles</u>. There are not many of these. As before, for each uniform title make "see from" references for references that you believe would be useful in a typical academic library catalog. If the authorized form of heading in the LC NAF is not in AACR2 form you will need to establish the heading using AACR2R and reference sources including the OCLC WorldCat. You will also need to establish appropriate references. The answers to this exercise appear in Appendix C, Part C.

The examples that have uniform titles as access points are:

<u>Example</u>	<u>Access Point</u>
121	Calvin and Hobbes
126	Publication (Group for the Advancement of Psychiatry)
143	Wycherley. Country wife
	Congreve. Way of the world
	Villiers. Rehersal
144	MacDonald. Empty copper sea
	Hallahan. Catch me, kill me
145	Simon. Cheap detective
148	Norton. Glossary of literary terms
155	Evans. American bibliography
160	King. Dark tower

Part II

SUBJECT ANALYSIS

CHAPTER SIX
Dewey Decimal Classification

Suggested Lecture Outline

A. History

B. Arrangement

    1. Order of Main Classes

    2. Summaries

    3. Schedules

    4. Relative Index

    5. Tables

        a. Table 1. Standard Subdivisions

        b. Table 2. Geographic Areas, Historical Periods, Persons

        c. Table 3. Subdivisions for the Arts, for Individual Literatures, for Specific Literary Forms

            (1) Table 3-A. Subdivisions for Works by or about Individual Authors

            (2) Table 3-B. Subdivisions for Works by or about More than One Author

            (3) Table 3-C. Notation to Be Added Where Instructed in Table 3-B, 700.4, 791.4. 808-809

        d. Table 4. Subdivisions of Individual Languages and Language Families

        e. Table 5. Racial, Ethnic, National Groups

        f. Table 6. Languages

        g. Table 7. Groups of Persons

C. Terminology

   1. Centered entries

   2. Dual headings

   3. Bracketed numbers

   4. Class-here notes; Including notes

   5. Class-elsewhere notes; Do-not use notes

   6. Preference order

   7. Add notes

   8. First-of-two rule; Rule of three

   9. Hierarchical force

  10. Number building

  11. Rule of zero

  12. Approximate the whole and Standing room

D. The MARC Record

   1. Field 082

   2. Field 092

Readings: Dewey, Melvil. *Dewey Decimal Classification and Relative Index.* Ed. 21. Albany, N.Y.: Forest Press, 1996.
  "Introduction to the Dewey Decimal Classification," p. xxxi-lvi.

Chan, Lois Mai; Comaromi, John P.; Mitchell, Joan S.; Satija, Mohinder P. *Dewey Decimal Classification: A Practical Guide.* 2nd ed., rev. for DDC 21. Albany N.Y.: Forest Press, 1996.

Comaromi, John P. *Book Numbers.* Littleton, Co.: Libraries Unlimited, 1981.
  or
Lehnus, Donald J. *Book numbers: History, Principles, and Application.* Chicago: American Library Association, 1980.

Resources: Cutter, Charles A. *Cutter-Sanborn Three-Figure Author Table.* Swanson-Swift rev. Littleton, CO: Libraries Unlimited, 1969.

TECHNIQUES USED IN THE DEWEY DECIMAL CLASSIFICATION

Access to the Scheme. There are two methods for finding a specific subject within the Dewey Decimal Classification (DDC). One approach is through the use of the summaries located at the beginning of volume 2 (2:ix-xx), the other is the use of the relative index.

Summaries. There are three summaries: the First Summary presents the class notation and headings for "The Ten Main Classes"; the Second Summary provides this information for "The Hundred Divisions"; while the Third Summary addresses "The Thousand Sections." It is possible to scan these summaries and identify an appropriate class or subclass as an entry point in the schedule for the further development of a classification number.

In addition to the summaries for the schedule as a whole, DDC also provides two types of summaries for parts of a class. The first of these is the "single-level" summary used at the schedules and tables whenever classes are encountered that have subdivisions covering four to forty pages. An example of this type of subdivision appears under Class 324 (The political process) and Class 658.1 (Organization and finance). The second type of summary is the "two-level" summary provided for each main class and division and for classes that have subdivisions extending over more than forty pages. Examples of multi-level summaries appear under Class 360 (Social problems and services; associations) and Class 780 (Music).

Relative Index. The use of the relative index generally is a more efficient and effective method of gaining access to a particular topic in the DDC schedules when the notation for the topic is unknown. This index shows the distribution of subjects among disciplines and provides the notation for these subjects used in the schedule and the tables. An example of an index presentation appears under "Soybeans"

Soybeans	583.74
agricultural economics	338.173 34
botany	583.74
commercial processing	
economics	338.476 648 05655
technology	664.805 655
cooking	641.656 55
field crop	633.34
food	641.356 55
garden crop	635.655

Here, information is given for seven different classes in which works on soybeans might be classified depending upon the subject content of the book. Although not present in this example, the relative index also uses "see also" references to indicate related topics.

Public service workers	352.63
see also Government workers	

Manual. The most striking change begun in DDC 20 and continued in DDC 21 is the provision of a manual to assist in the use of the classification. This manual is located following the relative index in volume 4. The manual describes policies and practices of the Decimal Classification Division of the Library of Congress, gives advice on classification in difficult areas, and detailed information on major revisions in the this edition of DDC. "See-Manual" references are provided in the schedules and tables for additional information needed when classifying including aid in choosing between numbers. Briefer notes are incorporated in the schedules and tables. These Manual and schedule notes help classifiers resolve problems and apply DDC more consistently.

Call Numbers. Call numbers for materials classified using the Dewey Decimal Classification generally consist of two elements: a DDC classification number and a book number (often referred to as a "Cutter" number after the 19th century librarian, C. A. Cutter, who developed a means of systematically assigning alpha-numeric notation for the surnames of individuals). The following call number might be assigned to the book *The Bethesda Weight Loss Diet* by Marilyn Lewis.

613.25   Classification number *[From DDC 21]*
L675b   Book number   *["L675" represents the surname of the main entry*
                          (Lewis). The "b," called a "work mark," represents
                          the first non-article word of the title (Bethesda).]

Because the DDC is widely used in North America for shelf arrangement, a book number and work mark are critical components in the development of a call number for they determine the shelving location of a document in relation to other documents in the same class. The development of book numbers is discussed in detail later.

Classification Numbers. The Dewey Decimal Classification uses a notation of Arabic numerals. The classification is based primarily on division by discipline rather than form. Classification numbers may be expanded decimally to provide for more specific aspects of general subjects or abridged to allow for grouping of works under a broader class.

One method of determining the meaning of a class number is to analyze its parts from the most basic element of the number to the most specific. An example of this type of analysis for the classification number 362.29883 assigned to the book *Sheltering Homeless Cocaine Abusers* follows:

3   Social sciences *[Class 300]*
36   Social problems and services; associations *[Class 360]*
           Specific social problems and *services*
           [Centered heading: 362-363]
362   Social welfare problems and services
362.2   Mental and emotional illnesses and disturbances
362.29   Substance abuse
362.298   Cocaine

362.29883   Provision of food, shelter, household assistance, clothing, other related necessities; recreation
[From 362-363]
      8   Remedial measures services, forms of assistance
    83   Provision of food, shelter, household assistance, clothing, other related necessities; recreation

This step-by-step method will be used throughout this chapter and Appendix D in the analysis of DDC classification numbers.

Number Building. The Dewey Decimal Classification employs several different techniques to provide greater specificity to a class number. Number building involves adding notation to a base number from (1) a table; (2) the entire schedule; or, (3) another part of the schedule. The paragraphs that follow discuss and illustrate a number of ways in which this is done.

Standard Subdivisions. Standard subdivisions (Table 1) make it possible to specify more exactly the form of the material being classified, i.e., dictionaries, serials, etc., or to indicate the treatment or viewpoint of the subject in the document, i.e., philosophy or history. If there is no range of numbers assigned or implied for the use of standard subdivisions in the schedule, the standard subdivision aspect is expressed using Table 1 (Standard Subdivisions). The book *Mineralogy: An Outline* is assigned the classification number 549.0202.

    5   Natural sciences and mathematics *[Class 500]*
    54   Chemistry and allied sciences *[Class 540]*
    549   Mineralogy
    549.0202   Synopses and outlines
           [From Table 1]
           -02 Miscellany
           -0202 Synopses and outlines

In some instances, one or more numbers that are standard subdivisions are given in the schedule. When this approach is taken, it is often to allow the schedule to identify one or more unique aspects of a standard subdivision specific to that subject not provided for in Table 1. The book *Alchemy*, assigned the class number 540.112, demonstrates this

    5   Natural sciences and mathematics *[Class 500]*
    54   Chemistry and allied sciences *[Class 540]*
    540.1   Philosophy and theory
    540.11   Ancient and medieval theories
    540.112   Alchemy

Note that in Table 1 the meaning of –011 is "Systems" rather than "Ancient and medieval theories" and that there is no standard subdivision in Table 1 for –0112

(Alchemy). These standard subdivisions were developed specifically for Class 540. When standard subdivisions are expressed in the schedule, the remaining standard subdivisions in Table 1 may still be used. Thus, the classification number for the book *Computer-Assisted Instruction in the World of Chemistry* (540.785) uses the standard subdivision from Table 1 for computer-assisted instruction (- 0785).

5	Natural sciences and mathematics *[Class 500]*
54	Chemistry and allied sciences *[Class 540]*
540.785	Computer-assisted instruction
	[From Table 1]
	-07 Education, research, related topics
	[Repeats what was stated in the schedule]
	-078 Use of apparatus and equipment in study and teaching
	-0785 Computer-assisted instruction

Sometimes a special range of numbers is provided to express standard subdivisions. Generally this involves the use of more than one zero for the standard subdivision. The classifier is informed that this approach is being used by the presence of a range of numbers for standard subdivisions in the schedules. For example, in Class 340 (Law) the standard subdivisions are indicated in the schedule with the notation .01, .02, .03-08, .09. Note that because the decimal number is given as part of the notation for the standard subdivision this number is added to "340" rather than appended to the base number "34". Thus, the book *An Outline of Law* is assigned the class number 340.0202.

3	Social sciences *[Class 300]*
34	Law *[Class 340]*
340.0202	Synopses and outlines
	-02 Miscellany
	[From the schedule]
	-0202 Synopses and outlines
	[From Table 1]

Another way that a range of numbers intended to be used as standard subdivisions is indicated in the schedules appears in Class 361 (Social problems and social welfare in general). In this class, the standard subdivisions are indicated by the allocation of the notation range ".001 - .008". The book *Social Welfare and Social Problems: A Synopsis* is assigned the class number 361.00202

3	Social sciences *[Class 300]*
36	Social problems and services; association *[Class 360]*
361	Social problems and social welfare in general
361.00202	Synopses and outlines
	[From Table 1]
	-02 Miscellany
	-0202 Synopses and outlines

Approximate the Whole. Standard subdivisions may be used only with works that approximate the whole. A work is said to approximate the whole if it

- is nearly coextensive with the topic of a DDC heading;
- covers more than half the content of the heading; or,
- covers representative examples from three or more subdivisions of a class (adapted from Chan p. 215)

The book *The Treatment of Hyperactive Students in Texas Public Schools* must be assigned the class number 371.93 rather than the more specific number 371.9009764 which adds the geographical standard subdivision for Texas (09764) because the work does not address all delinquent and problems students in Texas public schools but rather is limited to those who are hyperactive.

3	Social sciences [Class 300]
37	Education [Class 370]
371	Schools and their activities; special education
371.9	Special education
371.93	Delinquent and problem students

Topics such as this that do not approximate the whole are referred to as being in "standing room" in the number. For more on the concept of approximating the whole see the Manual (4:906).

Other Tables. The other six tables in DDC 21 may be used only when directed either in the schedules or under a standard subdivision. When their use is directed, the user always will be provided with a base number to which the number from the table is to be added. For example, under Class 398.9 (Proverbs), the classifier is directed to add to the base number "398.9," a number from Table 6 (Languages). Thus, the book *The Complete Yiddish Proverbs* would be assigned the class number 398.9391.

3	Social sciences *[Class 300]*
39	Customs, etiquette, folklore *[Class 390]*
398	Folklore
398.9	Proverbs
398.9391	Yiddish
	[From Table 6]
	-3 Germanic (Teutonic) languages
	-39 Other Germanic languages
	-391 Yiddish

Frequently, an aspect that could be expressed using one of the Tables 2 through 7 is present in the document being classified but cannot be expressed because DDC 21 does not direct that the relevant table may be used. In some instances, Tables 2 through 7 may be used indirectly through the use of Table 1. This indirect approach is frequently employed to allow for use of Table 2 (Geographic Areas, Historical Periods, Persons). For example, the standard subdivision "-09" (Historical, geographic, persons treatment) allows for the use of Table 2 with "-091" (Treatment by areas, regions, places in general) and "-093-099 (Treatment by specific continents, countries, localities,; extraterrestrial worlds). Similarly, the standard subdivision "-08809-0889" (Specific occupational and religious groups) allows Tables 7 (Groups of Persons) to be used.

"Add to" Directions. These directions are very similar to the number building process used for Tables 2 through 7. The difference is that instead of adding from a table, the classifier is given a base number and instructed to add to that number from another part of the schedule. A number that is related to another number as a result of being built with the same notation is called a "cognate" number. For example, under Class 359.1 to 359.2 (Naval life and resources), the classifier is instructed to add the numbers following "355" in the range 355.1-355.2 to the base number "359". Following these instructions, the class number 359.1336 would be assigned to the book *Naval Etiquette*.

3	Social sciences *[Class 300]*
35	Public administration and military science *[Class 350]*
359	Sea (Naval) forces and warfare
359.1336	Naval etiquette

        [As instructed under "359.1-.2" the numbers following "355 for etiquette (1336) are added to the base number "359".]

355.1	Military life and customs
355.13	Conduct and rewards
355.133	Regulation of conduct
355.1336	Etiquette

In some cases, an "add to" direction provides for addition from the entire classification schedule (volumes 2 and 3). For example, under Class 016 (Bibliographies and catalogs of works on specific subjects or in specific disciplines) it is possible to provide a class number for a bibliography on any subject by following the "add to . . . 001-999" directions. For *A Bibliography of Folklore*, the class number 016.398 would be assigned.

0	Generalities *[Class 000]*
01	Bibliography *[Class 010]*
	Bibliographies and catalogs of individuals, of works by specific classes of authors, of anonymous and pseudonymous works, of works from specific places, of works on specific subjects or in specific disciplines *[Centered heading: 012-106]*
016	Bibliographies and catalogs of works on specific subjects or in specific disciplines
016.398	Folklore

        [As instructed under "016," the number from the range "001-999" for folklore (398) is added to the base number "016".]

3	Social sciences *[Class 300]*
39	Customs, etiquette, folklore *[Class 390]*
398	Folklore

Book or Cutter Numbers. Smaller libraries often use an alphabetic representation of the main entry as a way to sub-arrange works in the same class. An example of this approach is illustrated by the call number for the book *Air Transportation* by Robert Bartlett.

387.7
Bar

This approach to shelf arrangement works well for smaller collections. Problems arise, however, when one encounters multiple works by the same person in the same class or works in the same class that use the same letters to represent the main entries, for example, three books on air transportation one by Bartlett, another by Barnes, and a third by Barrow. Generally, if a library anticipates significant growth or if many works are classified in a few classes because the library is specialized in its collection, an alphanumeric representation of the main entry generally is advised.

Currently, there are three sources widely used for this alphanumeric notation.

C. A. Cutter's Two-Figure Author Table
C. A. Cutter's Three-Figure Author Table
Cutter-Sanborn Three-Figure Author Table

Each of these tables provides an alphanumeric representation for a word, usually the main entry, but each results in a different number for the same name. For example, the name Judith Watkins would be assigned the following book numbers from these tables:

Cutter 2-Figure	Cutter 3-Figure	Cutter-Sanborn 3-Figure
W32	W325	W335

In 1998, OCLC released the OCLC Dewey Cutter Macro, a tool that provides for automated cutter number assignment for libraries using either the Cutter or Cutter-Sanborn tables. Unlike its predecessors, the OCLC Dewey Cutter Macro uses a four-figure cutter number. This reduces the need for catalogers to individually expand on the cutter number derived from the three-figure table to avoid number conflicts in heavily used portions of the Cutter table.

In addition to the notation derived from a Cutter table, most libraries use a letter of the alphabet in lower case to sub-arrange by title works by an author within a class. For the book *Organic Farming,* by Sheila Locke, the book number "L814o" would be assigned. The lowercase letter "o" represents the first non-article word of the title.

Special procedures for the assignment of books numbers for biographies, different editions of the same work, bibliographies, criticisms, translations, etc. are employed by libraries. The procedures vary from library to library, although there are general principles for the assignment of these numbers. See the works by Comaromi and Lehnus for more detailed discussion of assigning book numbers in these situations.

Prefix. A prefix often is used to indicate the location of a work in a special collection, for example, browsing, reference, oversized, or juvenile collections. The location or special collection symbol is generally placed at the head of the call number. For the *Concordance to the Works of Sir Walter Scott* by John Kerry, the prefix "R" is the location symbol in the call number indicates that the work is located in the Reference Collection.

> R
> 823.6
> S431k

OCLC/MARC Fields 082 and 092 – Dewey Decimal Call Number. The 082 field is used in the MARC bibliographic record to record Dewey call numbers assigned by the Library of Congress, the National Library of Canada, or other national agencies. For the book *Following in Father's Footsteps : Social Mobility in Ireland* by Michael Hout the DDC number, developed by the Library of Congress using DDC 20, would be formatted:

> 082 0 1   305.5/13/09415 ‡2 20

The first indicator in this field is used to report the edition of DDC used to develop the number – (0) full edition or (1)abridged edition. The second indicator reports whether LC assigned the DDC number (1) or an agency other than LC (4). Subfield "a" is used for the classification number and Subfield "2" to record the number of the edition used to develop the class number. The Library of Congress uses a prime mark (') to indicate logical places where a long DDC number could be abridged. OCLC and a number of other cataloging systems use a (/) to represent the prime mark.

The restriction of the use of MARC Field 082 to DDC numbers assigned by national library agencies necessitates that another field be used to record DDC numbers assigned by other libraries. OCLC uses Field 092 for this purpose. The First Indicator values are identical to those used in Field 082, the second indicator unused. The same subfields used for Field 082 are used with Field 092 although additional subfields are available. Typically, a subfield used very frequently with Field 092 and infrequently with Field 082 is Subfield "b.." This subfield is where the book number is recorded. The book *Getting Ready to Read*, by Diane Lynch-Fraser, classified using DDC 21, Field 092 would be formatted:

> 092 0   649.55 ‡b L987g ‡2 21

DEWEY DECIMAL CLASSIFICATION EXERCISES

Answers to these exercises appear in Appendix D

A.   The Relative Index. Indicate the appropriate classification number in the
       Relative Index for each of these titles.

1.   *Seed pictures and other dried natural arrangements.*

2.   *The varieties of cheese and how they are produced.*

3.   *The decorative arts of primitive peoples.*

4.   *The tactics of aerial warfare.*

5.   *Beginning typewriting: tests and drills.*

6.   *Book mending for libraries.*

7.   *Short-range weather forecasting.*

8.   *Doll furniture designs for the amateur craftsman.*

9.   *The inventions of J. S. Bach.*

B.   Analyzing DDC Numbers. Indicate the hierarchical development for the
        classification number provided with each title.

10.   *Library instruction in the elementary school.*

        027.8222

11.   *Cancer in Connecticut: incidence and characteristics.*

        616.994009746

12.   *Spare part surgery: transplants, the surgical practice of the future.*

        617.95

13.   *The farm beef herd.*

        636.213

14.   *Collective bargaining in the U. S. lithographic industry.*

        331.8904168623150973

15.   *Education for librarianship: the design of the curriculum of library schools in the
        United States.*

        020.71173

C.   Table 1: Standard Subdivisions. Classify the following document titles as specifically as possible.

16.   *The quarterly journal of technology.*

17.   *A short history of inventions.*

18.   *A dictionary of physics.*

19.   *Current methods in adult education research.*

20.   *Technology during the thirteenth century: a history.*

21.   *The encyclopedia of religion.*

22.   *Bookbinding as a profession.*

23.   *Biographies of 19th century mineralogists.*

24.   *The Pendant directory of mineralogists.*

D.   <u>Table 2: Area Tables</u>. Classify the following document titles as specifically as possible.

25.   *Patriotic societies of France.*

26.   *Library schools in Germany: a description.*

27.   *The books of bibliography of the University of Chicago Press: the definitive bibliography of all its published works.*
        [Located in Chicago, Illinois]

E.   <u>Tables 1 and 2</u>. Classify the following document titles as specifically as possible.

28.   *Orsini's directory of lawyers in Italy.*

29.   *Mining in 19th century Colorado: a history.*

30.   *Teaching engineering in Canadian universities.*

31.   *Engineers in Texas.*
        [A directory of engineers in Texas throughout the 20th century]

F.   <u>Table 4: Subdivisions of Individual Languages</u>. Classify the following
      document titles as specifically as possible.

32.   *Language today.*
        [A Canadian English language periodical]

33.   *Teaching the Romance languages.*

34.   *Teaching French in American secondary schools.*
        [Coverage limited to the U.S.]

35.   *Spanish words incorporated into the English language: an exhaustive list*

36. *The comprehensive French dictionary.*

37. *German-English, English-German dictionary.*

38. *German-Bulgarian, Bulgarian-German dictionary.*

39. *Papers of the East Slavic Languages Association.*
     [A bi-monthly publication of the international society]

G.   <u>800s and Tables 3A, 3B, and 3C: Literature (Belles Lettres) and Subdivisions of
     Individual Literatures</u>. Classify the following document titles as specifically as
     possible.

40. *The encyclopedia of English literature.*

41. *Pantheon anthology of English literature.*

42. *English fantasy.*
     [An anthology]

43. *English literature for boys.*
    [A collection]

44. *English literature of the pre-Elizabethan period: a criticism.*

45. *English drama: a critical study.*

46. *English drama of the Elizabethan period: a collection.*

47. *A collection of Welsh (Cymric) literature.*

48. *Drama of the 1960's.*
    [A collection of Estonian plays]

49. *18th century French literature.*
    [A collection]

50.   *19th century French poetry: a collection.*

H.   900s: Geography, History, and Auxiliary Disciplines.

51.   *Geography of Martha's Vineyard, Massachusetts.*

52.   *Travel in the British Isles during the Roman occupation.*

53.   *The exploration of Chile by Europeans.*

54.   *The history of medieval Austria.*

55.   *The Spanish-American War: the American perspective.*

56.   *The history of Pawtucket, Rhode Island.*

57.   *Outline of Eastern European history.*

58.   *History of the Burmese in New Zealand.*

59.   *World history of the Irish people.*

I.   Other Tables and "Add To" Directions.

60.   *Customs of the Huguenots.*

61.   *The management of agricultural museums.*

62.   *Visitor's guide to the Cobb Agriculture Museum, Butler County, Pennsylvania.*

63.   *The manufacture of football equipment.*
        [This is American football]

64.   *Congenital diseases of the scalp.*

65.   *Cheerleading at Indiana University basketball games.*
        [Indiana University is located in Bloomington (Monroe County), Indiana]

66.   *Materials for teaching science in elementary schools.*

67.   *Stamps of Ghana: a collector's guide.*

68.   *Atlas of France.*

69.   *Seventeenth century bookbinding.*

70.   *Ancient Roman coins: their description for collectors.*

71.   *Photography as a hobby: a guide for the amateur.*

72.   *Prospecting for gold in Colorado.*

73.   *Flagstone sidewalks: illustrations of their design and construction.*

74.   *Bibliography of folk literature.*

75.   *Solar houses in Southern California: a guide to architectural design.*

76.   *The Holy Bible.*
       [A modern version in Japanese]

77.   *The geography of Ethiopia.*

78.   *Design of interior furnishings for Glaxo-Wellcome, Inc., Research Triangle Park,*
       North Carolina.
       [A pharmaceutical firm in Durham County, North Carolina]

79.   *The natural sciences.*
       [A programmed learning text]

80.   *The anatomy of snakes.*

81.   *Research in medical toxicology.*

82.   *Travel in Trinidad today.*

83.   *The management of poplar forests.*

84.   *Books written by adolescents: a bibliography.*

85.   *Crime in Brazil.*

86.   *Norway's participation in the Korean War.*
       [The contributions of Norway extend beyond military participation]

CHAPTER SEVEN

Library of Congress Classification

Suggested Lecture Outline

    A. History

    B. Arrangement

        1. Order of Main classes

        2. Preface

        3. Synopses

        4. Outline

        5. Schedule

        6. Tables

        7. Index

        8. Adds and changes (A&C)

        9. Index to A&C

    C. Relationship to LC subject headings

    D. Techniques

        1. Class letter(s)/numbers

        2. Cutter numbers

            a. Double cutter numbers

            b. A-Z cutter numbers

            c. Reserve cutter numbers

            d. Reserve cutter number ranges

            e. Successive cutter numbers

        3. Arrange-like directions

        4. Tables

        5. Date

Immroth, John Phillip. *Immroth's Guide to the Library of Congress Classification.* 4th ed. by Lois Mai Chan. Englewood, CO.: Libraries Unlimited, 1990.

Resources: Library of Congress. *Classification.*
[See the "Introduction" of this workbook for a list of the current editions of the LC schedules that may have been used in this chapter's exercises.]

Library of Congress. Cataloging Policy and Support Office. *Subject Cataloging Manual: Shelflisting.* 2nd ed. Washington, DC: The Office, 1995. (SCM:SL)

Library of Congress. Office for Subject Cataloging Policy. *Subject Cataloging Manual: Classification.* 1st ed. Washington, DC: Cataloging Distribution Service, Library of Congress, 1992 (SCM:C)

TECHNIQUES USED IN THE
LIBRARY OF CONGRESS CLASSIFICATION

Call Numbers. Call numbers for the Library of Congress Classification generally consist of three elements: the classification number (using both letters of the alphabet and arabic numerals) , one or two cutter numbers and a date.

SB
435.52
.N6
S3
1989

Classification Numbers. The classification number represents the subject of a document. It is composed of from one to three uppercase letters and an arabic whole number of up to four digits (1-9999). This number also may have decimal extensions.

Cutter Numbers. Following the class number is a cutter or book number. The cutter number, usually representing the first non-article word of the main entry although the Library of Congress also does employ it to further represent the subject of the work. The cutter number provides for the alphabetical subarrangement of works within a class and enables a library to develop a unique call number for each work. In some situations LC may use two cutters numbers in a call number. These are called "double cutter" numbers.

A cutter number consists of a single letter of the alphabet preceded by a decimal point. The alphabetic character is followed by one or more arabic numerals. When a second cutter number is used, only the first is preceded by a decimal point.

The table issued by the Library of Congress for the development of cutter numbers appears on the next page. It has been taken from the *Subject Cataloging*

Manual: Shelflisting (SCM:SL), Instruction G 060. It should be noted that cutter numbers derived from this table are decimal in nature and relative. As such, they can be expanded to provide unique call numbers and locate any given document between two others. This process of adjusting cutter numbers is referred to as shelflisting. LC advises its catalogers when shelflisting to never end a cutter number with "0" or "1." The following examples illustrate how names within the C range of a given class might be assigned different cutter numbers:

Catton	.C3	Cox	.C69
Cecil	.C4	Crane	.C7
Cheever	.C44	Crider	.C75
Cicco	.C5	Cronin	.C76
Clint	.C55	Cullen	.C8
Corson	.C6	Cyert	.C9

Double cutter numbers. This technique is used throughout the classification scheme. It occurs most frequently when the first cutter number is used to indicate a topic, with the second cutter number most often used to alphabetize for the main entry. Usually no more than two cutter numbers are used in the LC classification to develop a call number. Double cutter numbers are used in some of the examples that follow.

Cutter Table

(1) **After initial** vowels

for the second letter:	b	d	l-m	n	p	r	s-t	u-y
use number:	2	3	4	5	6	7	8	9

(2) **After initial letter** S

for the second letter:	a	ch	e	h-i	m-p	t	u	w-z
use number:	2	3	4	5	6	7	8	9

(3) **After the initial letters** Qu
for the second

[i.e., third] letter:	a	e	i	o	r	t	y
use number:	3	4	5	6	7	8	9

For initial letters
Qa-Qt, use: 2-29

(4) **After other initial** consonants

for the second letter:	a	e	i	o	r	u	y
use number:	3	4	5	6	7	8	9

(5) **For** expansion

for the [third] letter:	a-d	e-h	i-l	m-o	p-s	t-v	w-z
use number:	3	4	5	6	7	8	9

A-Z Cutter Number Division. Cuttering is used throughout the LC classification to specify and subarrange topics in alphabetical order that would otherwise have been distributed alphabetically by main entry within the class. This technique incorporates a subject or topical arrangement function into the cutter element of a call number. When these topical elements are known, they are often listed in the schedule with their associated cutter number. The following use of A-Z cutter number divisions occurs in Subclass SF (Animal culture):

SF	Animal culture *[1996 ed.]*
	Feeds and feeding. Animal nutrition
98.A-Z	Individual feed constituents, compounds, and feed additives, A-Z
98.A2	Additives (General)
98.A34	Adrenergic beta agonists
98.A38	Amino acid chelates
98.A4	Amino acids
98.A44	Ammonia
98.A5	Antibiotics
98.A9	Azelaic acid
98.C45	Chromium
	. . . .
98.T7	Trace elements
98.U7	Urea
98.V5	Vitamins

Using this table of cuttered topics, the book *Amino Acids in Animal Nutrition*, by Boone (1983) would be assigned the call number

> SF98
> .A4
> B6
> 1983

In this call number, ".A4" is derived from the topical cutter number list in the schedule. Should a document being classified have a special topic that is not included in this list, it could be provided for within this alphabetic array. Although it is stated in the schedule, if a second cutter number has not been used already a cutter number is assigned for the main entry to subarrange within the special topic.

The A-Z technique is also used even when specific cutter numbers have not been pre-assigned to topics. Often this approach is used to subarrange subjects by country, state or other political divisions. For example, in Class S (Agriculture), the following appears:

S	Agriculture (General) *[1996 ed.]*
	Agricultural education.
	Agricultural extension work
	General and United States
544	General works
544.3.A-W	By state, A-W.
544.5.A-Z	Other regions or countries, A-Z

Using this schedule, the book *Agricultural Extension Activities in Canada,* by Lansing (1987) would be assigned the call number:

S544.5
.C3
L3
1987

The hierarchical breakdown of this call number is:

S	Agriculture *[1996 ed.]*
530-559.65	Agricultural education
544-545.53	Agricultural extension work
544.5.A-Z	Other regions or countries, A-Z
.C3	[Canada]
	[Cutter number for "Canada" from SCM:SL Instruction G 300]
L3	[Lansing]
	[Cutter number for the personal name main entry]
1987	[Date]

   Reserve cutter numbers. In some situations, a cutter number, or a range of cutter numbers, may be reserved for special purposes. Often the objective is to separate works by form or to further general treatment of a topic for more specific treatment. For example, in subclass SB (Plant Culture), the following appears:

SB	Plant culture *[1996 ed.]*
	Parks and public reservations
481.A1	Periodicals. Societies. Serials
481.A2	Congresses
481.A4-Z	General works

The periodical *Parks Monthly* would be assigned the call number

SB481
.A1
P3

The hierarchical structure of this call number is

S	Agriculture *[1996 ed.]*
SB	Plant culture
481-485	Parks and public reservations
481.A1	Periodicals. Societies. Serials
.P3	[Parks]
	[Cutter number for the first word of the title main entry]

Note that for this serial no date is provided in the call number. Library of Congress practice for the inclusion of dates in call numbers excludes their use for the call numbers of serials.

In Subclass SF (Animal Culture) the following appears:

SF	Animal Culture *[1996 ed.]*
	Veterinary medicine
	Veterinary parasitology
810.A3	General works
810.A4-Z	By parasite or pest, A-Z

All general works on veterinary parasitology would be assigned the reserve cutter number ".A3" followed by a cutter number for the main entry of the book. Thus, the book *Introductory Veterinary Parasitology*, by Jones (1998) would be assigned the call number

SF810
.A3
J6
1998

The hierarchical structure of this call number is:

S	Agriculture *[1996 ed.]*
SF	Animal Culture
600-1100	Veterinary medicine
810.A3-810.T75	Veterinary parasitology
.A3	General works
J6	[Jones]
	[Cutter number for the personal name main entry]
1998	[Date]

In this instance, following the reserve cutter number "A3," the classifier cuttered for the main entry. A second cutter number is then assigned provided that two cutter numbers have not been used already.

Reserve cutter number ranges. In some classes a range of numbers is reserved for a specific purpose. For example, in Subclass SH (Aquaculture. Fisheries. Angling) the following appears:

SH	Aquaculture. Fisheries. Angling *[1996 ed.]*
1	Periodicals. Societies. Serials
3	Congresses
	Documents
	United States
11.A1-A5	Federal
11.A6-Z	State

The cutter number range ".A1-5" is a shelflisting device. There is no way to determine the appropriate subarrangement within ".A1-5" without referring to either the local library's shelflist or searching the Library of Congress catalog. The LC catalog is available using the Internet. A call number search of that catalog will display how LC has used cuttering for SH11.

Successive cutter numbers. This is another technique using cutter numbers for the subarrangement to designate a subject subclass, indicate the form of material, or provide for further geographical subarrangement. In the schedules use of successive cutter numbers is indicated by the use of a number following a variable, for example, ".x3." or the presence of numbers enclosed within parentheses, for example, "(1)." It should be noted that not all numbers enclosed within parentheses in the schedules are successive cutter numbers. The different form of presentation of the use of successive cutter numbers is the result of the revision of individual LC schedules at different points in time. In Subclass SB (Plant Culture) the following is the use of a successive cutter number for geographical subdivision:

```
SB              Plant culture  [1996 ed.]
                    Flowers and flower culture.  Ornamental plants
                    Flower shows.  Exhibitions
                        . . .
     441                General works
     441.4              Judging
     441.5              Floral parades
                            For local, see SB441.7+
     441.6.A-Z          International.  By place, A-Z
                            Subarranged by year
                        National, state, and local
                          By region or country
                            United States
     441.7                  General works
     441.73.A-Z             By region or state, A-Z
                                Under each state:
                            .x          General works
                            .x2A-Z      By place, A-Z
```

The Milwaukee Flower Show: An Illustrated View by Solomon Neirhait (1987) would be assigned the call number:

```
SB441.73
.W62
M5
1987
```

The hierarchical structure of this call number is:

```
S              Agriculture  [1996 ed.]
  SB              Plant culture
    403-450.87      Flower and flower culture.  Ornamental plants
    441                Flower shows.  Exhibitions
                         National, state, and local
                           By region and country
      441.7-441.73           United States
        441.73.A-Z             By region or state, A-Z
          .W6                     [Wisconsin]
                                  [Cutter number from SCM:SL Instruction G
                                  302]
```

W62   By place, A-Z
M5   [Milwaukee]
                 [Cutter number derived from the LC cutter
                 table]
1987   [Date]

Note: *No cutter number could be provided for "Lares" because 2 cutter numbers were used as*
         part of the subject classification.

Date. In 1982, the Library of Congress has added the date to all call numbers
created for monographs. Prior to that year, a date was added only to the call number
when it was needed to identify another edition of that work. Generally, the date used
is the imprint date, although there are special situations where other dates are used.
For complete instructions on the assignment of dates see the SCM:SL Instruction G
140.

OCLC/MARC Fields 050 and 090 – Library of Congress Call Number. The 050
field is used in the MARC bibliographic record to record Library of Congress call
numbers assigned by the Library of Congress or other national library. For the book
The beginners book of side-saddle riding by Katherine Fairstein (1994) the LC call number,
developed by the Library of Congress, would be formatted:

050 0 1   SF309.27 ‡b .F3 1994

The first indicator in this field is used to report whether the work is in the Library of
Congress (0) or not in LC (1). The second indicator records whether LC assigned the
call number (1) or an agency other than LC (4). Subfield "a" is used for the
classification number and Subfield "b" to record the "item," i.e., cutter number.
Because LC call numbers may have more than one cutter number this will affect the
location of subfield b. That subfield precedes the second cutter number if there are
two with the first cutter number recorded in subfield a.

The restriction of the use of MARC Field 050 to LC call numbers assigned by LC
or another national library necessitates that another field be used to record LC call
numbers assigned by other libraries. OCLC uses Field 090 (Locally Assigned LC-type
Call Number) for this purpose. The book *Home Orchid Growing* by Taylor Givens
(1991) by LC call number assigned by a local library would be formatted:

090   SB409 ‡b .G5 1991

No indicators are used with Field 090. Subfield a is used to record the classification
number while Subfield b contains the "local cutter number."

LIBRARY OF CONGRESS CLASSIFICATION EXERCISES

Answers to these exercises appear in Appendix E.

A.   Assign LC call numbers to each of the following titles. Indicate the hierarchy
        for each call number.

1.   *How to catalog a rare book*, by Duncan. 1973.

2.   *How to grow asparagus*, by Unwin. 1922.

3.   *The woman's suffrage movement in the United States, 1870-1910*, by Sand. 1938.

4.   *The folklore of holy wells and springs*, by Ash. 1956.

5.   *How to train your homing pigeon*, by Walls. 1934.

6.   *The first book of astronomy*, by Clark. 1985.
            [A book for children]

7.   *The art of writing biographies,* by Queen. 1981.
         [A book of techniques]

8.   *A manual of archeology for the amateur archaeologist,* by Biddle. 1979.

9.   *The chemical analysis of rocks,* by Hruska. 1979.

10.   *Photography for children,* by Lytton. 1998.

11.   *Encyclopedia of science fiction,* by O'Rourke. 1996

12.   *Coins and coin collecting,* by Quiller. 1983.

13.   *Visiting Doctor Sue: A child's guide to what happens in an animal hospital,* by Ivers. 1986.

14.   *A history of 18th century astrology*, by Lewis. 1969.

15.   *The female worker: the vocational education for women*, by Tyrone. 1986.

16.   *A dictionary of philosophy*, by Ludlow. 1976.
      [In English]

17.   *"Bridge freezes before road": ice loads and bridge design*, by Womack. 1994.

B.   <u>A-Z directions</u>. Assign LC call numbers to each of the following titles.

18.   *Life on the stage : the biography of Helen Hayes*, by Loy. 1982.
      [The American actress born in 1900]

19.   *The National League*, by Gregg. 1922.
      [A history of the professional baseball league]

20.   *Go Cubs! a history of the Chicago Cubs,* by Rogers. 1994.
        [The professional baseball team]

21.   *School architecture in California,* by Salten. 1996.

22.   *Witchcraft in Alabama,* by Shick. 1961.

23.   *Cheesebox on a raft: the Union ironclad Monitor,* by Carr. 1919.
        [Centers on the activities of this ship during the American Civil War]

24.   *The Hogarth Press: the history of a great private press,* by Hull. 1966.

25.   *Techniques of writing mystery and detective stories,* by Fry. 1971.

26.   *The Honda Accord repair manual: 1994-1996,* by Ferry. 1996.

27.   *A bibliography of articles on motorcycles*, by Jansen. 1978.

28.   *North American Indian embroidery*, by Llewellyn. 1947.

29.   *Flowers in literature: a perspective*, by Escher. 1949.

30.   *How to win at the game Trivial Pursuit*, by Eastman. 1985.

31.   *Modern paper manufacture in Japan*, by Ervin. 1980.

C.   Fixed Successive Cutter Numbers. Assign LC call numbers to each of the
        following titles.

32.   *Kew Gardens: the British Royal Botanic Gardens*, by Mayfield. 1983.

33.   *Weighted in the balance: a history of the "Laboratory of the Government Chemist" an
        Australian institution*, by Blunt. 1992.

34. *Great buildings, great food: the architecture of the great restaurants of France,* by Marchand. 1989.

35. *Brasserie France: architecture with a Mediterranean flair,* by Bates. 1996.
   [This restaurant is in Marseilles]

36. *Latvian book publishing directory,* compiled by Solowicz. 1998.

37. *Walking tour of the bookdealers of Riga,* by Litinski. 1997.
   [Riga, Latvia]

38. *Philadelphians to the rescue: Philadelphia's volunteer fire companies of the early 19th century,* by Chestnut. 1984.

39. *Firehouse: the firehouses of Illinois,* by Barnard. 1999.

D.   Tables within the text. Double Cutter Numbers. Assign LC call numbers to
        each of the following titles.

40.   *Directory of school officials in Kentucky,* issued by the Kentucky Department of
        Public Instruction. 1977.

41.   *Directory of school officials in Preston County, W. Va.,* issued by the Preston
        County Board of Education. 1980.

42.   *Examination of the British drug scene,* by Hunter. 1971.

43.   *Psychedelic drug use in Vancouver,* by Steele. 1982.

44.   *The history of Brazil's libraries,* by Louis. 1955.

45.   *Libraries in the Tolna region of Hungary:* a history, by Case. 1952.

46.   *The Srečko Vilhar Public Library: an illustrated history,* by Smolič. 1994.
        [Located in Koper, Slovenia]

47.   *Caves of Scotland,* by MacDonald. 1977.

48.   *Made by ice: Wisconsin landforms created by the glaciers,* by Edison. 1946.

49.   *The beautiful valleys of Scotland,* by Lutz. 1981.

50.   *The handbook for publishers in France,* by La Mont. 1974.

51.   *The history of publishing in Czechoslovakia,* by Zdarsky. 1984.

52.   *Publishers and booksellers in Turkey: a comprehensive directory,* by Land. 1985.

E.   <u>Tables within the text</u>. Assign LC call numbers to each of the following titles. Use GV581+ (Sports : History).

53.   *The history of sports in Texas,* by Connelly. 1964.

54.   *The history of sports in Baton Rouge, La.*, by Quentin. 1921.

55.   *The history of sports in Ontario Province, Canada*, by Stone. 1932.

56.   *The history of sports in Mexico City, Mexico*, by Squires. 1970.

57.   *The history of sports in Bogota*, by Lares. 1968.
       [The city in Colombia, South America]

58.   *The history of sports in Ireland*, by O'Brien. 1949.

59.   *The history of sports in Dublin*, by McCaffrey. 1976.

F.   Class H. Assign LC call numbers to each of the following titles. Use HV 8157-8280.7 (Police).

60.   *The municipal police of Buenos Aires,* by Edwards. 1981.

61.   *The accountability of the English constable,* by Marshall. 1973.

62.   *The national police in Bulgaria,* by Raible. 1961.

63.   *The 20th century: a century of social reform in India,* by Natira. 1949.

64.   *A study of life in a Devonshire community,* by White. 1976.

65.   *Social problems in the Arab countries: a statistical report,* by Azeno. 1983.

66.   *A social history of 19th century Europe,* by Hill. 1935

67. *Power in Ica: the social structure of a Peruvian community*, by Lyle. 1966.

68. *Social mobility in Gibraltar*, by Wherry. 1981.

69. *The literature of social reform in China, 1830-1853*, compiled and translated by Ogden. 1927.

70. *Continuity and change: the social history of Spain since World War II*, by Ilian. 1978.

Use HG2701-3542.7 (Banking).

71. *La Banque de France: its history and influence*, by Andre. 1989.

72. *Banking and monetary control in South Africa*, by Koster. 1978.

73. *Annual report of the Banco de los Andes.*
    [Located in Bogata, Colombia]

74.   *Banking in Barcelona, Spain: 1840 to 1920,* by Voltes. 1962.

G.   <u>Class P: Forty-Nine Number Author</u>. Assign LC call numbers to each of the following titles.

75.   *The writings of Mark Twain (Samuel Langhorne Clemens).* Autographed [unedited] edition. 1899.

76.   *Huckleberry Finn, by Mark Twain.* London. 1844.

77.   *Le avventure di Tom Sawyer,* par Mark Twain ; traduzione di T. Orsi. 1930.
        [A translation into Italian]

78.   *Interpretations of The Adventures of Huckleberry Finn: a collection of essays,* edited by Abbott. 1938.

79.   *Twain's The mysterious stranger and the critics,* by Tuckey. 1968.
        [A criticism]

80. *Mark Twain: a profile*, by Kaplan. 1967.
     [A biography]

81. *Mark Twain's letters*, arranged with commentary by Paine. 1917.

H.   Class P: Nineteen Number Author. Assign LC call numbers to each of the following titles.

82. *The works of Herman Melville*, edited by Winchester. London, 1922-1924.

83. *Typee, or, A peep at Polynesian life*, by Herman Melville. 1957.

84. *Typee*, roman traduit de L'anglois par Verdier, Paris. 1945.
     [A translation into French]

85. *Rebel genius, the life of Herman Melville*, by Bixby. 1970.

86. *Studies in the minor and later works of Melville*, by Hull. 1970.

87.   *Melville's use of the Bible,* by Wright. 1949.

88.   *Melville's Israel Potter,* by Keyssar. 1969.
         [A criticism of that work]

89.   *The letters of Herman Melville,* edited by Davis. 1960.

I.   Class P: Cutter Number Author. Assign LC call numbers to each of the
         following titles.

90.   *The Faulkner reader: selections from the works of William Faulkner.* 1954.

91.   *The sound and the fury,* by William Faulkner. 1961.

92.   *Faulkner's The sound and the fury,* by Gold. 1964.
         [A criticism]

93.   *Requiem pour une Nonne, by William Faulkner;* translated by Coindreau. 1957.
       [A translation into French of Requiem for a nun]

94.   *Four studies of Faulkner,* by Overton. 1980.
       [A criticism]

CHAPTER EIGHT

Library of Congress Subject Headings

Suggested Lecture Outline

- A. History
- B. Word Forms
- C. Subject Headings in Card and Online Catalogs
- D. Entry Elements
    1. Headings
    2. LC Classification References
    3. Scope Notes
    4. Term Relationships
        a. "Use" References
        b. "Used For" Terms
        c. "Broader" Terms
        d. "Narrower" Terms
        e. "Related" Terms
        f. "See Also" Instructions
    5. Subdivisions
        a. Types
            (1) Topical
            (2) Form
            (3) Chronological
            (4) Geographic

b.   Free-Floating

(1)   Form and Topical of General Applicability

(2)   Persons, Corporate Bodies, Places, etc.

(3)   Controlled by Pattern Headings

E.   Headings Not Listed in the Controlled Vocabulary

Readings: Chan, Lois Mai. *Library of Congress Subject Headings: Principles and Application.* 3rd ed. Englewood, CO: Libraries Unlimited, 1995.

Library of Congress. Cataloging Policy and Support Office. *Library of Congress Subject Headings.* 22nd ed. Washington, DC: Library of Congress, Cataloging Distribution Service, 1999. "Introduction."

Resources: Library of Congress. Cataloging Policy and Support Office. *Library of Congress Subject Headings.* 22nd ed. Washington, DC: Library of Congress, Cataloging Distribution Service, 1999. (LCSH)

Library of Congress. Subject Cataloging Division. *Subject Cataloging Manual: Subject Headings.* 5th ed. Washington, DC: Library of Congress, 1988. (SCM:SH)

TECHNIQUES USED WITH
LIBRARY OF CONGRESS SUBJECT HEADINGS

The Library of Congress employs techniques in the use of its subject headings that are also used by a number of other controlled vocabularies to varied degrees. Specific guidelines for the use of its subject headings are published by the Library of Congress in its *Subject Cataloging Manual: Subject Headings* (SCM:SH).

Word Forms. Subject headings use a variety of word forms. A listing of the forms used by the Library of Congress, and some examples of each, appear below:

	Examples
Common nouns	Artillery
	Biscuits
	Carols
Phrases	Artificial satellites in navigation
	Copper in the body
	Education of the aged

Inverted headings	Artists, Blind Buildings, Plastic Dropout behavior, Prediction of
Glossed headings	Block building (Children's activity) Calypso (Game); Fire control (Gunnery)
Proper Nouns	Artistic Woodwork Strike, 1973 Bound Brook, Battle of, 1777 Canaan Mountain (W. Va.) *[Although there are a few proper names in LCSH, they primarily serve as examples. Proper names are added by an individual library as needed in the appropriate form, i.e., AACR2R, for the entry of the name as a heading.]*

Subject headings, with limitations, can be further divided using subdivisions to specify further the form or subject content of a document.

THE PRESENTATION OF SUBJECT HEADINGS

Catalog Card Format. Subject access points are traditionally the first added entries indicated in the tracings. The first letter of the first word of a subject heading or subject subdivision as well as the first letter of proper nouns and proper adjectives are capitalized (see SCM:SH Appendix B). When multiple subject added entries are assigned to a document, they are assigned in order of decreasing importance. In many instances, the first subject heading is closely representative of the class number assigned the document (see SCM:SH Instruction H 80). Each subject heading is preceded by an arabic numeral followed by a period and one space. Subject subdivisions are indicated by the placement of a dash (or two hyphens) before the subdivision. The following main entry card illustrates the placement of subject added entries in the tracings.

Main Entry Card

```
GT      Siefker, Phyllis.
4985         Santa Claus, last of the wild men : the origins and evolution
.S495    of Saint Nicholas, spanning 50,000 years / Phyllis Siefker. –
1997     Jefferson, N.C. : McFarland, c1997.
              vii, 219 p. : ill. ; 24 cm.

             Includes bibliographical references (p. 207-214) and index.
             ISBN 0-7864-0246-6 (lib. bdg. : alk. paper)


             1. Santa Claus–History.  2. Nicholas, Saint, Bp. of Myra–
         History.  3. Wild men–Folklore.  I. Title.
```

When a catalog card for a subject heading is produced it is generally typed in all upper case letters. A practice that began to disappear with computer production of catalog cards was the typing of subject heading added entries in upper and lower case in red. The three cards that follow are the added entry cards that would be produced for *Santa Claus, Last of the Wild Men*.

Subject Added Entry Cards

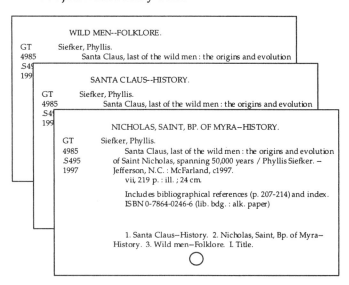

WILD MEN--FOLKLORE.

GT   Siefker, Phyllis.
4985   Santa Claus, last of the wild men : the origins and evolution
.S49
199

SANTA CLAUS--HISTORY.

GT   Siefker, Phyllis.
4985   Santa Claus, last of the wild men : the origins and evolution
.S4
199

NICHOLAS, SAINT, BP. OF MYRA–HISTORY.

GT   Siefker, Phyllis.
4985   Santa Claus, last of the wild men : the origins and evolution
.S495   of Saint Nicholas, spanning 50,000 years / Phyllis Siefker. –
1997   Jefferson, N.C. : McFarland, c1997.
             vii, 219 p. : ill. ; 24 cm.

             Includes bibliographical references (p. 207-214) and index.
             ISBN 0-7864-0246-6 (lib. bdg. : alk. paper)

             1. Santa Claus–History. 2. Nicholas, Saint, Bp. of Myra–
             History. 3. Wild men–Folklore. I. Title.

The OCLC/MARC Format. The 6xx range of fields is used with the OCLC/MARC bibliographic record to record subject added entries. As was the case with 1xx and 7xx fields, there are specific fields within that number range that are designed for use with different types of subject added entries. The fields used with subject headings from the Library of Congress are:

600   Personal Name
610   Corporate Name
611   Meeting Name
630   Uniform Title
650   Topical Term
651   Geographic Name

The OCLC/MARC fields used for Library of Congress call numbers and Dewey Decimal Classification numbers each have one field (050 or 082) that indicate that the classification number has been assigned by LC or another national library. Other fields (090 or 092) are used for locally assigned LC or DDC call numbers. The use of the Fields 600 to 651 is quite different. For these fields there is no indication of who assigned the subject added entries in these MARC fields. The field numbers only indicate that the term is a subject added entry. No greater specificity is provided by the second indicator which reports the controlled vocabulary from which the subject term was derived. The OCLC/MARC second indicators are:

0   Library of Congress subject heading
1   LC Annotated Card Program (AC)/Subject Heading for Children's
            Literature
2   National Library of Medicine (NLM) subject heading
3   National Agricultural Library (NAL) subject heading
4   Source not specified
5   Canadian subject heading/NLC authority file
6   Repetoire des vedettes-matiere/NLC authority file
7   Source is specified in subfield ‡2
8   Sears subject heading

The OCLC/MARC record for *Santa Claus, Last of the Wild Men* illustrates this practice.

020   0786402466 (lib. bdg. : alk. paper)
100 1   Siefker, Phyllis.
245 1 0   Santa Claus, last of the wild men : ‡b the origins and evolution
                of Saint Nicholas, spanning 50,000 years / ‡c Phyllis Siefker.
260   Jefferson, N.C. : ‡b McFarland, ‡c c1997.
300   vii, 219 p. : ‡b ill. ; ‡c 24 cm.
504   Includes bibliographical references (p. 207-214) and index.
650   0   Santa Claus ‡x History.
600 0 0   Nicholas, ‡c Saint, Bp. of Myra ‡x History.
650   0   Wild men ‡v Folklore.

The use of the first indicator for Fields 600-651 varies from field to field.

SUBJECT HEADING AUTHORITY INFORMATION

The display of subject headings in the print edition of the *Library of Congress Subject Headings* is illustrated well by the subject heading 'Communicable diseases."

> **Communicable diseases** *(May Subd Geog)*
> *[RA643-RA644 (Public health)]*
> *[RC109-RC216 (Internal medicine)]*
> UF Contagion and contagious diseases
>   *[Former heading]*
>   Contagious diseases
>   Infectious diseases
>   Microbial diseases in human beings
>   Zymotic diseases
> BT Diseases
>   Infection
>   Medical microbiology
> RT Epidemics
>   Quarantine
> SA *individual communicable diseases, e.g. Q fever*
> NT Bacterial diseases
>   Focal infection
>   Foodborne diseases
>   Foot--Infection
>   Heart--Infection
>   ...
>   Tick-borne diseases
>   Urinary tract infections
>   Virus diseases
>   Zoonoses

As was the case with bibliographic and name authority records, subject authority information is also available in MARC format. This information is used by OCLC and other bibliographic utilities and vendors but is displayed in a more readable way than it is presented on the MARC records issued by the Library of Congress. As was the case with LC name authority records, OCLC provides for two different displays of name authority records -- a tagged format and a mnemonic format that replaces some of the coding with labels. The example below is the LC subject authority record available from OCLC for the subject heading "Communicable diseases" in the mnemonic display format.

OCLC/MARC Subject Authority Record

ARN: 2023855   REC STAT: REVISED   ENTERED: 19860211

SUBJECT   ESTABLISHED HEADING   NOT EVALUATED
LC   INDIRECT

010	sh 85029015
040	DLC ‡c DLC ‡d DLC
005	19970325085456.8
053	RA643 ‡b RA644 ‡c Public health
053	RC109 ‡b RC216 ‡c Internal medicine
150 0	Communicable diseases
360	‡i individual communicable diseases, e.g. ‡a Q fever
450	Contagion and contagious diseases [EARLIER ESTABLISHED FORM]
450	Contagious diseases
450	Infectious diseases
450	Microbial diseases in human beings
450	Zymotic diseases
550	Diseases [BROADER TERM]
550	Infection [BROADER TERM]
550	Medical microbiology [BROADER TERM]
550	Epidemics
550	Quarantine

The definitions for these fields are:

ARN	[OCLC] Authority Record Number
010	Library of Congress Control Number
040	Cataloging Source
005	Date and Time of Last Transaction
1xx	Heading
360	Complex *See also from* reference—Subject
450	*See from* tracing—Topical term
550	*See also from* tracing—Topical term

In addition to the fields used on this record two other fields also frequently appear on subject authority records.

260	Complex *See from* reference—Subject
680	Public general note

Additional 4xx and 5xx fields can be used to create references for other than topical terms. Notice that the "NT" references in the print display for the subject heading are not present on the OCLC/MARC version. This will be addressed later in this chapter under the discussion of "Narrower Terms." Note also that in the OCLC/MARC subject authority example Fields 450 and 550 have the second indicator value blank. This reflects the decision by the Library of Congress to make the second indicator value (Number of Nonfiling Characters) obsolete. Although this practice has been implemented, the value "0" will continue to appear on many LC name authority records, including the source records from which these examples were derived because there are no plans to update existing records to conform to the new practice.

Instructions and other aids. The Library of Congress subject heading structure, whether in print or machine-readable format, provides several aids for the use and assignment of subject headings as well as an aid understanding the relationship of the subject headings to the Library of Congress Classification.

USE references. These are directions under an unauthorized heading referring users of the subject heading list to the authorized heading(s) for that subject. In the printed heading list the reference takes the following form.

> Contagious diseases
>   USE Communicable diseases

There is no equivalent to this type of reference in the OCLC/MARC subject authority file. Rather the terms in the 4xx fields are indexed so that when they are searched the authority record for the authorized heading for that subject is retrieved.

LC Classification references. Following some subject headings and subheadings are bracketed and italicized classification numbers derived from the Library of Congress Classification that represent an appropriate class or classes for the subject covered by that heading. These classification indications may be a single class, a range of classes, or several classes. When more than one class is given, each is followed by a term defining its scope. These classification numbers can serve as a form of index to the classification scheme. In the OCLC/MARC subject authority record these classification numbers are recorded in Field 053. When multiple classification numbers are used they are recorded in separate 053 fields.

Scope notes. A scope note defines the coverage or meaning of a heading within the controlled vocabulary. Scope notes provide for consistency in the application of a subject heading for a particular subject. The subject heading "Communicable diseases" does not use a scope note but the subject heading "Ballistic missiles" has the following note:

> **Ballistic missiles**
> Here are entered works on high-altitude, high-speed atomic missiles which are self-propelled and guided in the first stage of flight only, after which the trajectory becomes natural and uncontrolled. Works on conventional missiles are entered under Projectiles. Works on powered and guided missiles are entered under Rockets (Ordnance) and Guided missiles.

OCLC/MARC subject authority records have scope notes recorded in Field 680 (Public general note).

680   ‡i Here are entered works on high-altitude, high-speed atomic missiles which are self-propelled and guided in the first stage of flight only, after which the trajectory becomes natural and uncontrolled. Works on conventional missiles are entered under ‡a Projectiles. ‡i Works on powered and guided missiles are entered under ‡a Rockets (Ordnance) ‡i and ‡a Guided missiles.

In a card catalog this definitional information could be presented to users as on a card filed under "Ballistic missiles." In an online catalog the following display might be presented when a catalog user requests a "further description" of the subject "Ballistic missiles."

Online Catalog "Scope Note" Display

```
                                        LIBRARY_CATALOG

        HEADING:   Ballistic missiles
          SCOPE:   Here are entered works on high-altitude,
                   high-speed atomic missiles which are
                   self-propelled and guided in the first stage
                   of flight only, after which the trajectory
                   becomes natural and uncontrolled. Works
                   on conventional missiles are entered under
                   Projectiles. Works on powered and guided
                   missiles are entered under Rockets (Ordnance)
                   and Guided missiles.

   RELATED TERM:   Guided missiles
   RELATED TERM:   Rockets (Aeronautics)

       USED FOR:   Missiles, Ballistic
```

Term relationships. The purpose of any subject heading list or thesaurus is to create a controlled vocabulary that will save the time of the user by, according to Cutter, "find a book of which [the] … subject is known" and "show what the library has … on a given subject" To do this, the vocabulary must not only include the terms that can be used, but must also include the terms that can't be used and show the relationships between them. The structure of these relationships is called the "syndetic structure." This structure is an integral part of the subject heading system and is a part of the subject authority structure.

Syndetic structure. The relationships among the terms in a controlled vocabulary is indicated by its cross-references or syndetic structure. The Library of Congress uses a thesaurus format to present its syndetic structure. That format indicates broader, narrower, and related term relationships, as well as synonymous terms or concepts. For the subject heading "Communicable diseases" these references are indicated by "UF," "BT," "RT," and "NT" relationships.

In card catalogs references generally take the form of directions on cards for users to either "see" or "see also" other terms. These references are similar in structure to those used for name references. The directions given to users may be very simple or very detailed instructions depending on the local library's policy. In online catalogs a variety of methods can be used to represent this reference structure to the user, including the provision of an online thesaurus, forms of references similar to those used for names, and the automatic linking of some references.

"Used For" (UF) References. "Used for" (UF) references list unauthorized terms for the subject covered by the authorized term. These unauthorized terms are often synonyms or different word forms of the authorized heading. OCLC/MARC subject authority records use the 4xx fields to record "UF" terms. In the example for "Communicable Diseases," "Contagious diseases" is one of several terms that would be represented in the catalog by the subject heading "Communicable diseases." In a card catalog, references would be made from the "UF" headings to the authorized subject heading as follows:

> Contagious diseases
>   see
>   COMMUNICABLE DISEASES

In a card catalog one entry would be made for each "UF" term.
A directional reference in an online catalog might take the following form or it might be an invisible electronic link which would result in the display of the "Communicable diseases" entries in the catalog when the catalog user searched for "Contagious diseases."

Online Catalog "UF" Display

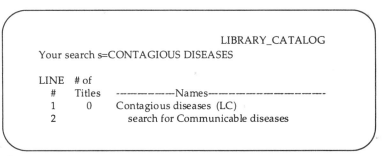

```
                              LIBRARY_CATALOG
         Your search s=CONTAGIOUS DISEASES

         LINE   # of
           #    Titles   ----------Names----------------------
           1      0      Contagious diseases  (LC)
           2                 search for Communicable diseases
```

"Broader Term" (BT) References. "Broader term" (BT) references indicate authorized subject headings that are broader in meaning than the subject heading under which they appear as a "BT." OCLC/MARC subject authority records use the 550 field to record "BT" terms. For the subject heading "Communicable diseases," the headings "Diseases" is one of several subject headings that is broader in meaning than "Communicable diseases." In a card catalog, references would be made from the "BT" headings to the authorized heading as follows:

> DISEASES
>   see also
>   COMMUNICABLE DISEASES

A directional reference in an online catalog might take the following form.

Online Catalog "BT" Display

```
                                            LIBRARY_CATALOG
      Your search s=DISEASES

   LINE   # of
     #    Titles   ----------Names--------------------
     1      88     DISEASES  (LC)
     2               for further description of this heading
     3               for related titles, also search for
                        COMMUNICABLE DISEASES
     4               for related titles, also search for EPIDEMICS
```

One card reference would be made from each of the "BT" subject headings to "Communicable diseases."

"Related Term" (RT) References. "Related term" (RT) references provide links between subject headings that are related in other than a hierarchical way. OCLC/MARC subject authority records use the 550 field to record "RT" terms similar to the way that field was used for "BT" relationships . For the subject heading "Communicable diseases," the "RT" subject heading "Epidemics" is considered neither broader nor narrower than the heading "Communicable diseases." Thus, in a card catalog, references would be made from the "RT" subject heading to the authorized subject heading and from the authorized subject heading to the "RT" subject headings. One part of this circular reference structure, from the subject heading being used to another subject heading, is similar to the reference structure used for "Narrower Term" references which is addressed in the next paragraph. As a result the "RT" references are included on the reference cards and online catalog displays for the "Narrower Term" references.

"Narrower Term" (NT) References. "Narrower term" (NT) references identify subject headings that are narrower in meaning than the subject heading under which they are listed. Unlike the print version of the subject headings, OCLC/MARC subject authority records do not record "NT" terms under a subject heading for which they are a narrower subject. Instead the terms that are listed as "NT" terms under a subject heading have that subject heading listed as a "BT" under the "NT" term. For the subject heading "Communicable diseases," the subject heading "Bacterial diseases" is but one of several subject headings that are more narrow in meaning than "Communicable diseases." In a card catalog, references would be made from the authorized heading to the "NT" subject headings.

COMMUNICABLE DISEASES
    see also
        EPIDEMICS
        BACTERIAL DISEASES
        FOCAL INFECTION
        FOODBORNE DISEASES
        FOOT--INFECTIONS
        HEART--INFECTIONS
        PARASITIC DISEASES
        PRION DISEASES
        SEPTICEMIA
        SEXUALLY TRANSMITTED DISEASES
        TICK-BORNE DISEASES
        URINARY TRACT DISEASES
        VIRUS DISEASES
        ZOONOSES

Note that in this example the first subject heading in the list, "Epidemics," is an "RT" relationship rather than an "NT" one. When either "RT" or "NT" references are made, catalogers must ensure that the references refer to subject headings that exist already in the catalog. If an entry does not exist in the catalog, that term would be excluded from the "see also" list. The excluded terms can be added later if the library acquires documents that are assigned that subject heading.

In an online catalog a "NT" relationship might be displayed as follows:

Online Catalog "NT" and "RT" Display

```
                                        LIBRARY_CATALOG
            Your search s=COMMUNICABLE DISEASES

            LINE   # of
             #    Titles   ---------Names----------------
             1      57     COMMUNICABLE DISEASES  (LC)
             2             for further description of this heading
             3             for related titles, also search for EPIDEMICS
             4             for related titles, also search for BACTERIAL
                               DISEASES
             5             for related titles, also search for FOCAL
                               INFECTION
             6             for related titles, also search for FOODBORNE
                               DISEASES
             7             for related titles, also search for FOOT-
                               INFECTIONS
            (More)
```

Note that this display the "RT" reference to "Epidemics" is again provided.

"See also" (SA) Instructions. "See also" (SA) instructions refer from a general heading to a more specific type of heading. This is different from the "NT" reference which refers from a general heading to a specific heading. The "SA" instruction used for "Communicable diseases" refers users to individual communicable diseases

through a general reference rather than attempting to list all individual diseases. If a library chooses to provide this type of instruction in a card catalog the reference is added to the "NT" reference card.

        COMMUNICABLE DISEASES
          see also
            Individual communicable diseases, e.g., Q fever
            EPIDEMICS
            BACTERIAL DISEASES
            FOCAL INFECTION
            FOODBORNE DISEASES
            FOOT--INFECTIONS
            HEART--INFECTIONS
            PARASITIC DISEASES
            PRIOR DISEASES
            SEPTICEMIA
            SEXUALLY TRANSMITTED DISEASES
            TICK-BORNE DISEASES
            URINARY TRACT DISEASES
            VIRUS DISEASES
            ZOONOSES

In the online catalog being used as the source for example in this chapter the display of "SA" references is provided when the user requests to see a "further description" of the heading.

Online Catalog "SA" Display

LIBRARY_CATALOG

HEADING: COMMUNICABLE DISEASES

SEARCH ALSO: Individual communicable diseases,
                  e.g., Q fever

RELATED TERM: DISEASES
RELATED TERM: INFECTION
RELATED TERM: MEDICAL MICROBIOLOGY
RELATED TERM: EIPDEMICS
RELATED TERM: QUARANTINE

USED FOR: Contagion and contagious diseases
USED FOR: Contagious diseases
USED FOR: Infectious diseases
USED FOR: Microbial diseases in human beings
USED FOR: Zymotic diseases

Whether used in a card or online catalog the cataloger must ensure that entries exist in the catalog for the subject headings given as examples in these references.

SUBJECT SUBDIVISIONS

Library of Congress subject headings may be divided by one or more aspects. These subdivisions further refine the nature of the subject headings and are indicative of a pre-coordinate indexing system. LC subject heading subdivisions are of four types:

(1) Topical
(2) Place
(3) Chronological
(4) Form

Topical subdivisions allow for greater identification of detail or specificity of a subject while the other three types simply divide a subject or a subject and its subdivisions by place, time, or form. Essentially subdivisions create more workable sub units of large subject files.

On a catalog card subject subdivisions are separated from the subject heading and from each other by either a long dash (−) or double hyphens (--).. On a MARC record subfields indicate the type of subdivision being used.

Topical	Subfield x
Chronological	Subfield y
Geographic	Subfield z
Form	Subfield v

The use of Subfield v for form subdivisions is relatively new having been introduced in 1998. Previously form subdivisions were coded as Subfield x. No retrospective code changes are planned by OCLC so pre-1999 bibliographic records will continue to have form subdivisions coded with Subfield x.

The Library of Congress has established two basic models for combining subject headings and subdivisions (See SCM:SH H 1075): That order is:

651   0   Geographic subject heading ‡x Topical subdivision

and

650   0   Topical subject heading ‡z Geographic subdivision

If the subject heading is a geographic the order of subdivisions is:

651   0   Geographic subject heading ‡x Topical ‡y Chronological ‡ v Form

If the subject heading is a topical subject heading the order of subdivisions can take one of two structures

650   0   Topical subject heading ‡z Geographic ‡x Topical ‡y
            Chronological ‡v Form

        or

650   0   Topical subject heading ‡x Topical ‡z Geographic ‡y
            Chronological ‡v Form

The assignment of topical, called "general" subdivisions in the OCLC/MARC
formatting documentation, geographic, chronological, and time subdivisions is
relatively straightforward. Special considerations for their use, however, are
presented in the next few paragraphs.

   Geographic subdivision. "May Subd Geog" is a parenthesized and italicized
statement in the print version of the *Library of Congress Subject Headings* immediately
following a main heading or a subdivision which indicates that further geographic
subdivision is both permitted and required if the subject is limited geographically in
the document. Unless this direction appears, names of geographic areas and political
divisions may not be added to a subject heading or subdivision. On an
OCLC/MARC Subject Authority Record the statement that a heading may be
subdivided geographically is indicated by the word "Indirect" or "direct" in the fixed
field area using the mnemonic display format or the values of "i" or "d" respectively
under "Geo subd" in the tagged display format.
   Geographic subdivision is done indirectly -- the larger political jurisdiction, i.e.,
country, is interposed between the heading or subheading and the specific place
name. For example, for the book *Contagious Diseases in Paris* the subject heading
assigned would be

650   0   Communicable diseases ‡z France ‡z Paris

while the book *Parisian Efforts at Contagious Disease Prevention* on would be assigned
the subject heading

650   0   Communicable diseases ‡z France ‡z Paris ‡x Prevention

In this latter situation, the geographic subdivision is placed before the topical
subdivision because an instruction "May Subd Geog" appears in the heading list
following "Communicable diseases " but no similar instruction appears following the
subdivision "Prevention." When the indication to subdivide geographically appears
after a subdivision, that instruction takes precedence over any instruction to
subdivide geographically following the main subject heading. Thus, the book *The
Transmission of Contagious Diseases in Paris* would be assigned the subject heading:

650   0   Communicable diseases ‡x Transmission ‡z France ‡z Paris

In this situation the instruction "May Subd Geog" that followed the subdivision
"Transmission" in the heading takes precedence over "May Subd Geog" following
"Communicable diseases." In applying this principle one must take care to ensure
that the context of the subject expression is accurate in relation to the document.

For three countries (Canada, Great Britain, and the United States), first-level political divisions (states, provinces, constituent countries and republics, respectively) are assigned directly without the interposition of the country name. These subdivisions may be further subdivided by the names of counties, cities, and other subordinate units.

650	0	Communicable diseases ‡z Ohio ‡z Columbus
650	0	Communicable diseases ‡z Nova Scotia ‡z Halifax
650	0	Communicable diseases ‡z England ‡z London

See SCM:SH Instructions H 810-H 870 for additional information on the use of geographic subdivisions.

Free -Floating Subdivisions. In each of the four categories of subdivisions there are some with relatively wide-spread usage that the Library of Congress has termed "free-floating" subdivisions. Five types of free floating subdivisions have been identified:

(1) form and topical subdivisions of general applicability
(2) subdivisions under classes of persons and ethnic groups
(3) subdivisions under name of individual corporate bodies, persons, and families
(4) subdivisions under place names
(5) subdivisions controlled by pattern subject headings

Form and Topical Free-Floating Subdivisions of General Applicability. This type of free-floating subdivision is the most frequently used. The following list identifies some of the more commonly assigned free-floating subdivisions.

Abstracts	Handbooks, manuals, etc.
Amateurs' manuals	History
Bibliography	Juvenile literature
Biography	Periodicals
Dictionaries	Popular works
Directories	Statistics
Fiction	Study and teaching

Other more specialized form and topical free-floating subdivisions include:

Adaptations	Mechanical properties
Development	Patents
Foreign influences	Toxicology
Lighting	Wounds and injuries

A complete listing of the free-floating subdivisions is given in SCM:SH Instruction H 1095 and in the LC publication *Free-Floating Subdivisions: An Alphabetical Index.*

Other Free-Floating Subdivisions. Some free-floating subdivisions are similar to form and topical free-floating subdivisions in their use except that they are more limited in the situations in which they can be applied. See the following SCM:SH

Instructions for specific guidance in using these specialized free-floating subdivisions:

H 1100	Free-Floating Subdivisions: Classes of persons
H 1103	Free-Floating Subdivisions: Ethnic groups
H 1105	Free-Floating Subdivisions: Corporate bodies
H 1110	Free-Floating Subdivisions: Names of persons
H 1120	Free-Floating Subdivisions: Names of families
H 1140	Free-Floating Subdivisions: Names of places
H 1145.5	Free-Floating Subdivisions: Bodies of water

Free-Floating Subdivisions Controlled by Pattern Headings. Free-floating subdivisions controlled by pattern headings are standardized sets of topical and form subdivisions for certain categories of subject headings. Rather than repeat these subdivisions for every subject heading in these special categories, representative or "pattern" subject headings are developed with a standardized set of subdivisions that can be applied to any heading falling under the category. Some examples of pattern subject headings are the following:

Category	Pattern Heading (SCM:SH Instruction)
Chemicals	Copper; Insulin (H 1149)
Diseases	Cancer; Tuberculosis (H 1150)
Educational institutions	
Individual institutions	Harvard University (H 1151)
Types of	Universities and colleges (H 1151.5)
Industries	Construction industry; Retail trade (H 1153)
Languages	English language; French language; Romance language (H 1154)
Materials	Concrete; Metals (H 1158)
Musical instruments	Piano (H 1161)
Plants and crops	Corn (H 1180)
Wars	United States--History--Civil War, 1861-1865; World War, 1939-1945 (H 1200)

SCM:SH Instructions H 1146 to H 1200 cover use of free-floating subdivisions for subject headings controlled by pattern subject headings.

LIBRARY OF CONGRESS SUBJECT HEADINGS EXERCISES

For each of the works assign Library of Congress subject heading(s) and subdivisions that best describe the documents. Additionally, assign the appropriate OCLC/MARC fields, indicators and subfield codes. When needed consult the *Subject Cataloging Manual: Subject Headings*. Answers to these exercises appear in Appendix F.

A.   <u>Simple Subject Headings</u>. Assign the most appropriate subject heading(s) for the following titles.

1.   *Plea Bargaining: is it fair?*

2.   *An introduction to machine-shop mathematics.*

3.   *Water-borne power projection: naval policy and a nation's destiny.*

4.   *Ocean drilling vessels.*

5.   *What are the effects of agricultural chemicals on plants?*

6.   *Windmills: the clean, free power source.*

7.   *Your solar heated home.*

8.   *An introduction to industrial psychology.*

9.   *The story of orchestration.*

10.   *The Sopwith Camel.*
           [A type of fighter plane]

11.   *Danish Christmas carols.*

12.   *Rats and the diseases they carry.*

13.   *The Battle for Guadalcanal.*
           [A World War Two series of battles]

14.   *Requirements for controlled atmospheres in space.*

15.   *Infant welfare.*

B.   Subject Headings with Topical Subdivisions. Assign the most appropriate
      subject heading(s) for the following titles.

16.   *The 1956 Anglo-French intervention in Egypt.*

17.   *Ride down that road again: recycling road building materials.*

18.   *How to breed roses.*

19.   *When did Buddha die? The controversy continues.*

20.   *Gasoline pipelines.*

21.   *Light filters in photography.*

22.   *Crabgrass, dandelions, and other green lawn disasters: weed control in the lawns of
      suburbia.*

23.   *Aircraft collision avoidance systems: the state of the art.*

24.   *Quality processing for top quality photos.*

25.   *Operation Overlord: D-Day, 1944.*
        [Accounts of the invasion]

C.   <u>Subject Headings with Geographical Subdivisions</u>. Assign the most
      appropriate subject heading(s) for the following titles.

26.   *The courts of Scotland.*
        [Addresses the legal courts]

27.   *Taxation of artists in the Republic of Ireland: the laws and commentary.*

28.   *Children of working parents: the Minneapolis experience.*

29.   *Crack abuse in Cleveland: the report of the 1989 survey.*

30.   *Electronic spying by the United States.*
        [The collection of foreign non-communication electromagnetic
        radiations by agencies of the U.S. government]

31.   *Labor unions in the tire industry of Akron, Ohio.*

32.   *Political activities of artisans in Mexico City.*

33.   *The pre-Lenten carnivals of Baton Rouge, Louisiana.*

34.   *Dog laws of Washington, D.C.*

35.   *Bog men of England and Denmark.*

36.   *The new way to get the job done in the U.S.: contracting for services.*

37.   *Nineteenth century magazine illustration in Great Britain.*

38.   *Costume in 17th and 18th century France: a definitive history.*

39.   *Mandatory retirement laws in Georgia.*

40.   *Depression glass of East Liverpool, Ohio.*

41.   *What family? The problem of family abandonment in Indiana.*

D.   Subject Headings with Form and Topical Free-Floating Subdivisions. Assign
      the most appropriate subject heading(s) for the following titles.

42.   *The history of the Dewey Decimal Classification.*

43.   *Soil density in Zurich, Switzerland: a bibliography.*

44.   *The effects of drugs on the newborn: a compilation of essays.*

45.   *Minority employment in the states of California and New York: a comparative
       statistical report.*

46.   *U. S. copyright law for musical works: abstracts.*

47.   *Fox hunting in Albemarle County, Virginia: an historical view.*

48.   *Fire towers and fire spotters of North and South Carolina: a directory.*

49.   *Physics: a basic textbook.*

50.   *Macroeconomics for the layman.*

51.   *Railroad collisions in late 19th century Pennsylvania.*

52.   *Zeppelins: an illustrated history.*
       [The text of this work is richly illustrated with photographs. They constitute approximately
       two-thirds of this work. This work deals with airships throughout the world rather than being
       limited to German zeppelins.]

53.   *Yearbook of industrial mental health.*

54.   *Tennessee's campsites: a directory.*

55.   *Nursing home care and the Federal commitment*

56.   *Japanese history, 1919 to 1945: a source book.*

57.   *House repair for the homeowner.*

E.   Subject Headings with Pattern and Other Free-Floating Subdivisions. Assign
       the most appropriate subject heading(s) for the following titles.

58.   *Thomas Alva Edison: a definitive biography.*

59.   *The travelers' guide to Peru.*
      [Provides information on facilities, accommodations and items of interest]

60.   *Genealogy of the Carpenter family of Massachusetts.*

61.   *Control of the color fading of apples.*

62.   *Edgar Allan Poe as a character in mystery novels: review essays.*

63.   *Camping and backpacking in the Great Lakes area.*

64.   *Japan and France: a review of their foreign relations.*
      [The foreign relations between these two countries primarily from the Japanese perspective]

65.   *At the tip of the continent: the Strait of Magellan along the Chilean coast.*
      [A general geography text not a work designed for travelers]

66.   *They fell for the Union: Pennsylvanian's who died for their country in the Civil War.*
      [A listing]

67.   *Lord Peter: English dilettante or true detective?*
      [A character created by Dorothy L. Sayers]

68.   *Tunnel vision: innovations in the diagnosis of retinitis pigmentosa in the United States.*

69.   *The incidence of diseases in lambs in Greene County, Pennsylvania: a statistical evaluation.*

70.   *Lost with the Titanic.*
       [A novel about the loss of the R.M.S. Titanic in 1912]

71.   *Henry Ford's contributions to the automobile industry.*
       [This work concentrates on his contributions to the U.S. auto industry rather than his life or the Ford Motor Company.]

72.   *The West Virginia University: pictorial views of campus.*

73.   *Women in the fiction of Ernest Hemingway.*

74.   *Recruiting practices of the Central Intelligence Agency.*

F.   Miscellaneous Subject Heading Situations. Assign the most appropriate subject heading(s) for the following titles.

75.   *How to catalog a rare book.*

76.   *How to grow asparagus.*

77.   *The conservation of museum collections.*

78.   *Sacred waters: the folklore of holy wells and holy springs in Europe.*

79.   *How to train your homing pigeon.*

80.   *The first book of astronomy.*
       [A book for children]

81.   *The art of writing biographies.*
       [A book of techniques]

82.   *The essential manual of archeology for the amateur archaeologist.*

83.   *The chemical analysis of rocks.*

84.   *Photography for children.*

85.   *Lawyers as characters in modern fiction.*

86.   *Coins and coin collectors.*

87.   *Veterinary hospitals: a survey.*

88.   *The history of 18th century astrology.*

89.   *Vocational education for women.*

90.   *The complete dictionary of philosophy.*
        [In English]

91.   *Children's furniture building for the home craftsman.*

92.   *Life on the stage: the biography of Helen Hayes.*
        [The American actress born in 1900]

93.   *The National League.*
        [A history of the professional baseball league]

94.   *Go Cubs! a history of the Chicago Cubs.*
         [The professional baseball team]

95.   *School architecture in California.*

96.   *Witchcraft in Alabama.*

97.   *Cheesebox on a raft: the Union ironclad Monitor.*
         [Centers on the activities of this ship during the Civil War]

98.   *The Hogarth Press: the history of a great private press.*

99.   *Techniques of writing mystery and detective stories.*

100. *A repair manual for the Buick automobile.*

101. *"The open road": A bibliography of articles on motorcycles.*

102. *North American Indian embroidery.*

103. *Flowers in literature.*

104. *How to win at the game Trivial Pursuit.*

105. *Modern paper manufacture in Japan: the industry and the craft.*

APPENDICES

Answers to the Exercises

APPENDIX A

Answers to the
Descriptive Cataloging Exercise

N.B. In the answers and accompanying explanations that follow, AACR2R related aspects are addressed first followed by OCLC/MARC formatting issues. Because these answers are formatted using the OCLC formatting standards, the subfield delimiter and subfield code for Subfield "a" is not recorded for the first occurrence of that subfield in a field.

1.

020	0987643210	
245 _ _	House design for modern living / ‡c by Robert Grogan ; with illustrations by Patty Brown.	
250	3rd ed.	
260	New York : ‡b Albatross Press, ‡c 1979.	
300	xii, 306 p., [12] p. of plates : ‡b ill. (some col.) ; ‡c 22 cm.	

Area 1
  Title proper — Rule 1.1B1
  [The wording, order and spelling of the title proper are retained, but not the capitalization.]
  Rule A.4A1
  [The first word is capitalized and other words that would be capitalized in the language of the title.]

  Statement of responsibility — Rule 1.1F1
  Rule 1.1F6
  [The individuals perform different functions. Multiple statements of responsibility are recorded in the order in which they appear on the chief source of information.]

Area 2
  Edition statement — Rule 1.2B1
  Rule C.8A
  [Numbered editions are recorded as ordinal numbers in this form.]
  Rule B.9
  [Abbreviations must be used when available.]

Area 4
  Place — Rule 1.4C1
  [Only the 1st named place in the country of the cataloging agency is recorded.]

  Publisher — Rule 1.4D1 & Rule 1.4D2
  [In recording the "shortest form" possible, terms of incorporation are usually not recorded.]

Date   Rule 1.4F6
                                  *[With no evidence to the contrary, the title page date is
                                  accepted as the publication date. The copyright date is not
                                  recorded because it is the same as the date of publication
                                  which is the preferred date.]*
                                  Rule 2.4G2
                                  *[Unless this optional addition is applied, the date of printing
                                  is not recorded.]*
Area 5
  Pagination   Rule 2.5B1 & Rule 2.5B2
                                  *[The last numbered page of each numbered sequence is
                                  recorded. This book has 2 sequences, iii-xii and 1-306.]*
  Plates   Rule 2.5B10
                                  *[Because the plates are unnumbered, the total number of
                                  plates is enclosed within square brackets. The color of plates
                                  cannot be mentioned here.]*
  Illustrative matter   Rule 2.5C1 & Rule 2.5C3
                                  *["Ill. (some col.)" is recorded to account for both the colored
                                  plates and the black and white photographs. The word
                                  "photographs" does not appear in the list of types of
                                  illustrations in Rule 2.5C2 nor does it appear to be an
                                  appropriate term to be added at the cataloger's discretion.]*
                                  Rule B.9
                                  [Abbreviations must be used when available.]
  Dimensions   Rule 2.5D1
                                  *[Only the height is recorded, in centimeters, unless the
                                  book's width is (1) less the ½ the height or, (2) greater than
                                  the height. In the latter two situations, both the height and
                                  width are recorded in that order.]*
Area 8
  Standard number   Rule 1.8B1

OCLC/MARC Formatting
  010   Library of Congress Control Number
                                  *[Areas 1 though 8 of the bibliographic description do not
                                  include provision of this element typically it would be
                                  provided as part of a complete MARC record If this element
                                  had been recorded in this record it would have appeared as:
                                      010   79-192064*
  020   International Standard Book Number
                                  [The number is recorded with no hyphens.]

2.

245 _ _   Environmental effects of the use of asbestos / ‡c Horace
             Lemper, Justine McCabe ; introduction by J. Wells Sinclair ;
             photographs by Ann Reed & Ella Julianno.
250   2nd rev. ed.
260   London ; ‡a New York : ‡b Osgood Pub. Co., ‡c c1969.
300   398 p. : ‡b ill. ; ‡c 23 cm.
504   Includes bibliographical references (p. [361]- 388) and index.

Area 1

Title proper   Rule 1.1B1
                                 [The wording, order and spelling of the title proper are retained, but not the capitalization.]
                                 Rule A.4A1
                                 [The first word is capitalized and other words that would be capitalized in the language of the title.]

Statement of responsibility   Rule 1.1F1
                                 [In transcribing the statement of responsibility, the statement is recorded in the form in which it appears in the item, including ampersands, etc.]
                                 Rule 1.1F7
                                 [Qualifications, i.e., degrees, are not recorded.]
                                 Rule 1.1F6
                                 [The individuals perform different functions. Multiple statements of responsibility are recorded in the order in which they appear on the chief source of information. Because the cataloger is transcribing what appears on the document, the "&" used as the conjunction is recorded rather than substituting the word "and."]

Area 2

Edition statement   Rule 1.2B1
                                 [Brackets are not used because the edition statement is taken from a prescribed source of information for Area 2, i.e., a preliminary -- the title page verso.]
                                 Rule C.8A
                                 [Numbered editions are recorded as ordinal numbers in this form.]
                                 Rule B.9
                                 [Abbreviations must be used when available.]

Area 4

Place   Rule 1.4C4
                                 [Only the first named place not in the country of the cataloging agency, and a later named place in that country, are recorded.]

Publisher   Rule 1.4D1 & Rule 1.4D2
                                 Rule B.9
                                 [Abbreviations must be used when available.]

Date   Rule 1.4F6
                                 [The date of publication of the 2nd rev. ed. is unknown. The copyright date is recorded in its place.]

Place of printing, name   Rule 2.4G2
of printer, date of   *[This information is recorded as an option only when the place and name of the printer are known. In this case, only the place of printing is known. Unless this optional addition is applied, the date of printing is not recorded.]*
printing

Area 5

Pagination   Rule 2.5B1 & Rule 2.5B2
                                 [The last numbered page of each numbered sequence is recorded. Although both roman and arabic numerals are used, there is only one numbering sequence, i [i.e., 1] to 398.]

Illustrative matter   Rule 2.5C1
                                 [Tables are considered text, not illustrations.]
                                 Rule B.9
                                 [Abbreviations must be used when available.]

Dimensions	Rule 2.5D1
	[The height is recorded to the next whole centimeter.]
Area 7	
Contents	Rule 2.7B18
	[Informal contents note using the style of the Library of Congress. Pagination of a single bibliography is enclosed within parentheses. Because the 1st page of the bibliography is unnumbered, the number is enclosed in square brackets. Generally, the pagination of an index is not recorded.]
Area 8	
Standard number	Rule 1.8B1

OCLC/MARC Formatting

020	International Standard Book Number
	[The number is recorded with no hyphens.]
504	Bibliography, etc. note
	[This field is used to note information about bibliographic sources even when combined with an index note. An index note by itself would be recorded in a 500 field.]

3.

020	0234598701
020	0234598712 (pbk.)
245 _ _	The problems of earth : ‡b readings in ecology / ‡c by Adam Smith ... [et al.].
260	Bloomington, Ind. : ‡b Ecology Association Press, ‡c 1993, c1992.
300	296 p. : ‡b maps ; ‡c 24 cm.
4_ _	Environmental sciences series ; ‡v no. 9
504	Includes bibliographical references.

....

Area 1	
Title proper	Rule 1.1B1
	[The wording, order and spelling of the title proper are retained, but not the capitalization.]
	Rule A.4A1
	[The first word is capitalized and other words that would be capitalized in the language of the title.]
	Rule A.27A1
	["Earth" was not capitalized because its use in the title is not in conjunction with the names of other planets.]
Other title information	Rule 1.1E1
Statement of responsibility	Rule 1.1F1
	Rule 1.1F5
	[With more than 3 persons performing the same function, only the first named is recorded. The others are represented by the mark of omission and "[et al.]".]

Area 4
  Place   Rule 1.4C1
                                     Rule B.14A
  Publisher   Rule 1.4D1
  Date   Rule 1.4F1
                                     [The publication date, 1993, is recorded.]
                                     Rule 1.4F5
                                     [The "optional addition" of recording the latest copyright
                                     date, if it is different from the publication date, was
                                     exercised.]
  Date of printing   Rule 2.4G2
                                     [Unless this optional addition is applied, the date of printing
                                     is not recorded.]
Area 5
  Pagination   Rule 2.5B1 & Rule 2.5B2
                                     [The last numbered page of the only numbered sequence was
                                     recorded.]
                                     Rule 2.5B3
                                     [The unnumbered pages were not recorded because they do
                                     not constitute a "substantial part" of the work and are not
                                     referred to in a note.]
  Illustrative matter   Rule 2.5C2
                                     [This option was exercised. The illustrations are of only 1
                                     type -- maps and are considered to be important.]
  Dimensions   Rule 2.5D1
                                     [The height of a book is recorded in centimeters.]
Area 6
  Title proper of series   Rule 1.6B1
                                     Rule A.9A1
                                     [The series title is capitalized according to the rule for a title
                                     proper (see Rule A.4).]
  Statement of responsibility   Rule 1.6E1
    relating to the series   *[The series editor was not recorded because that*
                                     Information was not necessary for the identification of the
                                     series.]
  Numbering within the series   Rule 1.6G1
                                     Rule B.9
                                     [Abbreviations must be used when available.]
                                     Rule A.9B1
                                     [The abbreviation "no." is not capitalized.]
                                     Rule C.2B1
                                     [Arabic numerals are substituted for roman numerals in the
                                     Series Area.]
Area 7
  Contents   Rule 2.7B18
                                     [Informal contents note using the style of the Library of
                                     Congress. Page numbers are not recorded when there are
                                     multiple bibliographies in different locations.]
Area 8
  Standard number   Rule 1.8B1
                                     Rule 1.8B2
                                     [With multiple ISBNs, the one pertaining to the item being
                                     described must be recorded. Applying the option to this rule
                                     allows for recording the second ISBN along with a
                                     qualification. When recording multiple ISBNs, LC policy
                                     calls for recording the ISBN for the item in hand first.]

Qualification   Rule 1.8E2
                                       Rule B.9
                                       [Abbreviations must be used when available.]

OCLC/MARC Formatting
    020   International Standard Book Number
                                       *[The number is recorded with no hyphens. When is more
                                       than one ISBN, OCLC/MARC formatting requires that each
                                       ISBN be entered in a separate 020 field.]*
    4__   Series
                                       *[Only 4__ has been recorded rather than a more specific
                                       field number, i.e., 440 or 490, because the decision on which
                                       field should be used is based on whether or not to make an
                                       access point for the series and how that access point, if made,
                                       would be written -- not issues covered by the AACR2R
                                       chapters for description. OCLC/MARC formatting does not
                                       require parenthesis around the series statement. For catalog
                                       cards, this would be provided as a print constant.]*
    504   Bibliography, etc. note
                                       *[This field is used to note information about bibliographic
                                       sources.]*

4.

020	0567890123	
245 _ _	American book illustrators : ‡b a bibliography / ‡c by Karen Gale. American binders : a bibliography / by Hugo Ellis.	
246 _ 8	American illustrators and binders	
260	Pittsburgh, Pa. : ‡b Gambit Press, ‡c c1987.	
300	116, 125 p. ; ‡c 28 cm. + ‡e 120 slides (col.)	
4__	Books for collectors	
500	Slides in pocket in back of book.	
500	Includes topical index to slides.	

Area 1
    Title proper   Rule 1.1B1
                                       *[The wording, order and spelling of the title proper are
                                       retained, but not the capitalization.]*
                                       Rule A.4A1
                                       *[The first word is capitalized and other words that would be
                                       capitalized in the language of the title.]*
                                       Rule 1.1G2 and Rule 1.1G3
                                       *[When an item, (1) lacks a collective title, (2) neither work
                                       predominates, and (3) the work is described as a unit, the
                                       titles are recorded in the order in which they appear on the
                                       title page.]*

Statement of responsibility	Rule 1.1F1
	Rule 1.1G3
	[When an item lacks a collective title, neither work predominates, and the work is described as a unit, the statements of responsibility are recorded following the work with which they are associated.]
Area 4	
Place	Rule 1.4C1
	Rule 1.4C3
	[When the name of the state appears in the source of information it is recorded if considered necessary for identification or to distinguish one place from others with the same name. In this case, the name of the state is provided because of the latter condition.]
	Rule B.14A
Publisher	Rule 1.4D1 & Rule 1.4D2
Date	Rule 1.4F7
	[With no known date of publication, the copyright date is recorded instead.]
Area 5	
Pagination	Rule 2.5B1 & Rule 2.5B2
	[The last numbered page of each numbered sequence is recorded.]
Dimensions	Rule 2.5D1
	[Height is recorded to the next whole centimeter.]
Area 6	
Title proper of series	Rule 1.6B1
	Rule A.9A1
	[The series title is capitalized according to the rule for a title proper (see Rule A.4).]
Area 7	
Variations in title	Rule 2.7B4
	[See Field 246 under OCLC/MARC formatting.]
	Rule A.10A
	[A variant title is capitalized according to the rule for a title proper (see Rule A.4.]
Accompanying material	Rule 2.7B11
	[Location of the accompanying material.]
Contents	Rule 2.7B18
	[Informal contents note using the style of the Library of Congress. The particular type of index is identified at the discretion of the cataloger.]
Area 8	
Standard number	Rule 1.8B1
OCLC/MARC Formatting	
020	International Standard Book Number
	[The number is recorded with no hyphens.]
245	Title Statement
	[Subfields "a" and "b" are not repeatable. All subsequent title and statement of responsibility information is recorded in Subfield "c" (Remainder of title page transcription/statement of responsibility).]

246   Varying Form of Title
                                       *[Field 246 produces a note if the 1st Indicator value is either
                                       "0" or "1." The decision on which to use is based on
                                       whether the varying title is to be an access point or not. The
                                       2nd Indicator value "8" produces the Print Constant "Spine
                                       title:" for the note.]*
4_ _   Series
                                       *[Only 4_ _ has been recorded rather than a more specific
                                       field number, i.e., 440 or 490, because the decision on which
                                       field is used is based on whether to make an access point for
                                       the series and how that access point would be written -- not
                                       issues covered by the AACR2R chapters for description.
                                       OCLC/MARC formatting does not require parenthesis
                                       around the series statement. For catalog cards, this would be
                                       provided as a print constant.]*

5.

245 _ _   The official guide to post-service employment opportunities /
               ‡c Department of the Navy, Office of Retirement Affairs.
260   [Washington, D.C.] : ‡b The Office, ‡c [1996]
300   96 p. ; ‡c 22 cm.
500   Cover title.
500   Compiled by Nelson F. Halleck.
500   Revision of: The reference guide to post-service employment
               opportunities for naval personnel.
500   "May 1996."
504   Includes bibliographical references and index.
500   "ORA P-19913."

Area 1
  Title proper   Rule 1.1B1
                                       *[The wording, order and spelling of the title proper are
                                       retained, but not the capitalization.]*
                                       Rule A.4A1
                                       *[The first word is capitalized and other words that would be
                                       capitalized in the language of the title.]*
  Statement of responsibility   Rule 1.1F1
                                       *[The statement of responsibility is recorded as it appears on
                                       the title page substitute. Halleck cannot be recorded as a
                                       statement of responsibility in Area 1, even if enclosed in
                                       square brackets, because the statement does not come from a
                                       prescribed source of information for either Area 1 or 2, i.e.,
                                       title page, other preliminaries, or colophon. Note that the
                                       page illustrated the page following the table of contents and
                                       thus, not a preliminary. If transcribed at all, this statement
                                       of responsibility would be given in a note.]*
                                       Rule 1.1F3
                                       *[In the description, the statement of responsibility is
                                       transposed to follow the title proper.]*

Area 4
    Place   Rule 1.4C6
                                           [No place of publication is stated. The country of publication is assumed with confidence given the nature of the work.]
    Publisher   Rule 1.4D1
                                           [Often with corporate works, statements of responsibility and statements of publication are stated only once, but serve a dual purpose.]
                                         Rule 1.4D4
                                         [Because the name of the publisher appears in a recognizable form in the statement of responsibility, it is given in Area 4 in the shortest form possible.]
    Date   Rule 1.4F6
                                           [The date on the title page is a transmittal date. These dates are most often associated with works from corporate bodies and contain the month and sometimes day of the month, in addition to the year. The Library of Congress does not consider a transmittal date as the date of publication. A transmittal date can be recorded as a probable date of publication, enclosed in square brackets. The transmittal date itself, is recorded as a quoted note.]

Area 5
    Pagination   Rule 2.5B1 & Rule 2.5B2
                                         [The last numbered page of each numbered sequence is recorded. This book has 1 numbered sequence.
                                         Rule 2.5B3
                                         [The unnumbered preliminary pages were not recorded because they do not constitute a "substantial part" of the work.]
    Dimensions   Rule 2.5D1
                                           [Height is recorded to the next whole centimeter.]

Area 7
    Source of title proper   Rule 2.7B3
                                         [The cover was used as the chief source of information. See also rule 1.1B1.]
    Statement of responsibility   Rule 2.7B6
    Edition and history   Rule 2.7B7
                                         Rule A.10A
                                         [A related title is capitalized according to the rule for a title proper (see Rule A.4.]
    Publication, distribution, etc. Rule 2.7B9
                                         [The Library of Congress records a transmittal date as a quoted note.]
    Contents   Rule 2.7B18
                                         [Informal contents note using the style of the Library of Congress.]
    Numbers   Rule 2.7B19
                                         [This number is not a standard number, but might be useful in identifying the item.]

OCLC/MARC Formatting
    504   Bibliography, etc. Note
                                         [Notes are recorded in the order of the AACR2R note rules, not in the numerical order of the MARC note field values.]

6.

        245 _ _ The right of women : ‡b our struggle for the vote / ‡c by Alice Faberman.
        250   1st ed.
        260   Philadelphia : ‡b Feminist Issues Press, ‡c 1995.
        300   xiii, 389 p., [1] leaf of plates : ‡b port. ; ‡c 23 cm.
        4_ _   The feminist struggle series ; ‡v v. 7
        500   Originally published: Philadelphia : Lippincott, 1911.
        500   "Limited to 500 copies"--T.p. verso.
        500   "A Susan Ebert/Karen Norris book."
        590   "Copy 173"--T.p. verso.

Area 1
  Title proper   Rule 1.1B1
                                [The wording, order and spelling of the title proper are retained, but not the capitalization.]
                                  Rule A.4A1
                                  [The first word is capitalized and other words that would be capitalized in the language of the title.]
  Statement of responsibility Rule 1.1F1
Area 2
  Edition statement   Rule 1.2B1
                                  Rule 1.2B1
                                  [Brackets are not used because the edition statement is taken from a prescribed source of information for Area 2, i.e., a preliminary -- the title page verso.]
                                  Rule C.8A
                                  [Numbered editions are recorded as ordinal numbers in this form.]
                                  Rule B.9
                                  [Abbreviations must be used when available.]
Area 4
  Place   Rule 1.4C1
  Publisher   Rule 1.4D1 & Rule 1.4D2
                                  [In recording the "shortest form" possible, initial articles are usually not recorded.]
  Date   Rule 1.4F6
                                  [The date on the title page is the date of publication.]
Area 5
  Pagination   Rule 2.5B1 & Rule 2.5B2
                                  [The last numbered page of each numbered sequence is recorded. This book has 2 sequences, i-xiii and 1-389.]
  Plates   Rule 2.5B10
                                  [The frontispiece is a plate. Because it is printed on only 1 side, it is referred to as a leaf. The number appears in square brackets because the leaf is unnumbered.]
  Illustrative matter   Rule 2.5C2
                                  [This option was exercised. The frontispiece is the only illustration in the work. It is of one type -- a portrait and was considered to be important.]
                                  Rule B.9
                                  [Abbreviations must be used when available.]

Dimensions	Rule 2.5D1
	[The height of a book is recorded in centimeters.]
Area 6	
Title proper of series	Rule 1.6B1
	Rule 1.6B2
	[Because series title on the title page differs from the series title on the series title page, the form that appeared on the 1st of the prescribed sources of information for Series Area, i.e., the series title page, (see Rule 2.0B2)was transcribed.]
	Rule A.9A1
	[The series title is capitalized according to the rule for a title proper (see Rule A.4).]
Numbering within series	Rule 1.6G1
	Rule B.9
	[Abbreviations must be used when available.]
	Rule A.9B1
	[The abbreviation "." is not capitalized.]
	Rule C.2B1
	{Numbers represented by words are converted to numerals.]
Area 7	
Edition and history	Rule 2.7B7
	[This is the style used by the Library of Congress for this note.]
	Rule 1.7A3
	[The order for data in a note should correspond to the ISBD order and punctuation used in the area related to those data. The location of the original copy is generally not mentioned in the description.]
	Rule 2.7B7
	[A limited production statement is considered a form of edition statement and is generally given as a quoted note by the Library of Congress.]
	Rule 1.7A3
	[The source of a quoted note must be given if that source is other than the chief source of information.]
Series	Rule 2.7B12
	[It is Library of Congress policy to reject as a series, a phrase naming in-house editors or another official of the firm. This information is recorded instead, as a quoted series note.]
Copy being described	Rule 2.7B20
	[This number is unique to the library's copy.]
OCLC/MARC Formatting	
500	General Note
	[Notes are recorded in the order of the AACR2R note rules.]
4__	Series
	[Only 4__ has been recorded rather than a more specific field number, i.e., 440 or 490, because the decision on which field is used is based on whether to make an access point for the series and how that access point would be written -- not issues covered by the AACR2R chapters for description. OCLC/MARC formatting does not require parenthesis around the series statement. For catalog cards, this would be provided as a print constant.]
590	Local Note

7.

020	0513634982 (set)
020	0513634991 (v. 1)
245	Wilson's history of computer processing.
250	3rd ed. / ‡b revised by B. Cameron.
260	New York : ‡b Bull's Eye Book Co., ‡c 1996-
300	v. : ‡b ill. ; ‡c 27 cm.
504	Includes bibliographical references and index.
505 0 ⋫	v.1. The early years

Area 1
  Title proper   Rule 1.1B1
                                            [The wording, order and spelling of the title proper are retained, but not the capitalization.]
                                            Rule A.4A1
                                            [The first word is capitalized and other words that would be capitalized in the language of the title.]
                                            Rule 1.1B2
                                            [The statement of responsibility is an integral part of this title proper.]
  Statement of responsibility   Rule 1.1F1
                                            [Generally, a person responsible for design of the cover is not transcribed in the statement of responsibility.]
                                            Rule 1.1F13
                                            [When the name associated with responsibility for the item has been named in the title proper, a statement of responsibility is recorded for that name only if there is a separate responsibility statement on the chief source of information.]

Area 2
  Edition statement   Rule 1.2B1
                                              Rule C.8A
                                            [Numbered editions are recorded as ordinal numbers in this form.]
                                            Rule B.9
                                            [Abbreviations must be used when available.]
  Statement of responsibility   Rule 1.2C1
  relating to the edition
                                            Rule 1.1F7
                                            [Qualifications are not transcribed.]
                                            Rule B.4A
                                            [Abbreviations in a statement of responsibility are limited to those found in the prescribed sources of information and the abbreviations "i.e." and ""et al.". The other abbreviations in Rule B.9 cannot be used.]

Area 4
  Place   Rule 1.4C1
  Publisher   Rule 1.4D1 & Rule 1.4D2

Date

Rule 1.4F8

[The date on the title page is the publication date. For multipart works not yet complete, the earliest date of publication is recorded followed by a hyphen.]

Place of manufacture and name of manufacturer

Rule 1.4G4

[The "optional addition" of recording the place of manufacture and name of the manufacturer, when that name differs from the name of the publisher, has not been exercised.]

Area 5

Extent of item

Rule 1.5B5

[For multipart works not yet complete, three spaces are recorded, followed by "v.". Although AACR2R calls for the placement of 3 blank spaces preceding the "v.", the OCLC-MARC format specifies that these spaces not be input -- they are system supplied.]

Pagination

Rule 2.5B20 or Rule 2.5B21

[The pagination of multi-volume works is not recorded if the work is incomplete because the final pagination is unknown.]

Plates

Rule 2.5B10

[Plates are not recorded for multi-volume works. Rule 2.5B10 comes under the heading for "single volumes" (see p. 72 in AACR2R). The physical description rules for multi-volume works begin on p. 75 of AACR2R..]

Illustrative matter

Rule 2.5C1

[The plates are the illustrations by definition.]

Rule B.9

[Abbreviations must be used when available.]

Dimensions

Rule 2.5D1

[The height of a book is recorded in centimeters.]

Area 7

Contents

Rule 2.7B18

[Informal contents note using the style of the Library of Congress.]

Rule 2.7B18

[Contents note in the formal structure used by the Library of Congress.]

Rule A.10A

[Titles are capitalized according to the rule for a title proper (see Rule A.4.]

Area 8

Standard number

Rule 1.8B1

Qualification

Rule 1.8B2

[Qualifications are given if there are 2 or more standard numbers.]

OCLC/MARC Formatting

020

International Standard Book Number

[The number is recorded with no hyphens. When is more than one ISBN, OCLC/MARC formatting requires that each ISBN be entered in a separate 020 field.]

504

Bibliography, etc. note

[This field is used to note information about bibliographic sources even when combined with an index note. An index note by itself would be recorded in a 500 field.]

505   Formatted Contents Note
                                       *[The 505 field produces a complete contents note if the 1st
                                       Indicator value is "0" and the Print Constant "Contents:".
                                       The 2nd Indicator value of "ƀ " results in the contents note
                                       being "basic" rather than "enhanced." The "enhanced"
                                       format was not chosen because it appears from the first
                                       volume that the titles of the individual volumes will not be
                                       particularly distinctive.*

APPENDIX B

Answers to the
Choice of Access Points Exercise

In the answers that follow, the new information that would be added to the catalog record already in Chapter 1 to provide for access points appears in boldface. Indicators that deal with the form of the heading rather than the creation of the access point have not been included, similar to the practice used with the examples in Chapter 2. In recording the Field 245 only subfield ‡a data have been recorded to conserve space.

For each access point the rule that applies is given on the right-hand column. Rather than repeat the same rule each time the following "General Rules" also apply:

Personal authorship main entry	**21.4A2**
Corporate body main entry	**21.1B2**
Corporate body not the main entry	**21.1B3**
Title main entry	**21.1C1**

Similarly, unless otherwise stated, the following rules were used, although not given with the answers:

Title added entries:	**21.30J1**
Series added entries	**21.30L1**

1. *Nothing could be finer than a crisis that is minor in the morning.*

    100   Osgood, Charles.   *[Rule 21.4A1]*
    245 1 0   Nothing could be finer than a crisis that
                is minor in the morning /

2. *Lucy's bones, sacred stones, & Einstein's brain: the remarkable stories behind the great objects and artifacts of history, from antiquity to the modern era.*

    100   Rachlin, Harvey.   *[Rule 21.6C1]*
    245 1 0   Lucy's bones, sacred stones, & Einstein's
                brain :
    **246 3 ƀ Lucy's bones, sacred stones, and Einstein's
                brain**
                *[When a symbol appears in the first five
                words of the title proper, it is LC policy also
                to provide access to the title with the word
                represented by the symbol written out.]*

3. *Carnegie Library of Pittsburgh: a brief history and description.*

    100   Munn, Ralph.   *[Rule 21.4A1]*
    245 1 0   Carnegie Library of Pittsburgh :

4.   *Seminary addresses & other papers.*

      100   **Schechter, Solomon.**   *[Rule 21.4A1]*
      245 **1** **0** Seminary addresses & other papers /
      246 **3** **ƀ** **Seminary addresses and other papers**
                            [When a symbol appears in the first five
                            words of the title proper, it is LC policy to
                            also provide access to the title with the word
                            represented by the symbol written out.]
      440   **0** Religion in America

5.   *Isn't that just like a man! Oh, well, you know how women are.*

      100   **Rinehart, Mary Roberts.**   *[Rule 21.7C1]*
      245 **1** **0** Isn't that just like a man! /
      700   **Cobb, Irvin S. ‡t Oh, well, you know**   *[Rule 21.7C1]*
                   how women are.
                            [This is a name-title access point because
                            Cobb is the main entry for this work]

6.   *The principles, origin and establishment of the Catholic school system in the United States.*

      100   **Burns, J. A.**   *[Rule 21.4A1]*
      245 **1** **4** The principles, origin and establishment of
                   the Catholic school system in the United States /

7.   *Deutsch für Amerikaner.*

      100   **Goedsche, C. R.**   *[Rule 21.6C1]*
      245 **1** **0** Deutsch für Amerikaner /
      700   **Spann, Meno.**   *[Rule 21.6C1]*

8.   *Decimal classification and relativ index.*

      100   **Dewey, Melvil.**   *[Rule 21.4A1]*
      245 **1** **0** Decimal classification and relativ [sic.] index /
      246 **3** **ƀ** **Decimal classification and relative index**
                              [This additional title access for the normal
                            spelling of "relativ" follows LC policy
                            where a word occurs in the first five words
                            of a title proper that has [sic.] appearing
                            after the word.]

                            [No access points were provided for the
                            editors because they are not named
                            prominently in the work, i.e., they were
                            named only in the foreword (Rule
                            21.30D1).]

9.   *The fun book of fatherhood, or, How the animal kingdom is helping to raise the wild kids in our house.*

100		**Cammarata, Jerry.**	*[Rule 21.46B1]*
245	1 4	The fun book of fatherhood, or, How the animal kingdom is helping to raise the wild kids in our house /	
246	3 0	**Fun book of fatherhood**	
246	3 0	**How the animal kingdom is helping to raise the wild kids in our house**	

[These 246 title access points reflect LC policy regarding title access to works with alternative titles.]

700		**Leighton, Frances Spatz.**	*[Rule 21.6B1]*

10.   *Chaucer's major poetry.*

100		**Chaucer.**	*[Rule 21.4A1]*
245	1 0	Chaucer's major poetry /	
700		**Baugh, Albert C.**	*[Rule 21.30D1]*

[No title access point using Field 246 was provided for "Major poetry." It was not considered a useful title.]

11.   *Van Nostrand Reinhold manual of film-making.*

100		**Callaghan, Barry.**	*[Rule 21.4.A1]*
245	1 0	Van Nostrand Reinhold manual of film-making /	
246	3 0	**Manual of film-making**	
246	3 0	**Manual of film making**	
710		**Van Nostrand Reinhold.**	*[Rule 21.30H1]*

[The access point for Van Nostrand Reinhold is borderline as to its usefulness. It would be more important in divided catalogs and online catalogs with separate indexes. The second 246 field allows for differences in how local computers would handle the use of a hyphen in a word.]

12.   *William Alanson White.*

100		**White, William A.**	*[Rule 21.4A1]*
245	1 0	William Alanson White /	
440	0	Historical issues in mental health	

13. *Three from the 87th.*

100		**McBain, Ed.**	*[Rule 21.4A1]*
245 1 0		Three from the 87th /	
246 3 ♭		**3 from the 87th**	

        [It is LC policy to provide additional title access for a number represented by a word in the first five words of the title proper if it is assumed that a catalog user would reasonably expect that the numeral form was used in the title. Accepting this assumption for the word "three," this access point was provided. It was assumed that no user would expect "87th" to have been spelled-out.]

740 0 2	**Hail, hail, the gang's all here.**	*[Rule 21.30M1]*
740 0 2	**Jigsaw.**	*[Rule 21.30M1]*
740 0 2	**Fuzz.**	*[Rule 21.30M1]*

        [Field 740 provides for an uncontrolled, i.e., non-uniform title, related/analytical title access point for independent works contained within the item. The provision of access points for the individual titles is a local library option.]

14. *Triglavski Narodni Park = Triglav National Park*

100	**Bizak, James.**	*[Rule 21.24A]*
245 1 0	Triglavski Nardoni Park = Triglav National Park /	
246 3 1	**Triglav National Park**	*[Rule 21.30J1]*
700	**Klemenc, Stane.**	*[Rule 21.24A]*

        [This work appears to be the collaboration of an writer and an artist rather than a text to which an artist had added illustrations. Thus the use of Rule 21.24a rather than 21.11A1. This would be difficult to judge, however, without being able to examine the work.]

15. *Murallas de San Juan = Forts of San Juan.*

245 0 0	Murallas de San Juan = Forts of San Juan /	*[Rule 21.5A]*
246 3 1	**Forts of San Juan**	*[Rule 21.30J1]*

16. *The wild boy of Burundi: a study of an outcast child.*

100	**Lane, Harlan.**	*[Rule 21.6C1]*
245 1 4	The wild boy of Burundi :	
700	**Pillard, Richard.**	*[Rule 21.6C1]*

        [Generally, no access point is provided for the author of a foreword.]

17.   *Birds of North America: a guide to field identification.*

    100   **Robbins, Chandler S.**   *[Rule 21.6C1]*
    245 **1** **0** Birds of North America :
    700   **Bruun, Bertel.**   *[Rule 21.6C1]*
    700   **Zim, Herbert S.**   *[Rule 21.6C1]*
    700   **Singer, Arthur.**   *[Rule 21.30K2]*
                       [The illustrations were considered an important feature of this work. This would be difficult to judge, however, without being able to examine the work.]

18.   *Gray lady down: original title, Event 1000: a novel.*

    100   **Lavallee, David.**   *[Rule 21.4A1]*
    245 **1** **0** Gray lady down :
    740 **0** **2** **Event 1000.**
    740 **0** **2** **Event one thousand.**
                       [Field 740 provides for an uncontrolled, i.e., non-uniform title, related/analytical title access point for independent works contained within the item. The provision of these latter two access points is a local library option.]

19.   *1066 and all that: a memorable history of England.*

    100   **Sellar, Walter Carruthers.**   *[Rules 21.6C1 & 21.11A1]*
    245 **1** **0** 1066 and all that :
                       [For a single year written in arabic numerals, LC policy calls for no additional access point for the date in spelled-out form.]
    700   **Yeatman, Robert Julian.**   *[Rule 21.6C1]*
                       [No access point was provided for the illustrator because the illustrations were not considered an important feature of this work (Rule 21.30K2) This would be difficult to judge, however, without being able to examine the work.]

20.   *Solitaire & Double solitaire.*

    100   **Anderson, Robert.**   *[Rule 21.4A1]*
    245 **1** **0** Solitaire ; ‡b & Double solitaire /
    246 **3** **b** **Solitaire & Double solitaire**
    246 **3** **b** **Solitaire and Double solitaire**
                       [When a symbol appears in the first five words of the title proper, it is LC policy also to provide access to the title with the word represented by the symbol written out.]
    246 **3** **0** **Solitaire**

[Continued on next page]

246 3 0 Double solitaire
> *[These four 246 access points reflect LC policy for works that lack a collective title. The first 246 field was provided because "Double solitaire was in Subfield b of Field 245 and thus not searchable in most online catalogs.]*

21. *Lake Wobegon days.*

    100   **Keillor, Garrison.**   *[Rule 21.4A1]*
    245 **1 0** Lake Wobegon days /

22. *Against the wind.*

    100   **Freedman, J. F.**   *[Rule 21.4A1]*
    245 **1 0** Against the wind /

23. *"And I was there.": Pearl Harbor and Midway--breaking the secrets.*

    100   **Layton, Edwin T.**   *[Rule 21.6B1]*
    245 **1 0** "And I was there." :
    700   **Pineau, Roger.**   *[Rule 21.6B1]*
    700   **Costello, John.**   *[Rule 21.6B1]*

24. *Digging up the past.*

    100   **Woolley, Leonard.**   *[Rule 21.4A1]*
    245 **1 0** Digging up the past.

25. *Famous speeches of the eight Chicago anarchists.*

    245 0 **0** Famous speeches of the eight Chicago   *[Rule 21.7B1]*
           anarchists /
> *[It is LC policy to provide additional title access for a number represented by a word in the first five words of the title proper if it is assumed that a catalog user would reasonably expect that the numeral form was used in the title. Rejecting this assumption for the word "eight" no access point was provided.]*

    246 1 8 Speeches of the eight Chicago anarchists
    440   **0** Mass violence in America
    700   **Parsons, Lucy.**   *[Rule 21.7B1]*
> *[No access point was provided for the first named contributor, Spies, because he was not named on the chief source of information (Rule 21.7B1).]*

26. *A journal of the plague year: being observations or memorials . . .*

      100   **Defoe, Daniel.**   *[Rule 21.4A1]*
                  [Rule 21.5C does not apply because the
                  author is known.]
     245 1 2 A journal of the plague year :
     490 1   The Shakespeare Head edition of the novels
                & selected writings of Daniel Defoe
      800   **Defoe, Daniel. ‡t The Shakespeare Head**
                edition of the novels & selected writings of
                Daniel Defoe.
                  [This is a name-title series entry because the
                  personal author is responsible for all the
                  works in the series.]

27. *Red Lobster, white trash and the Blue lagoon.*

      100   **Queenan, Joe.**   *[Rule 21.4A1]*
     245 1 0 Red Lobster, white trash and the Blue
                lagoon :

28. *The best of Robert Benchley.*

      100   **Benchley, Robert.**   *[Rule 21.4A1]*
     245 1 4 The best of Robert Benchley /

29. *Outdoor education.*

     245 0 0 Outdoor education /   *[Rule 21.6C2]*
      700   **Smith, Julian W.**   *[Rule 21.6C2]*

30. *Irving Wallace: a writer's profile.*

      100   **Leverence, John.**   *[Rule 21.4A1]*
     245 1 0 Irving Wallace :
      440   **0**   Profiles in popular culture ; ‡v no. 1
                  [The contributions of Weidman, Grogg and
                  Browne were not considered significant
                  enough to warrant the provision of access
                  points for them.]

31. *The rights of woman.*

      100   **Wollstonecraft, Mary.**   *[Rule 21.7C1]*

      245 1 4   The rights of woman /

      440   **0**   Everyman's library ; ‡v no. 825. Science

      700   **Mill, John Stuart. ‡t Subjection of women.**   *[Rule 21.7C1]*

      700   **Catlin, G. E. G.**   *[Rule 21.30F1]*

                    [An access point was provided for the
                    author of the introduction because it was
                    considered an important feature of this
                    work. This would be difficult to judge,
                    however, without being able to examine the
                    work.]

32. *Pictorial treasury of U.S. stamps.*

      245 0 0   Pictorial treasury of U.S. stamps /   *[Rule 21.6C2]*

      440   **0**   Collectors Institute reference library

      700   **Marzulla, Elena.**   *[Rule 21.30D1]*

      710   **Collectors Institute.**   *[Rule 21.30E1]*

33. *An introduction to historical bibliography.*

      100   **Binns, Norman E.**   *[Rule 21.4A1]*

      245 1 3   An introduction to historical bibliography /

34. *Two thousand years of science: the wonders of nature and their discoverers.*

      100   **Harvey-Gibson, R. J.**   *[Rule 21.12A1]*

      245 1 0   Two thousand years of science :

      246 3 ƀ   **2000 years of science**

                    [It is LC policy to provide additional title
                    access for a number represented by a word
                    in the first five words of the title proper if it
                    is assumed that a catalog user would
                    reasonably expect that the numeral form
                    was used in the title. Accepting this
                    assumption for the words "thousand" this
                    access point was provided.]

      700   **Titherley, A. W.**   *[Rule 21.12A1]*

35. *The happy critic and other essays.*

      100   **Van Doren, Mark.**   *[Rule 21.4A1]*

      245 1 4   The happy critic and other essays /

36. *Brian Friel.*

100		**Maxwell, D. E. S.**
245	**1 0**	Brian Friel /
440	**4**	The Irish writers series

[Rule 21.4A1]

37. *Strictly speaking: will America be the death of English?*

100		**Newman, Edwin.**
245	**1 0**	Strictly speaking :

[Rule 21.4A1]

38. *The 13th valley: a novel.*

100		**Del Vecchio, John M.**
245	**1 4**	The 13th valley :
246	**3 b**	**Thirteenth valley**

[Rule 21.4A1]

> [It is LC policy to provide additional title access for a word represented by a number in the first five words of the title proper.]
>
> [Initial articles are deleted in Field 246. This field has no indicator assigned to handle non-filing characters.]

39. *Reading and reasoning.*

100		**Downing, John.**
245	**1 0**	Reading and reasoning /

[Rule 21.4A1]

40. *Kennedy and Roosevelt: the uneasy alliance.*

100		**Beschloss, Michael R.**
245	**1 0**	Kennedy and Roosevelt :

[Rule 21.4A1]

> [Generally, no access point is provided for the writer of a foreword.]

41. *Printed books, 1481-1900, in the Horticultural Society of New York: a listing.*

110		**Horticultural Society of New York.**

[Rule 21.4B1]

> [An administrative work (Rule 21.1B2a). It lists resources of the corporate body.]

245	**1 0**	Printed books, 1481-1900, in the Horticultural Society of New York :

> [For a span of years written in arabic numerals, LC policy calls for no additional access point for the dates in a spelled-out form.]

700		**Hall, Elizabeth Cornelia.**

[Rule 21.30C1]

42.   *Secrecy and power: the life of J. Edgar Hoover.*

    100   **Powers, Richard Gid.**   *[Rule 21.4A1]*
    245 **1** **0**   Secrecy and power :

43.   *Rare, vanishing & lost British birds.*

    100   **Hudson, W. H.**   *[Rule 21.12A1]*
    245 **1** **0**   Rare, vanishing & lost British birds /
    246 **3** **ƀ** **Rare, vanishing and lost British birds**
                [When a symbol appears in the first five
                words of the title proper, it is LC policy to
                also provide access to the title with the word
                represented by the symbol written out.]
    700   **Hudson, W. H. ǂb Lost British birds.**   *[Rule 21.30G1]*
                [The provision of an access point for the
                previous title would be a local library
                option. It is a name-title access point
                because Hudson is the main entry for that
                work.]
    700   **Gardiner, Linda.**   *[Rule 21.12A1]*
    700   **Gronvold, H.**   *[Rule 21.30K2]*
                [The illustrations were considered an
                important feature of this work. This would
                be difficult to judge, however, without being
                able to examine the work.]

44.   *Raising laboratory animals: a handbook for biological and behavioral research.*

    100   **Silvan, James.**   *[Rule 21.4A1]*
    245 **1** **0**   Raising laboratory animals :
    710   **American Museum of Natural History.**   *[Rule 21.30E1]*

45.   *David Brinkley: 11 presidents, 4 wars, 22 political conventions, 1 moon landing, 3 assassinations, 2,000 weeks of news and other stuff on television and 18 years of growing up.*

    100   **Brinkley, David.**   *[Rule 21.4A1]*
    245 **1** **0**   David Brinkley :

46.   *Patty Jane's House of Curl: a novel.*

    100   **Landvik, Lorna.**   *[Rule 21.4A1]*
    245 **1** **0**   Patty Jane's House of Curl :

47.   *Shipwrecks in Puerto Rico's history.*

    100   **Cardona Bonet, Walter A.**   *[Rule 21.4A1]*
    245 **1** **0**   Shipwrecks in Puerto Rico's history /

48. *Tunnel war.*

    100   **Poyer, Joe.**   *[Rule 21.4A1]*
    245 **1 0** Tunnel war /

49. *Principles of bibliographical description.*

    100   **Bowers, Fredson.**   *[Rule 21.4A1]*
    245 **1 0** Principles of bibliographic description /

50. *Eat the rich.*

    100   **O'Rourke, P. J.**   *[Rule 21.4A1]*
    245 1 0 Eat the rich /

51. *Golden mists.*

    100   **Author of Poppet.**   *[Rule 21.5C]*
                     [Assumes the identity of this person is
                     unknown]
    245 **1 0** Golden mists /
    440   **4** The family story-teller

52. *A history of book publishing in the United States.*

    100   **Tebbel, John.**   *[Rule 21.4A1]*
    245 **1 2** A history of book publishing in the
            United States /
    740 0 2 **Creation of an industry, 1630-1865.**   *[Rule 21.30M1]*
    740 0 2 **Expansion of an industry, 1865-1919.**   *[Rule 21.30M1]*
    740 0 2 **Golden age between two wars, 1920-1940.** *[Rule 21.30M1]*
    740 0 2 **Great change, 1940-1980.**   *[Rule 21.30M1]*
                     [Field 740 provides for an uncontrolled, i.e.,
                     non-uniform title, related/analytical title
                     access point for independent works
                     contained within the item. The provision of
                     access points for the titles of the individual
                     volumes is a local library option.]

53. *Doors and windows.*

    245 **0 0** Doors and windows /   *[Rule 21.6C2]*
    440   **0** Home repair and improvement
    710   **Time-Life Books.**   *[Rule 21.30E1]*

54. *Whose broad stripes and bright stars: the trivial pursuit of the Presidency, 1988.*

        100   **Germond, Jack W.**   *[Rule 21.6C1]*
        245 **1 0** Whose broad stripes and bright stars :
        700   **Witcover, Jules.**   *[Rule 21.6C1]*

55. *Technical services: a syllabus for training leading to certification of library assistants.*

        245 **0 0** Technical services :   *[Rule 21.6C2]*
                         [This was not considered an administrative work (Rule 21.1B2a and 21.1B3). This would be difficult to judge, however, without being able to examine the work.]
        710   **Pennsylvania State Library. Bureau of**   *[Rule 21.30E1]*
                      Library Development.

56. *Daniel Deronda.*

        100   **Eliot, George.**   *[Rule 21.4A1]*
        245 **1 0** Daniel Deronda /
        440   **4** The world's classics
        490 **0**   Oxford paperbacks   *[Rule 21.30L1]*
                         [Usually no access point would be provided for this series-- the works are related only by common physical characteristics.]
        700   **Handley, Graham.**   *[Rule 21.30D1]*

57. *French for cats.*

        100   **Beard, Henry.**   *[Rule 21.6B1]*
        245 **1 0** French for cats :
        700   **Boswell, John.**   *[Rule 21.6B1]*
        700   **Zamchick, Gary.**   *[Rule 21.30K2]*
                         [The illustrations were considered an important feature of this work. This would be difficult to judge, however, without being able to examine the work.]

58. *The Doonesbury chronicles.*

        100   **Trudeau, G. B.**   *[Rule 21.4A1]*
        245 **1 4** The Doonesbury chronicles /
                         [Generally, no access point is provided for the writer of an introduction.]

59. *Trees, shrubs and vines: a pictorial guide to the ornamental woody plants of the Northern United States exclusive of conifers.*

      100   **Viertel, Arthur T.**   *[Rule 21.4A1]*

      245 **1 0** Trees, shrubs and vines :

60. *OCLC communications & access planning guide.*

      245 **0 0** OCLC communications & access planning   *[Rule 21.6C2]*
               guide.

                    [This was not considered an administrative work (Rule 21.1B2a and 21.1B3). This would be difficult to judge, however, without being able to examine the work.]

      246 3 b **OCLC communications and access**
               planning guide

                    [When a symbol appears in the first five words of the title proper, it is LC policy to also provide access to the title with the word represented by the symbol written out.]

      710   **OCLC.**   *[Rule 21.30E1]*

61. *Library of Congress rule interpretations.*

      110   **Library of Congress. Office for**   *[Rule 21.1B2a]*
               Descriptive Cataloging Policy

      245 **1 0** Library of Congress rule interpretations /

                    [In its cataloging LC did not consider this to be an administrative work (Rule 21.1B2a), although one can see how others might -- it states LC cataloging policies. Thus, LC was made the main entry.]

                    [No access point would be provided for the editor because he is not named prominently in the work, i.e., he was named in the preface (Rule 21.30D1).]

62. *Lucy: the beginnings of humankind.*

      100   **Johanson, Donald C.**   *[Rule 21.6C1]*

      245 **1 0** Lucy :

      700   **Edey, Maitland A.**   *[Rule 21.6C1]*

63. *The makers of Florence: Dante, Giotto, Savonarola, and their city.*

    100   **Oliphant, Mrs.**   *[Rule 21.11A1]*
    245 **1 4** The makers of Florence :
                      *[No access point was provided for the
                      illustrator because the illustrations were not
                      considered an important feature of this work
                      (Rule 21.30K2) This would be difficult to
                      judge, however, without being able to
                      examine the work.].]*

64. *Was this Camelot?: excavations at Cadbury Castle, 1966-1970.*

    100   **Alcock, Leslie.**   *[Rule 21.4A1]*
    245 **1 0** Was this Camelot? :
    440   **0** New aspects of archaeology
    710   **Camelot Research Committee.**   *[Rule 21.30E1]*

65. *The complete works of O. Henry.*

    100   **Henry, O.**   *[Rule 21.4A1]*
    245 **1 4** The complete works of O. Henry /
                      *[Generally, no access point is provided for
                      the writer of an foreword.]*

66. *The organic chemistry of palladium.*

    100   **Maitlis, Peter M.**   *[Rule 21.4A1]*
    245 **1 4** The organic chemistry of palladium /
    440   **0** Organometallic chemistry
    740 0 2 **Metal complexes.**   *[Rule 21.30M1]*
    740 0 2 **Catalytic reactions.**   *[Rule 21.30M1]*
                      *[Field 740 provides for an uncontrolled, i.e.,
                      non-uniform title, related/analytical title
                      access point for independent works
                      contained within the item. The provision of
                      access points for the titles of the individual
                      volumes is a local library option.]*

67. *West's New York digest, 4th.*

    245 **0 0** West's New York digest, 4th /   *[Rule 21.34C]*
    246 3 0 **New York digest, 4th**
                      *[No additional title access point was
                      provided for the word "4th" spelled out. It
                      was assumed that no user likely would have
                      expected that.]*
    710   **West Publishing Company.**   *[Rule 21.34C]*

68.   *Russia under the autocrat, Nicholas the First.*

      100   **Golovine, Ivan.**   *[Rule 21.4A1]*
      245 1 0 Russia under the autocrat, Nicholas the First
      440   **0** Praeger scholarly reprints. ‡p Source books
              in Russian and Soviet history
                     [Generally no title access is provided for the
                     title from which a work has been
                     translated.]

69.   *She walks in beauty.*

      100   **Shankman, Sarah.**   *[Rule 21.4A1]*
      245 1 0 She walks in beauty /
      490 0   G.K. Hall large print book series
                     [Usually no access point would be provided
                     for this series-- the works are related only by
                     common physical characteristics.]

70.   *Burning down the house: MOVE and the tragedy of Philadelphia.*

      100   **Anderson, John.**   *[Rule 21.6C1]*
      245 1 0 Burning down the house :
      700   **Hevenor, Hilary.**   *[Rule 21.6C1]*

71.   *Why Wisconsin.*

      100   **Bowman, Francis Favill.**   *[Rule 21.4A1]*
      245 1 0 Why Wisconsin /

72.   *Men of Dunwich: the story of a vanished town.*

      100   **Parker, Rowland.**   *[Rule 21.4A1]*
      245 1 0 Men of Dunwich :

73.   *The secret life of Walter Kitty.*

      100   **Goodman, Joan Elizabeth.**   *[Rule 21.4A1]*
      245 1 4 The secret life of Walter Kitty /
      490 0   A big little golden book
                     [Usually no access point would be provided
                     for this series-- the works are related only by
                     common physical characteristics.]

74.   *Greek art.*

    100   **Boardman, John.**   *[Rule 21.4A1]*
    245 **1** 0   Greek art /
    440   0   Praeger world of art series
    490 0   Books that matter
                  [Usually no access point would be provided
                  for this series-- the works are related only by
                  common physical characteristics.]

75.   *Gods' man: a novel in woodcuts.*

    100   **Ward, Lynd.**   *[Rule 21.4A1]*
    245 **1** 0   Gods' man :

76.   *Sacred cows—and other edibles.*

    100   **Giovanni, Nikki.**   *[Rule 21.4A1]*
    245 **1** 0   Sacred cows—*and other edibles* /

77.   *Reader's Digest complete do-it-yourself manual.*

    245 0 0   Reader's Digest complete do-it-yourself   *[Rule 21.6C2]*
                  manual /
    246 **3** **0**   **Complete do-it-yourself manual**
    710   **Reader's Digest Association.**   *[Rule 21.30E1]*

78.   *Records management: controlling business information.*

    100   **Place, Irene.**   *[Rule 21.6C1]*
    245 **1** 0   Records management :
    700   **Hyslop, David J.**   *[Rule 21.6C1]*

79.   *Using the new AACR2: an expert systems approach to choice of access points.*

    245 0 0   Using the new AACR2 :   *[Rule 21.6C2]*
    700   **Smith, David.**   *[Rule 21.6C2]*
    730   **Using AACR2.**   *[Rule 21.30G1]*
                  [The provision of an access point for the
                  previous title would be a local library
                  option. This access point is under title
                  rather than name-title because this work
                  was also the more or more than 3 authors.]

80.   *American railroads.*

          100   **Stover, John F.**   *[Rule 21.4A1]*
          245 **1 0**   American railroads /
          440   **4**   The Chicago history of American civilization

81.   *Role of vitamin B6 in neurobiology.*

          245 **0 0**   Role of vitamin B6 in neurobiology /   *[Rule 21.7B1]*
          440   **0**   Advances in biochemical
                         pyschopharmacology ; ‡v v. 4
          700   **Ebadi, Manuchair S.**   *[Rule 21.7B1]*
          700   **Costa, Erminio.**   *[Rule 21.7B1]*

82.   *The creation of an industry, 1630-1865.*

          100   **Tebbel, John.**   *[Rule 21.4A1]*
          245 **1 4**   The creation of an industry, 1630-1865 /
                         [For a span of years written in arabic
                         numerals, LC policy calls for no additional
                         access point for the dates in spelled-out
                         form.]
          490 1   A history of book publishing in the United
                         States ‡v v.1
          800   **Tebbel, John. ‡t A history of book publishing**
                         in the United States ; v.1.
                         [This is a name-title series entry because the
                         personal author is responsible for all the
                         works in the series. See Example 51.]

83.   *Settlement and politics in three classic Maya polities.*

          100   **Montmollin, Olivier de.**   *[Rule 21.4A1]*
          245 **1 0**   Settlement and politics in three Maya
                         polities /
          440   **0**   Monographs in world archaeology,
                         ‡x 1055-2316 ; ‡v no. 24

84.   *The Fourth of July valley: glacial geology and archeology of the Timberline ecotone.*

          100   **Benedict, James B.**   *[Rule 21.4A1]*
          245 **1 4**   The Fourth of July valley :
[Continued on next page]

246 3 0 **4th of July valley**
                  [It is LC policy to provide additional title
                  access for a number represented by a word
                  in the first five words of the title proper if it
                  is assumed that a catalog user would
                  reasonably expect that the numeral form
                  was used in the title. Accepting this
                  assumption for the word "fourth" this
                  access point was provided.]

490 1 Research report / Center for Mountain
         Archeology ; ‡v no. 2

830   0 **Research report (Center for Mountain**
         Archeology) ; ‡v no. 2.
         [The development of the form of this access
         point with the parenthetical qualifier is
         addressed in Chapter 5 of this text.]

85.   *The graffiti of Tikal.*

     100   **Trik, Helen.**   *[Rule 21.6C1]*
     245 1 4 The graffiti of Tikal /
     440   0 Tikal report ; ‡v no. 31
     440   0 University Museum monograph ; ‡v 57
     700   **Kampen, Michael E.**   *[Rule 21.6C1]*

86a. *The quintessence of Irving Langmuir.*
       [Both series as access points]

     100   **Rosenfeld, Albert.**   *[Rule 21.4A1]*
     245 1 4 The quintessence of Irving Langmuir /
     440   4 The Commonwealth and international
                library. ‡p Selected readings in physics
     440   0 Men of physics
     700   2 **Langmuir, Irving. ‡t Collected works of**   *[Rule 21.30G1]*
                Irving Langmuir.
                [The provision of an access point for the
                companion work is a local library option. It
                is a name-title access point because
                Langmuir is the main entry for that work.]

86b. *The quintessence of Irving Langmuir,*
       [Neither series as an access point]

     100   **Rosenfeld, Albert.**   *[Rule 21.4A1]*
     245 1 4 The quintessence of Irving Langmuir /
     490 0   The Commonwealth and international
                library. ‡p Selected readings in physics.
     490 0   Men of physics
     700   2 **Langmuir, Irving. ‡t Collected works of**   *[Rule 21.30G1]*
                Irving Langmuir.

87.   *Michels retinal detachment.*

100		**Wilkinson, Charles P.**	*[Rule 21.6C1]*
245	1 0	Michels retinal detachment /	
700		**Rice, Thomas A.**	*[Rule 21.6C1]*
700		**Michels, Ronald G. ‡t Retinal detachment.**	*[Rule 21.30G1]*

[The provision of an access point for the original work is a local library option. It is a name-title access point because Michels is the main entry for that work.]

88.   *Victoria.*

100		**Weintraub, Stanley.**	*[Rule 21.4A1]*
245	1 0	Victoria /	

89.   *Essay on rime.*

100		**Shapiro, Karl.**	*[Rule 21.4A1]*
245	1 0	Essay on rime.	

90.   *Confessions of Felix Krull: confidence man : the early years.*

100		**Mann, Thomas.**	*[Rule 21.4A1]*
245	1 0	Confessions of Felix Krull :	

[Generally no title access is provided for the title from which a work has been translated.]

91.   *Greening the government: a guide to implementing executive order 12873.*

245	0 0	Greening of the government :	*[Rule 21.6C1]*
246	**3 0**	**Closing the circle**	

[Given the ambiguity of the representation of the title on the title page substitute it appears it would be useful to provide title access to this other title.]

710	**Office of the Vice President.**	*[Rule 21.30E1]*

[This was not considered an administrative work reporting recommendations of the corporate body (Rule 21.1B2c and 21.1B3). This would be difficult to judge, however, without being able to examine the work.]

92.   *What you should know about selling and salesmanship.*

      100   **Burstein, Milton B.**   *[Rule 21.4A1]*
      245 **1 0** What you should know about selling and
                salesmanship /
      246 **1 4** Selling and salesmanship
      440   **0** Business almanac series ; ‡v no. 18

93.   *Great men of American popular song.*

      100   **Ewen, David.**   *[Rule 21.4A1]*
      245 **1 0** Great men of American popular song /

94.   *Classification. Class KJ-KKZ, law of Europe.*

      110   **Library of Congress. Processing Services.** *[Rule 21.4B1]*
                 Subject Cataloging Division.
                    [This was considered an administrative
                    work (Rule 21.1B2a).]
      245 **1 0** Classification. Class KJ-KKZ, law of Europe /
      246 **1 4** Law of Europe
                    [No access point was provided for Goldberg
                    because she was not named prominently in
                    the work, i.e., not in a prescribed source for
                    Area 1 or 2 (Rule 21.30D1).]

95.   *Foreign diplomacy in China, 1894-1900: a study in political and economic*
      relations with China..

      100   **Joseph, Philip.**   *[Rule 21.4A1]*
      245 **1 0** Foreign diplomacy in China, 1894-1900 :
                    [Generally no series access point would be
                    provided for the series in of which the
                    original work was a part.]

96.   *Old Mr. Boston de luxe official bartender's guide.*

      245 **0 0** Old Mr. Boston de luxe official bartender's *[Rule 21.6C2]*
                 guide /
      246 **3 b** **Old Mister Boston de luxe official bartender's**
                 guide
      246 **3 b** **Old Mr. Boston deluxe official bartender's**
                 guide

[Continued on next page]

246 3 b̸ **Old Mister Boston deluxe official bartender's
guide**

> *[It is LC policy to provide additional title
> access for a word represented by an
> abbreviation in the first five words of the
> title proper if it is assumed that a catalog
> user would reasonably expect that the full
> form of the word was used in the title.
> Additionally, title access points for the
> more common spelling of "deluxe" were
> provided because it was assumed that a
> catalog user would reasonably expect that
> that spelling had been used.]*

700   **Cotton, Leo.**   *[Rule 21.30D1]*

> *[This was considered to be a work produced
> under editorial direction rather than a work
> of personal authorship. This would be
> difficult to judge, however, without being
> able to examine the work.]*

> *[A access point for "Mr. Boston" a
> corporate body could also have been made
> under Rule 21.30E1.]*

97.   *Defense Intelligence Agency organization, mission and key personnel.*

110   **Defense Intelligence Agency.**   *[Rule 21.4B1]*

> *[This was considered an administrative
> work (Rule 21.1B2a). This would be
> difficult to judge, however, without being
> able to examine the work.]*

245 1 0   Defense Intelligence Agency organization,
mission and key personnel /

> *[The Directorate for Human Resources is
> part of the Defense Intelligence Agency and
> produced this work for the entire agency.
> Thus, is was not deemed appropriate for
> them to be the main entry no have an access
> point provided.]*

98.   *Early Renaissance fifteenth century Italian painting.*

100   **Gould, C. H. M.**   *[Rule 21.4A1]*

245 1 0   Early Renaissance fifteenth century
Italian painting /

246 3 b̸ **Early Renaissance 15th century Italian
painting**

> *[It is LC policy to provide additional title
> access for a number represented by a word
> in the first five words of the title proper if it
> is assumed that a catalog user would
> reasonably expect that the numeral form
> was used in the title.]*

440   0   Color slide program of the world's art

99.   *The road ahead.*

    100   **Gates, Bill.**   *[Rule 21.6B1]*
    245 1 4 The road ahead /
    700   **Myhrvold, Nathan.**   *[Rule 21.6B1]*
    700   **Rinearson, Peter.**   *[Rule 21.6B1]*

100.   *Death of a schoolboy.*

    100   **Koning, Hans.**   *[Rule 21.4A1]*
    245 1 0 Death of a schoolboy /

101.   *Bubba talks of life, love, sex, whiskey, politics, foreigners, teenagers, movies, food,*
    football, and other matters that occasionally concern human beings.

    100   **Jenkins, Dan.**   *[Rule 21.4A1]*
    245 1 0 Bubba talks of life, love, sex, whiskey,
              politics, foreigners, teenagers, movies, food,
              football, and other matters that occasionally
              concern human beings /

102.   *Alexander and the terrible, horrible, no good, very bad day.*

    100   **Viorst, Judith.**   *[Rule 21.24A]*
    245 1 0 Alexander and the terrible, horrible, no
              good, very bad day /
    700   **Cruz, Ray.**   *[Rule 21.24A]*

103.   *Rumpole and the age of miracles.*

    100   **Mortimer, John.**   *[Rule 21.4A1]*
    245 1 0 Rumpole and the age of miracles /
              [No access points were provided for the
              titles in the contents note -- they are short
              stories.]

104.   *Shakespeare: lectures on five plays.*

    245 0 0 Shakespeare: lectures on five plays /   *[Rule 21.7B1]*
    440   0 Carnegie series in English ; ‡v no. 4
    700   **Sochatoff, A. Fred.**   *[Rule 21.7B1]*
              [No access points were provided for the
              titles in the contents note -- they are essays.]

105.   *Plays from the Circle Repertory Company.*

    245 0 0 Plays from the Circle Repertory Company.   *[Rule 21.7B1]*
    246 1 4 Plays from the Circle Rep

106. *Annoying the Victorians.*

    100   **Kincaid, James R.**   *[Rule 21.4A1]*
    245 **1 0** Annoying the Victorians /

107. *Internal Revenue Service: computer readiness for 1988 filing season: report to the Chairman, Joint Committee on Taxation, U.S. Congress.*

    110   **United States General Accounting Office.** *[Rule 21.4B1]*
                    [This was considered both an administrative work (Rule 21.1B2a) and a work reporting the collective thought of the corporate body (Rule 21.1B2c). This would be difficult to judge, however, without being able to examine the work.]
    245 **1 0** Internal Revenue Service :
    710   **Joint Committee on Taxation.**   *[Rule 21.30E1]*

108. *A child's book of wildflowers.*

    100   **Kelly, M. A.**   *[Rule 21.24A]*
    245 **1 2** A child's book of wildflowers /
    700   **Powzyk, Joyce.**   *[Rule 21.24A]*

109. *Letter to Loren.*

    100   **Thomas, Dylan.**   *[Rule 21.4A1]*
    245 **1 0** Letter to Loren /
                    [Generally, no access point is provided for the writer of an introduction and notes.]

110. *Hot air: all talk, all the time.*

    100   **Kurtz, Howard.**   *[Rule 21.4A1]*
    245 **1 0** Hot air :

111. *Andrew Carnegie.*

    100   **Wall, Joseph Frazier.**   *[Rule 21.4A1]*
    245 **1 0** Andrew Carnegie /

112. *No ordinary time: Franklin and Eleanor Roosevelt: the home front in World War II.*

    100   **Goodwin, Doris Kearns.**   *[Rule 21.4A1]*
    245 **1 0** No ordinary time :

113. *501 Latin verbs fully conjugated in all the tenses in a new easy-to-learn format*
      alphabetically arranged.

    100   **Prior, Richard E.**   *[Rule 21.6C1]*

    245 **1 0** 501 Latin verbs fully conjugated in all the
                tenses in a new easy-to-learn format
                alphabetically arranged /

    246 **3 ƀ** **Five hundred one Latin verbs fully conjugated**
                in all the tenses in a new easy-to-learn format
                alphabetically arranged
                    [It is LC policy to provide additional title
                    access for a word represented by a number
                    in the first five words of the title proper.]

    246 **3 ƀ** **Five hundred and one Latin verbs fully**
                conjugated in all the tenses in a new easy-to-
                learn format alphabetically arranged
                    [A variation on the way the numbers would
                    be pronounced and thus written as words.]

    700   **Wohlberg, Joseph E.**   *[Rule 21.6C1]*

    700   **Wohlberg. Joseph E. ‡t 201 Latin verbs fully** *[Rule 21.30G1]*
                conjugated in all tenses, alphabetically
                arranged.
                    [The provision of an access point for the
                    previous title would be a local library
                    option. It is a name-title access point
                    because Wohlberg is the main entry for that
                    work.]

114. *Dead souls.*

    100   **Gogol, Nikolai.**   *[Rule 21.4A1]*
    245 **1 0** Dead souls /
    440   **0**   **Russian classics**
    700   **English, Christopher.**   *[Rule 21.30K1]*
                    [No access point was provided for the editor
                    because she was not named on the chief
                    source of information, however, it would not
                    be been inappropriate to have provided one.]

115. *Angela's ashes: a memoir.*

    100   **McCourt, Frank.**   *[Rule 21.4A1]*
    245 **1 0** Angela's ashes :

116. *Revegetation equipment catalog.*

    100   **Larson, John E.**   *[Rule 21.4A1]*
    245 **1 0** Revegetation equipment catalog /
    246 **1 4** Catalog, revegetation equipment
    710   **Equipment Development Center.**   *[Rule 21.30H1]*
    711   **Vegetative Rehabilitation and**
                Equipment Workshop.   *[Rule 21.30H1]*

117. *Men who matched the mountains: the Forest Service in the Southwest.*

100	**Tucker, Edwin A.**	*[Rule 21.6C1]*
245 **1 0**	Men who matched the mountains :	
700	**Fitzpatrick, George.**	*[Rule 21.6C1]*
710	**U.S. Dept. of Agriculture, Forest Service, Southwestern Region.**	*[Rule 21.30H1]*

118. *Handbook for eastern timber harvesting.*

100	**Simmons, Fred C.**	*[Rule 21.4A1]*
245 **1 0**	Handbook for eastern timber harvesting /	
700	**Simmons, Fred C. ‡t Northeastern loggers' handbook.**	*[Rule 21.30G1]*
	[The provision of an access point for the original work is a local library option. It is a name-title access point because Simmons is the main entry for that work.]	
710	**U.S. Dept. of Agriculture, Forest Service, Northeastern Area, State & Private Forestry.**	*[Rule 21.30H1]*

APPENDIX C

Answers to the
Forms of Headings and References Exercise

The answers below show an abbreviation form of the name authority record for each access point. "See from" (Field 4xx) and "see also from" (Field 5xx) references are also shown. It is very possible that you may have thought of additional references that would have been equally useful to have used or decided that you would not have used some that were suggested.

In addition to the name heading and the references, the OCLC Authority Record Number (ARN) and the Library of Congress Control Number (Field 010) also have been retained. The ARN can be used to search the LC NAF using OCLC should you wish to see the entire authority record.

In all cases the heading is in AACR2R form. Unless otherwise indicated by "non-LC", the authority information is an abridgement of the LC name authority record. The answers reflect information in the LC NAF as of the latter part of 1998. Other names and additional authority files may have been added to the file which may change a few of the answers.

It is current LC practice to end name headings in authority records with a period only if the heading ends with an initial or with an abbreviation. There are a number of records in the NAF that do not conform to that policy. Those periods have been removed in the answers to this exercise.

Part A. Persons

119. *A gentle madness: bibliophiles, bibliomanes, and the eternal passion for books.*

Basbanes

ARN	3662210
010	n 94077608
100 1 0	**Basbanes, Nicholas A., ‡d 1943-**

120. *Management principles and practice: a guide to information sources.*

Bakewell

ARN	51438
010	n 50015977
100 1 0	**Bakewell, K. G. B.**
400 1 0	Bakewell, Kenneth Graham Bartlett

121   *The essential Calvin and Hobbes: a Calvin and Hobbes treasury.*

>   **Watterson**
>
>   ARN   1937426
>   010   n 87934510
>   100 1 0   **Watterson, Bill**

122.   *Mr. Dooley in the hearts of his countrymen.*

>   **Dunne**
>
>   ARN   321909
>   010   n 79089538
>   100 1 0   **Dunne, Finley Peter, ‡d 1867-1936**
>   400 0 0   F. P. D. ‡q (Finley Peter Dunne), ‡d 1867-1936
>   400 1 0   D., F. P. ‡q (Finley Peter Dunne), ‡d 1867-1936

123.   *Library of Congress classification adapted for children's books.*

>   **Perkins**
>
>   ARN   45208
>   010   n 50009692
>   100 1 0   **Perkins, John W., ‡d 1917-**
>   *[There are several persons in the LC NAF with the name "John W.*
>   *Perkins" or with an expansion of the middle name. Be careful that*
>   *you choose the correct one for this work.]*

>   **Clingen**
>
>   100 1 0   **Clingen, Paul N.** [non-LC]

>   **Jones**
>
>   100 1 0   **Jones, Paul C.** [non-LC]

127.   *South Carolina journals and journalists: proceedings of the Reynolds Conference,*
       University of South Carolina, May 17-18, 1974.

>   **Meriwether**
>
>   ARN   241865
>   010   n 79007743
>   100 1 0   **Meriwether, James B.**

130. *The autobiography of Alice B. Toklas.*

   Stein
   ARN   241108
   010   n 79006977
   100 1 0 **Stein, Gertrude, ‡d 1874-1946**

   Toklas
   ARN   49341
   010   n 50013863
   100 1 0 **Toklas, Alice B.**

131. *Mrs. Bridges' upstairs downstairs cookery book.*

   Bailey
   ARN   53395
   010   n 50017950
   100 1 0 **Bailey, Adrian, ‡d 1928-**
            [There are several persons in the LC NAF with the name "Adrian
            Bailey." Be careful that you choose the correct one for this work.]

   Hedgecoe
   ARN   298623
   010   n 79065706
   100 1 0 **Hedgecoe, John**

132. *The economic reports of the President as transmitted to the Congress, January*
      1949, January 1947, July 1947, January 1948, July 1948, together with the Joint
      Congressional Committee reports of 1947 & 1948.

   Truman
   ARN   263406
   010   n 79029742
   100 1 0 **Truman, Harry S., ‡d 1884-1972**
   400 1 0 Truman, Harry S., ‡c Pres. U.S., ‡d 1884-1972 [OLD CATALOG
            HEADING]
   400 1 0 Truman, Harry, ‡d 1884-1972
   510 1 0 United States. ‡b President (1945-1953 : Truman)

133. *President Wilson's state papers and addresses.*

Wilson

ARN	279672
010	n 79046299
100 1 0	**Wilson, Woodrow, ‡d 1856-1924**
400 1 0	Wilson, Thomas Woodrow, ‡d 1856-1924
400 1 0	Wilson, Woodrow, ‡c Pres. U.S., ‡d 1856-1924 [OLD CATALOG HEADING]
400 1 0	Wilson, T. W. ‡q (Thomas Woodrow), ‡d 1856-1924
510 1 0	United States. ‡b President (1913-1921 : Wilson)
510 1 0	New Jersey. ‡b Governor (1911-1913 : Wilson)

[These two 510 fields assume that the library already has other entries in the catalog under these headings. If not, it is likely that they would have been made as 410 references.]

Shaw

ARN	1459432
010	n 85158395
100 1 0	**Shaw, Albert, ‡d 1857-1947**

[There are several persons in the LC NAF with the name "Albert Shaw" with or without a middle name/initial. Be careful that you choose the correct one for this work.]

134. *Profiles in courage.*

Kennedy

ARN	288416
010	n 79055297
100 1 0	**Kennedy, John F. ‡q (John Fitzgerald), ‡d 1917-1963**
400 1 0	Kennedy, John Fitzgerald, ‡c Pres. U.S., ‡d 1917-1963 [OLD CATALOG HEADING]
400 1 0	Kennedy, John Fitzgerald, ‡d 1917-1963
400 1 0	Kennedy, Jack, ‡d 1917-1963
510 1 0	United States. ‡b President (1961-1963 : Kennedy)

[This 510 field assumes that the library already has an entry in the catalog under this heading. If not, it is likely that it would have been made a 410 reference.]

135. *The notion-counter: a farrago of foibles: being notes about nothing.*

Nobody

100 0 0	**Nobody** [non-LC]

[Although there are at least four entries in the LC NAF for the name "Nobody" none is believed to be for the author of this work. Because the other entries are already qualified by a date it was not considered necessary to qualify this name to make it unique.]

136. *The schoolmistress of Herondale, or, Sketches of life among the hills.*

    Author of The mountain refuge

        100 0 0   **Author of The mountain refuge** [non-LC]
        400 2 4   The mountain refuge, Author of [non-LC]

137. *The copyright dilemma: proceedings of a conference held at Indiana University, April 14-15, 1977.*

    White

        ARN   872498
        010   n 82213701
        100 1 0   **White, Herbert S.**

138. *The vital balance: the life process in mental health and illness.*

    Menninger

        ARN   72236
        010   n 50036990
        100 1 0   **Menninger, Karl A. ‡q (Karl Augustus), ‡d 1893-**
                  [There are several persons in the LC NAF with the name "Karl Menninger" with or without a middle name/initial. Be careful that you choose the correct one for this work.]

    Mayman

        100 1 0   **Mayman, Martin** [non-LC]

    Pruyser

        ARN   55536
        010   n 50020105 ‡z n 79003064
        100 1 0   **Pruyser, Paul W.**

139. *Destination disaster: from the tri-motor to the DC-10: the risk of flying.*

    Eddy

        ARN   67285
        010   n 50031929
        100 1 0   **Eddy, Paul, ‡d 1944-**
                  [There are several persons in the LC NAF with the name "Eddy, P" with or without the forename written out. Be careful that you choose the correct one for this work.]

[Continued on next page]

Potter

```
ARN      55275
010      n 50019843
100 1 0  Potter, Elaine
```

Page

```
ARN      86780
010      n 50051844
100 1 0  Page, Bruce
```
            [There are several persons in the LC NAF with the name "Bruce
            Page." Be careful that you choose the correct one for this work.]

140. *A dictionary of basic geography.*

Schmieder

```
100 1 0  Schmieder, Allen A. [non-LC]
```

141. *Headhunter.*

Slade

```
ARN      1212134
010      n 84182198
100 1 0  Slade, Michael
500 1 0  Clarke, Jay
500 1 0  Banks, John
500 1 0  Covell, Richard
```
            [There are several persons in the LC NAF with the name "Michael
            Slade." Be careful that you choose the correct one for this work.]

            [The 500 Fields assumes the catalog also has works written by these
            authors under their real names.]

142. *The feminist papers: from Adams to de Beauvoir.*

Rossi

```
ARN      398281
010      n 80015846
100 1 0  Rossi, Alice S., ‡d 1922-
```

143. *Three Restoration comedies.*

Falle

```
100 1 0  Falle, G. G. [non-LC]
```
                              [Continued on next page]

Wycherley

```
ARN      299551
010      n 79066666
100 1 0  Wycherley, William, ‡d 1640-1716
```

Congreve

```
ARN      324837
010      n 79092555
100 1 0  Congreve, William, ‡d 1670-1729
```
> [There are several persons in the LC NAF with the name "William Congreve." Be careful that you choose the correct one for this work.]

Villiers

```
ARN      76540
010      n 50041360
100 1 0  Buckingham, George Villiers, ‡c Duke of, ‡d 1628-1687
400 1 0  Villiers, George, ‡c Duke of Buckingham, ‡d 1628-1687
400 1 0  Buckingham, George Villiers, ‡c 2d Duke of, ‡d 1628-1687 [OLD
         CATALOG HEADING]
400 1 0  Buckingham, ‡c Duke of ‡q (George Villiers), ‡d 1628-1687
```
> [There are quite a few persons in the LC NAF with the name "George Villiers." Be careful that you choose the correct one for this work.]

144.   *The last Sherlock Holmes story.*

Dibdin

```
ARN      131063
010      n 77014601
100 1 0  Dibdin, Michael
```

MacDonald

```
ARN      278595
010      n 79045202 ‡z n 88104149 ‡z sh 86005102 ‡z sh 86003045
100 1 0  MacDonald, John D. ‡q (John Dann), ‡d 1916-1986
400 1 0  Farrell, John Wade, ‡d 1916-1986
400 1 0  O'Hara, Scott, ‡d 1916-1986
400 1 0  Reed, Peter, ‡d 1916-1986
400 1 0  MacDonald, John Dann, ‡d 1916- [OLD CATALOG HEADING]
```
> [There are several persons in the LC NAF with the name "John D. MacDonald" or with an expansion of the middle name. Be careful that you choose the correct one for this work.]

[Continued on next page]

Hallahan

ARN	54120
010	n 50018681
100 1 0	**Hallahan, William H.**

145. *The cheap detective.*

Grossbach

100 1 0   **Grossbach, Robert** [non-LC]

Simon

ARN	298492
010	n 79065574
100 1 0	**Simon, Neil**
400 1 0	Simon, Marvin Neil

146. *Esdaile's manual of bibliography.*

Esdaile

100 1 0   **Esdaile, Arundell, ‡d 1880-1956** [non-LC]
400 1 0   Esdaile, Arundell James Kennedy, ‡d 1880-1956. [COMPATIBLE]

> *[The form of name in the LC NAF (ARN: 91861) for "Arundell James Kennedy Esdaile" is termed "Compatible" meaning that it is not exactly in accord with AACR2. Accordingly, that form of name was not used for the heading. The name he commonly used in his works was "Arundell Esdaile." Please be aware that many libraries in reality would have used the compatible form. The use of dates for Field 100 is optional.]*

Stokes

100 1 0   **Stokes, Roy, ‡d 1915-** [non-LC]
400 1 0   Stokes, Roy Bishop, ‡d 1915- [COMPATIBLE]

> *[The form of name in the LC NAF (ARN: 397804) for "Roy Stokes" is termed "Compatible" meaning that it is not exactly in accord with AACR2. Accordingly, that form of name was not used for the heading. The name he commonly used in his works was "Roy Stokes." Please be aware that many libraries in reality would have used the compatible form. The use of dates for Field 100 is optional.]*

147.   *A glossary of literary terms.*

> **Abrams**
>
> 100 1 0   **Abrams, M. H.** [non-LC]
> > *[Based on the name he used in his works this is the proper form of name. The OCLC WorldCat does show that LC had established a form of name for him (Abrams, M. H. ‡q (Meyer Howard), ‡d 1912-) under earlier rules. It would be correct to have added the qualifier and the date to this name.]*
>
> **Norton**
>
> 100 1 0   **Norton, Daniel S.** [non-LC]
> 400 1 0   Norton, Daniel Silas, ‡d 1908-1951. [EARLIER RULES]
> > *[The form of name in the LC NAF (ARN: 58238) for "Dan S. Norton" is based on an earlier set of rules not AACR2. Accordingly, that form of name was not used for the heading.*

148.   *"Gentlemen prefer blondes": the illuminating diary of a professional lady.*

> **Loos**
>
> ARN   78589
> 010   n 50043422
> 100 1 0   **Loos, Anita, ‡d 1894-1981**
> 400 1 0   Emerson, John, ‡c Mrs., ‡d 1894-1981
> 400 1 0   Loos, Corine Anita, ‡d 1894-1981
>
> **Barton**
>
> ARN   2454092
> 010   n 89606660
> 100 1 0   **Barton, Ralph, ‡d 1891-1931**

149.   *Winnie ille Pu.*

> **Milnei**
>
> ARN   448603
> 010   n 80067053
> 100 1 0   **Milne, A. A. ‡q (Alan Alexander), ‡d 1882-1956**
> 400 1 0   Milne, Alan Alexander, ‡d 1882-1956 [OLD CATALOG HEADING]
> > *[There are several persons in the LC NAF with the name "A. A. Milne." Be careful that you choose the correct one for this work.]*
>
> **Lenardo**
>
> 100 1 0   **Leonard, Alexander** [non-LC]
> 400 1 0   Lenardo, Alexandro [non-LC]
> > *[The OCLC WorldCat reveals that this author has written works under "Alexander Leonard." The use of the Latin form of name in this work was likely done to create a feeling for the Latin just as the place of publication and publisher appear in the Latin form.]*

150.   *Gustav Mahler: memories and letters.*

Mahler, A.

ARN   38135
010   n 50002491
100 1 0   **Mahler, Alma, ‡d 1879-1964**
400 1 0   Werfel, Alma Schindler Mahler [OLD CATALOG HEADING]
400 1 0   Schindler, Alma Maria, ‡d 1879-1964
400 1 0   Gropius, Alma, ‡d 1879-1964
400 2 0   Mahler-Werfel, Alma, ‡d 1879-1964
400 1 0   Werfel, Alma, ‡d 1879-1964
400 1 0   Mahlerová, Alma, ‡d 1879-1964
400 2 0   Schindler-Mahler, Alma, ‡d 1879-1964
                    [This is a very generous use of references for this name. Many
                    libraries likely have chosen to have made few or none of them.]

Mahler, G.

ARN   448654
010   n 80067106
100 1 0   **Mahler, Gustav, ‡d 1860-1911**
400 1 0   Maler, Gustav, ‡d 1860-1911
400 1 0   Maler, G. ‡q (Gustav), ‡d 1860-1911

Mitchell

ARN   68909
010   n 50033572
100 1 0   **Mitchell, Donald, ‡d 1925-**
                    [There are several persons in the LC NAF with the name "Donald
                    Mitchell" with or without an expansion of the middle name. Be
                    careful that you choose the correct one for this work.]

151.   *Beethoven's letters: a critical edition.*

Beethoven

ARN   339691
010   n 79107741 ‡z no 98056029 ‡z no 98056518
100 1 0   **Beethoven, Ludwig van, ‡d 1770-1827**
400 1 0   Van Beethoven, Ludwig, ‡d 1770-1827

Kalischer

ARN   2541436
010   no 89007870
100 1 0   **Kalischer, Alfred Christlieb, ‡d 1842-1909**
400 1 0   Kalischer, Alfred Christlieb Salomo Ludwig, ‡d 1842-1909 [OLD
                    CATALOG HEADING]
400 1 0   Kalischer, A. C. ‡q (Alfred Christlieb), ‡d 1842-1909
400 1 0   Kalischer, Alf C. ‡q (Alf Christlieb), ‡d 1842-1909

152. *The gardens of Louisiana: places of work and wonder.*

Meek

ARN   1682285
010   n 85313761
100 1 0 **Meek, A. J.**

Turner

ARN   4240222
010   n 96123003
100 1 0 **Turner, Suzanne, ‡d 1950-**
            *[There are several persons in the LC NAF with the name "Suzanne
            Turner" with or without an expansion of the middle name. Be
            careful that you choose the correct one for this work.]*

153. *Conversations with Shelby Foote.*

Foote

ARN   291610
010   n 79058551
100 1 0 **Foote, Shelby**
400 1 0 Foote, Shelby Dade

Carter

ARN   152957
010   n 78016528
100 1 0 **Carter, William C.**
            *[There are several persons in the LC NAF with the name "William
            C. Carter" with or without an expansion of the middle name. Be
            careful that you choose the correct one for this work.]*

154. *Speak for England: an oral history of England, 1900-1975, based on interviews
      with the inhabitants of Wigton, Cumberland.*

Bragg

ARN   78422
010   n 50043252
100 1 0 **Bragg, Melvyn, ‡d 1939-**

155. *Supplement to Charles Evans' American bibliography.*

Bristol

ARN   2239168
010   n 87836812
100 1 0 **Bristol, Roger P. ‡q (Roger Pattrell), ‡d 1903-1974**
400 1 0 Bristol, Roger Pattrell [OLD CATALOG HEADING]
[Continued on next page]

Evans

ARN   44524
010   n 50009001
100 1 0   **Evans, Charles, ‡d 1850-1935**
              *[There are quite a number of persons in the LC NAF with the name
              "Charles Evans" with or without an expansion of the middle name.
              Be careful that you choose the correct one for this work.]*

156.   *The compleat angler, 1653-1967: a new bibliography.*

Horne

100 1 0   **Horne, Bernard S.** [non-LC]
              *[An examination of the OCLC WorldCat reveals that the "Bernard
              Shea Horne" in the LC NAF is not the author of this work. The
              name LC established for the author of this work under earlier rules
              added dates to the form of name. It would be appropriate to use them
              here too.]*

157.   *40 million schoolbooks can't be wrong: myths in American history.*

Ellis

100 1 0   **Ellis, L. Ethan** [non-LC]
400 1 0   Ellis, Lewis Ethan [EARLIER RULES]
              *[Based on the name he used in his works the name in Field 100 is the
              proper form of name.]*

158.   *Paul Hogarth's walking tours of old Philadelphia: through Independence Square,
         Society Hill, Southwark, and Washington Square.*

Hogarth

ARN   241088
010   n 79006956
100 1 0   **Hogarth, Paul, ‡d 1917-**

159.   *The United States and China.*

Fairbank

ARN   251882
010   n 79018027
100 1 0   **Fairbank, John King, ‡d 1907-** [COMPATIBLE]
400 1 0   Fairbank, John K. ‡q (John King), ‡d 1907-
              *[The form of name in the LC NAF (ARN: 251882) for "John K.
              Fairbank" is termed "Compatible" meaning that it is not exactly in
              accord with AACR2. An examination of the records for his works in
              the OCLC WorldCat reveals that he appears to use the form of name
              "John K. Fairbank" and "John King Fairbank" interchangeably in
              his works with no latest use of name apparent. Accordingly, the
              "Compatible" form of name was used for this heading.]*

160. *The waste lands.*

    King

      ARN   296711
      010   n 79063767 ‡z n 87125504
      100 1 0 **King, Stephen, ‡d 1947-**
      500 1 0 Bachman, Richard

                  *[There are quite a number of persons in the LC NAF with the name
                  "Stephen King" with or without an expansion of the middle name.
                  Be careful that you choose the correct one for this work.]*

161. *Victorian bookbindings.*

    Allen

      ARN   2555678
      010   n 89637799
      100 1 0 **Allen, Sue**

                  *[There are a number of persons in the LC NAF with the name "Sue
                  Allen" or "Susan Allen" with or without an expansion of the middle
                  name. Be careful that you choose the correct one for this work.]*

Part B. Corporate Bodies

123. *Library of Congress classification adapted for children's books.*

    Inglewood Public Library

      ARN   111321
      010   n 50077645
      110 2 0 **Inglewood Public Library**
      410 1 0 Inglewood (Calif.). ‡b Public Library

124. *ALA membership directory, 1996-1997.*

    American Library Association

      ARN   295892
      010   n 79062941
      110 2 0 **American Library Association**
      410 2 0 ALA
      410 2 0 A.L.A.

125. *The library code.*

Pennsylvania

ARN   256684
010   n 79022911 ‡z n 79022910 ‡z sh 85099515
151   0   **Pennsylvania**
          [Technically this is a geographic name rather than a corporate name
          and as such is covered by the rules in AACR2R Chapter 23 rather
          than Chapter 24.]

Pennsylvania State Library

ARN   506634
010   n 80126172
110 2 0   **Pennsylvania State Library**
410 1 0   Pennsylvania. ‡b State Library, Harrisburg [OLD CATALOG
          HEADING]
410 1 0   Pennsylvania. ‡b Dept. of Education. ‡b Pennsylvania State Library
410 1 0   Pennsylvania. ‡b Dept. of Public Instruction. ‡b Pennsylvania State
          Library
410 1 0   Pennsylvania. ‡b Pennsylvania State Library
410 1 0   Harrisburg (Pa.). ‡b Pennsylvania State Library
510 2 0   State Library of Pennsylvania [LATER HEADING]

126. *The child and television drama: the psychosocial impact of cumulative viewing.*

Committee on Social Issues

ARN   844926
010   n 82148887
110 2 0   **Group for the Advancement of Psychiatry. ‡b Committee on Social**
          Issues
410 2 0   Committee on Social Issues (Group for the Advancement of
          Psychiatry) [non-LC]

127. *South Carolina journals and journalists: proceedings of the Reynolds Conference,*
      University of South Carolina, May 17-18, 1974.

Reynolds Conference

ARN   252586
010   n 79018739
111 2 0   **Reynolds Conference**

Southern Studies Program

ARN   254835
010   n 79021034
110 2 0   **University of South Carolina. ‡b Southern Studies Program**
410 1 0   South Carolina. ‡b University. ‡b Southern Studies Program [OLD
          CATALOG HEADING]

128. *The Firesign Theatre's big book of plays.*

    Firesign Theatre

      ARN   616534
      010   n 81071220
      110 2 0 **Firesign Theatre (Performing group)**
      410 2 0 Firesign Theater

129. *A programmed introduction to PERT: program evaluation and review technique.*

    Federal Electric Corporation

      110 2 0 **Federal Electric Corporation** [non-LC]
      410 2 0 International Telephone and Telegraph Corporation. ‡b Federal
                Electric Corporation [non-LC]
                [This assumes that an authority record and heading already exist for
                "International Telephone and Telegraph Corporation and that a
                reference has been made from "ITT" and "I.T.T."]

132. *The economic reports of the President as transmitted to the Congress, January
     1949, January 1947, July 1947, January 1948, July 1948, together with the Joint
     Congressional Committee reports of 1947 & 1948.*

    United States. President (Truman)

      ARN   263425
      010   n 79029761
      110 1 0 **United States. ‡b President (1945-1953 : Truman)**

    Joint Economic Committee

      ARN   273557
      010   n 79040066
      110 1 0 **United States. ‡b Congress. ‡b Joint Economic Committee**
      410 2 0 Joint Economic Committee Congress of the United States
      410 1 0 United States. ‡b Congress. ‡b Joint Committee on the Economic
                Report [EARLIER HEADING]

    Council of Economic Advisors

      ARN   581693
      010   n 81036048
      110 2 0 **Council of Economic Advisers (U.S.)**
      410 1 0 United States. ‡b Council of Economic Advisers [OLD CATALOG
                HEADING]
      410 1 0 United States. ‡b Executive Office of the President. ‡b Council of
                Economic Advisers
      410 2 0 President's Council of Economic Advisers (U.S.)
      410 2 0 Council of Economic Advisors (U.S.)

133.   *President Wilson's state papers and addresses.*

    United States. President (Wilson)

       ARN   279674
       010   n 79046301
       110 1 0   **United States. ‡b President (1913-1921 : Wilson)**

135.   *The copyright dilemma: proceedings of a conference held at Indiana University,
April 14-15, 1977.*

    Indiana University Graduate Library School

       ARN   152550
       010   n 78016120
       110 2 0   **Indiana University. ‡b Graduate Library School**
       410 1 0   Indiana. ‡b University. ‡b Graduate Library School [OLD CATALOG
                 HEADING]
       410 2 0   Indiana University. ‡b Division of Library Science [EARLIER
                 HEADING]
       510 2 0   Indiana University, Bloomington. ‡b Graduate Library School [LATER
                 HEADING]

155.   *Supplement to Charles Evans' American bibliography.*

    Bibliographical Society of America

       ARN   240663
       010   n 79006523
       110 2 0   **Bibliographical Society of America**

    Bibliographical Society of the University of Virginia

       ARN   252418
       010   n 79018569
       110 2 0   **University of Virginia. ‡b Bibliographical Society**
       410 2 0   Bibliographical Society of the University of Virginia
       410 1 0   Virginia. ‡b University. ‡b Bibliographical Society [OLD CATALOG
                 HEADING]

Part C. Uniform Titles

*AACR2R requires that when a name-title access point is provided the title must be in the
form of a uniform title for that work. Accordingly name authority records have been
made for all the name-title access points in this assignment. Please note that in addition
to the uniform title name authority record one must also have a name authority record for
the personal name. These were provided in Part A of this assignment.*

121   *The essential Calvin and Hobbes: a Calvin and Hobbes treasury.*

        Calvin and Hobbes (Comic strip)

        ARN   2604739

        010   n 88190847 ‡z n 88099741

        100 1 0 **Watterson, Bill. ‡t Calvin and Hobbes (Comic strip). ‡k Selections**

        400 1 0 Watterson, Bill. ‡t Essential Calvin and Hobbes

126.   *The child and television drama: the psychosocial impact of cumulative viewing.*

        Publication (Group for the advancement of Psychiatry)

        ARN   18919

        010   n 42020291

        130   0 **Publication (Group for the Advancement of Psychiatry)**

        410 2 0 Group for the Advancement of Psychiatry. ‡t Publication

        410 2 0 Group for the Advancement of Psychiatry. ‡t Publication - Group for
                  the Advancement of Psychiatry [OLD CATALOG HEADING]

        530   0 Report (Group for the Advancement of Psychiatry) [EARLIER
                  HEADING]

        530   0 Report (Group for the Advancement of Psychiatry : 1984) [LATER
                  HEADING]

                *[These two 530 references would only have been made if the library also
                has entries for the series under the earlier and later headings.]*

143.   *Three Restoration comedies.*

        Wycherley. Country wife.

        100 1 0 **Wycherley, William, ‡d 1640-1716. ‡t Country wife** [non-LC]

        Congreve. Way of the world.

        100 1 0 **Congreve, William, ‡d 1670-1729. ‡t Way of the world** [non-LC]

        Villiers. Rehersal.

        100 1 0 **Buckingham, George Villiers, ‡c Duke of, ‡d 1628-1687. ‡t Rehersal**
                [non-LC]

144.   *The last Sherlock Holmes story.*

        MacDonald. Empty copper sea

        100 1 0 **MacDonald, John D. ‡q (John Dann), ‡d 1916-1986. ‡t Empty copper
                sea** [non-LC]

        Hallahan. Catch me, kill me

        100 1 0 **Hallahan, William H. ‡t Catch me, kill me** [non-LC]

145. *The cheap detective.*

Simon. Cheap detective
    100 1 0 **Simon, Neil. ‡t Cheap detective** [non-LC]

147. *A glossary of literary terms.*

Norton. Glossary of literary terms.
    100 1 0 **Norton, Daniel S. ‡t Glossary of literary terms** [non-LC]

155. *Supplement to Charles Evans' American bibliography.*

Evans. American bibliography.
    100 1 0 **Evans, Charles, ‡d 1850-1935. ‡t American bibliography** [non-LC]

160. *The waste lands.*

King. Dark tower.
    ARN   1995572
    010   n 84743102
    100 1 0   King, Stephen, ‡d 1947- ‡t Dark tower
    430   0   Dark tower

APPENDIX D

Answers to the
Dewey Decimal Classification Exercise

A.   The Index. *[The number in square brackets is the fully developed class number for that work.]*

1.   *Seed pictures and other dried natural arrangements.*

      745.928   *Index entry: Seed arrangements | decorative arts*   [745.928]

2.   *The varieties of cheese and how they are produced.*

      637.3   *Index entry: Cheese | processing*   [637.35]

3.   *The decorative arts of primitive peoples.*

      745   *Index entry: Decorative arts or Arts | decorative*   [745.441]

4.   *The tactics of aerial warfare.*

      358.4   *Index entry: Aerial warfare or Air warfare*   [358.4142]

5.   *Beginning typewriting: tests and drills.*

      652.3   *Index entry: Typewriting or Typing*   [652.3024]

6.   *Book mending for libraries.*

      025.7   *Index entry: Book restoration | library science*   [025.7]

7.   *Short-range weather forecasting.*

      551.6362   *Index entry: Short-range weather forecasting*   [551.6362]
                              or
      551.63   *Weather Forecasting*

8.   *Doll furniture designs for the amateur craftsman.*

      745.5923   *Index entry: Doll furniture | handicrafts*   [745.5923]

9.   *The inventions of J. S. Bach.*

      784.1874   *Index entry: Inventions (Musical forms)*   [784.1874]

N.B.: In the sections that follow, information enclosed within square brackets indicates that it was not derived directly from the classification schedules or was derived from a centered heading. Similarly, to aid readability, if a number added to a base number has its own hierarchical development, that development is shown under the full number added to the base number.

B.   <u>Analyzing DDC Numbers.</u>

10.   *Library instruction in the elementary school.*

      027.8222

0	Generalities *[Class 000]*
02	Library and information sciences *[Class 020]*
	Specific kinds of institutions
	[Centered heading: 026-027]
027	General libraries, archives, information centers
027.8	School libraries
027.82	Specific levels and specific libraries
027.822	Specific levels
027.8222	Elementary level

11.   *Cancer in Connecticut: incidence and characteristics.*

      616.994009746

6	Technology (Applied sciences) *[Class 600]*
61	Medical sciences. Medicine *[Class 610]*
616	Diseases
616.9	Other diseases
616.99	Tumors and miscellaneous communicable diseases
616.994	Cancers
616.994009	Historical, geographic, persons treatment
	[Standard subdivision derived initially from instructions under "618.1-618.8" as modified under "616.1-616.9."]

616.994009746	Connecticut
	[From Table 2. As instructed under standard subdivision "-093-099,", the number from Table 2 for "Connecticut" (-746) is added to "-09."]

	-7	North America
		Countries and localities
		[Centered heading: -71-79]
		Specific States of the United States
		[Centered heading: -74-79]
		Northeastern and southeastern United States
		[Centered heading: -74-75]
	-74	Northeastern United States (New England and Middle Atlantic states)
	-746	Connecticut

12. *Spare part surgery: transplants, the surgical practice of the future.*

617.95

6	Technology (Applied sciences) *[Class 600]*
61	Medical sciences. Medicine *[Class 610]*
617	Miscellaneous branches of medicine. Surgery
617.9	Operative surgery and special fields of surgery
	Operative surgery and special fields of surgery
	[Centered heading: 617.91-617.96]
617.95	Cosmetic and restorative plastic surgery, transplantation of tissue and organs, implantation of artificial organs

13. *The farm beef herd.*

636.213

6	Technology (Applied sciences) *[Class 600]*
63	Agriculture and related technologies *[Class 630]*
636	Animal husbandry
	Specific kinds of domestic animals
	[Centered heading: 636.1-636.8]
636.2	Ruminants and Camelidae. Bovidae. Cattle
636.21	Cattle for specific purposes
636.213	Animals raised for food
	[As instructed under "636.21," the number following "636.088" for "food animals" (3) is added to the base number "636.21."]

14.   *Collective bargaining in the U. S. lithographic industry.*

    331.8904168623150973

3	Social sciences *[Class 300]*
33	Economics *[Class 330]*
	Economics of labor, finance, land, energy
	[Centered heading: 331-333]
331	Labor economics
331.8	Labor unions (Trade unions), labor-management (collective) bargaining and disputes
331.89	Labor-management (Collective) bargaining and disputes
331.8904	Labor-management (Collective) bargaining and disputes by industry and occupation
331.89041	Labor-management (Collective) bargaining and disputes in industries and occupations other than extractive, manufacturing, construction
331.890416862315	Planographic (Flat-surface)
	[As instructed under "331.89041001 - 331.89041999," the number from "001-999" for "lithography" (686.2315) is added to the base number "331.89041."]
	6 Technology (Applied sciences)
	68 Manufacture of products for specific uses
	686 Printing and related activities
	686.2 Printing
	686.23 Presswork (Impression)
	686.231 Mechanical techniques
	686.2315 Planographic (Flat-surface)
331.89041686231509	Historical, geographic, persons treatment
	[From Table 1]
331.8904168623150973	United States
	[From Table 2. As instructed under standard subdivision "-093-099," the number from Table 2 for "United States" (-73) is added to "-09."]
	-7 North America
	Countries and localities
	[Centered heading: -71-79]
	-73 United States

15.   *Education for librarianship: the design of the curriculum of library schools in the United States.*

    020.71173

0	Generalities *[Class 000]*
02	Library and information sciences *[Class 020]*

020.711   Higher education
                     [From Table 1]
                              -07 Education, research, related topics
                              -071   Education
                              -0711   Higher education
020.71173   United States
                     [From Table 2. As instructed under standard subdivision "-0711,"
                     the number From Table 2 for "United States" (-73) is added to
                     "-0711."]
                              -7   North America
                                   Countries and localities
                                   [Centered heading:
                                   -71-79]
                              -73   United States

*N.B. In sections C-H that follow, on the same line as the classification number is the
index term that should have been consulted in the relative index to find a starting point
to classify the document. Following that term is the DDC class number for it from the
index. Additional index terms that would be useful in the further development of the
number are also provided. While the index is always the best place to start, it is **only a
starting point**.*

C.   Table 1: Standard Subdivisions.

16.   *The quarterly journal of technology.*

605   *Index entry: Technology   600*

       6   Technology (Applied sciences) *[Class 600]*
       605   Serial publications *[Class 600]*
                      *[Although taken from the schedule, this is a standard subdivision
                      equivalent to "-05" in Table 1.]*

17.   *A short history of inventions.*

609   *Index entry: Inventions   608*

       6   Technology (Applied sciences) *[Class 600]*
       609   Historical, geographic, persons treatment *[Class 600]*
                      *[Although taken from the schedule, this is a standard subdivision
                      equivalent to "-09" in Table 1.]*

18.   *A dictionary of physics.*

530.03   *Index entry:*   *Physics   530*
                                          Dictionaries | specific subject   T1 -03

         5   Natural sciences and mathematics   *[Class 500]*
         53   Physics   *[Class 530]*
         530.03   Dictionaries, encyclopedias, concordances
                        *[From Table 1. In the schedule the range ".03-.09" is given for standard
                        subdivisions.]*

19.   *Current methods in adult education research.*

374.0072   *Index entry:*   *Adult education   374*

         3   Social sciences   *[Class 300]*
         37   Education   *[Class 370]*
                        Specific levels of education
                        [Centered heading: 372-374]
         374   Adult education
         374.007   Education, research, related topics
                          *[Although given in the schedule, "374.007" is a standard
                          subdivision equivalent to '-07" in Table 1.]*
         374.0072   Research; statistical methods
                          [From Table 1]

20.   *Technology during the thirteenth century: a history.*

609.022   *Index entry:*   *Technology   600*
                                          Historical periods   T1 –0901-0905

         6   Technology (Applied sciences) *[Class 600]*
         609   Historical geographical, persons treatment   *[Class 600]*
                        *[Although taken from the schedule, this is a standard subdivision
                        equivalent to "-09" in Table 1.]*
         609.022   13th century, 1200-1299
                        [From Table 1]
                            -0902   6th-15th centuries, 500-1499
                            -09022   13th century, 1200-1299

21.   *The encyclopedia of religion.*

200.3   *Index entry:*   *Religion   200*
                                          Encyclopedias   T1 –03

         2   Religion   *[Class 200]*
         200.3   Dictionaries, encyclopedias, concordances   *[Class 200]*
                        *[From Table 1. In the schedule the range ".2-.3" is given for standard
                        subdivisions.]*

22.   *Bookbinding as a profession.*

     686.30023   *Index entry:*   *Bookbinding*   *686.3*
                                     Professions   *T1 –023*

       6   Technology (Applied sciences) *[Class 600]*
      68   Manufacture of products for specific uses *[Class 680]*
     686   Printing and related activities
     686.3   Bookbinding
     686.30023   The subject as a profession, occupation, hobby
                             [From Table 1. In the schedule the range "686.3001-686.3009" is
                             given for standard subdivisions.]
                             -02 Miscellany
                                   -023   The subject as a profession, occupation,
                                            hobby

23.   *Biographies of 19th century mineralogists.*

     549.0922   *Index entry:*   *Mineralogists*   *549.092*

       5   Natural sciences and mathematics *[Class 500]*
      54   Chemistry and allied sciences *[Class 540]*
     549   Mineralogy
     549.0922   Collected persons treatment
                             [From Table 1. Note table of preference on 1:4.]
                             -09 Historical, geographic, persons treatment
                           -092   Persons
                           -0922   Collected persons treatment

24.   *The Pendant directory of mineralogists.*

     549.025   *Index entry:*   *Mineralogy*   *549*
                                    [The index entry for "Mineralogists" is not used
                                    because it is for biographical works about
                                    mineralogists (549.092).]
                                    Directories   *T1 –025*

       5   Natural sciences and mathematics *[Class 500]*
      54   Chemistry and allied sciences *[Class 540]*
     549   Mineralogy
     549.025   Directories of persons and organizations
                           [From Table 1]
                           -02 Miscellany
                             -025   Directories of persons and organizations

D.   Table 2: Area Tables.

25.   *Patriotic societies of France.*

369.244   *Index entry: Patriotic societies   369.2*
                                         France   T2 -44

3   Social sciences *[Class 300]*
36   Social problems and services; associations *[Class 360]*
369   Miscellaneous kinds of associations
369.2   Hereditary, military, patriotic societies
                    Specific continents, countries, localities
                    [Centered heading: 369.23-.29]
369.244   France and Monaco
                    *[From Table 2. As instructed under "369.23-29," the number
                    from Table 2 for "France" (-44) is added to the base number
                    "369.2."]*
                        -4   Europe. Western Europe
                        -44   France and Monaco

26.   *Library schools in Germany: a description.*

020.71143   *Index entry: Library science   020*
                                         Germany   T2 -43

0   Generalities *[Class 000]*
02   Library and information sciences *[Class 020]*
020.7   Education, research, related topics
                    *[Although taken from the schedule, "020.7" is a standard subdivision
                    equivalent to "-07" in Table 1.]*
020.711   Higher education
                    [From Table 1]
                        -07 Education, research, related topics
                        -071   Education
                        -0711   Higher education
020.71143   Central Europe. Germany
                    *[From Table 2. As instructed under standard subdivision "-
                    0711," the number from Table 2 for "Germany" (-43) is added to
                    "-0711."]*
                        -4   Europe. Western Europe
                        -43   Central Europe. Germany

27.   *The books of bibliography of the University of Chicago Press: the definitive
       bibliography of all its published works.*
          [Located in Chicago, Illinois]

015.77311054   *Index entry:*   *Books | bibliographies   011*
                                           Chicago   T2 -77311

          0   Generalities   *[Class 000]*
          01   Bibliography   *[Class 010]*
                       Bibliographies and catalogs of individuals, of works by
                       specific classes of authors, of anonymous and
                       pseudonymous works, of works from specific places, of
                       works on specific subjects or in specific disciplines
                       [Centered heading: 012-016]
          015   Bibliographies and catalogs of works from specific
                           places
          015.77311   Chicago
                               *[From Table 2. As instructed under "015," the number from Table
                               2 for "Chicago" (-77311) is added to the base number "015."]*
                                   -7   North America
                                         Countries and localities
                                         *[Centered heading:
                                         -71-79]*
                                   -77   North Central United Sates. Lake states
                                             Lake states
                                             [Centered heading: -771-776]
                                   -773   Illinois
                                   -7731   Cook County
                                   -77311   Chicago
          015.77311054   Publications of university and college presses
                               *[As instructed under "015," a "0" is added following
                               "015.77311." Then, the numbers following "011" in "011.1-
                               011.7" for "publications of university and college presses" (54)
                               are added to "015.773110"]*
                                   5   General bibliographies of works issued by
                                         specific kinds of publishers
                                   54   Publications of university and college
                                             presses

E.   <u>Tables 1 and 2.</u>

28.   *Orsini's directory of lawyers in Italy.*

340.02545   *Index entry:*   *Law   340*
                                           *[The index entry for "Lawyers" is not used because
                                           it is for biographical works about lawyers (340.092).]*
                                           Directories   T1 -025
                                           Italy   T2 -45

          3   Social sciences   *[Class 300]*
          34   Law   *[Class 340]*

340.025   Directories of persons and organizations
                   [From Table 1]
                        -02 Miscellany
                             [Although taken from the schedule, "340.02" is a standard
                             subdivision equivalent to "-02" in Table 1.]
                        -025   Directories of persons and organizations
340.02545   Italian peninsula and adjacent islands. Italy
                   [From Table 2. As instructed under standard subdivision "-025," the
                   number from Table 2 for "Italy" (-45) is added to "-025."]
                             -4   Europe
                             -45   Italian peninsula and adjacent islands. Italy

29. *Mining in 19th century Colorado: a history.*

622.0978809034   *Index entry: Mining   622*
                   *   Colorado   T2 -788*
                   *   Historical periods   T1 –0901-0905*

6   Technology (Applied sciences) *[Class 600]*
62   Engineering and allied operations *[Class 620]*
622   Mining and related operations
622.09   Historical, geographic, persons treatment
                       [From Table 1]
622.09788   Colorado
                       [From Table 2. As instructed under standard subdivision "-093-
                       099," the number from Table 2 for "Colorado" (-788) is added to
                       "-09."]
                            -7   North America
                                  Countries and localities
                                  [Centered heading:
                                  -71-79]
                            -78   Western United States
                                     Rocky Mountains states
                                     [Centered heading: -786-789]
                            -788   Colorado
622.0978809034   19th century, 1800-1899
                       [From Table 1. See the note under "-093-099" that allows for
                       the use of "09 Historical, geographic persons treatment."]
                            -09 Historical, geographic, persons treatment
                            -0903 Modern period, 1500-
                            -09034   19th century, 1800-1899

30. *Teaching engineering in Canadian universities.*

620.0071171   *Index entry: Engineering   620*
                   *   Higher education   T1 -0711*
                   *   Canada   T2 –71*

6   Technology (Applied sciences) *[Class 600]*
62   Engineering and allied operations *[Class 620]*

620.00711   Higher education

[From Table 1. In the schedule the range ".001-.009" is given for standard subdivisions.]

      -07 Education, research, related topics
      -071   Education
      -0711   Higher education

620.0071171   Canada

[From Table 2. As instructed under standard subdivision "-0711," the number from Table 2 for "Canada" (-71) is added to "-0711.']

      -7 North America
      -71   Canada

31.   *Engineers in Texas.*

[A directory of engineers in Texas throughout the 20th century]

620.0025764   *Index entry: Engineering   620*

[The index entry for "Engineers" is not used because it is for biographical works about engineers (620.0092).]

Texas   T2 -764

6   Technology (Applied sciences) *[Class 600]*
62   Engineering and allied operations *[Class 620]*
620.0025   Directories of persons and organizations

[From Table 1]

      -02 Miscellany

[Although taken from the schedule, "620.002," is a standard subdivision equivalent to "-02" in Table 1.]

      -025   Directories of persons and organizations

620.0025764   Texas

[From Table 2. As instructed under standard subdivision "-025," the number from Table 2 for "Texas" (-764) is added to "-025."]

      -7 North America
      -76   South Central United States. Gulf Coast states
      -764   Texas

[Of the three standard subdivisions present (Directories; Treatment by specific continents, countries, localities, extraterrestrial worlds; Historical periods), Directories is the first in the table of preference for Table I (1:4). Directories (-025) may only be subdivided by geographic treatment based on the instructions given under that number in Table 1. Hence, historical period, cannot be expressed in the class number.]

F. Table 4: Subdivisions of Individual Languages.

32. *Language today.*
   [A Canadian English language periodical]

   420.5   *Index entry: English language   420*
                                                 Serials   T1 –05

                4   Language *[Class 400]*
                                   Specific languages
                                   [Centered heading: 420-490]
                                      Specific Indo-European languages
                                      [Centered heading: 420-491]
                42   English and Old English (Anglo-Saxon) *[Class 420]*
                                         ["42" is the base number for the English language.]
                420.5   Serial publications
                                         [From Table 1. The range for standard subdivisions ("-05-08") is
                                         from Table 4.]

33. *Teaching the Romance languages.*

   440.071   *Index entry: Romance languages   440*
                                                 Teaching   T1 –071

                4   Language
                                   Specific languages *[Class 400]*
                                   [Centered heading: 420-490]
                                      Specific Indo-European languages
                                      [Centered heading: 420-491]
                44   Romance languages. French *[Class 440]*
                440.071   Education
                                         [From Table 1. In the schedule the ranges ".01-.03" and ".05-.09"
                                         are given for the standard subdivisions of Romance languages.]
                                            -07 Education, research, related topics
                                            -071   Education

34. *Teaching French in American secondary schools.*
   [Coverage limited to the U.S.]

   440.71273   *Index entry: French language   440*
                                                 Secondary schools   T1 –0712
                                                 United States   T2 –73

                4   Language *[Class 400]*
                                   Specific languages
                                   [Centered heading: 420-490]
                                      Specific Indo-European languages
                                      [Centered heading: 420-491]
                44   Romance languages. French *[Class 440]*
                                         ["44" is the base number for the French language.]

440.712	Secondary education
	[From Table 1. In the schedule the range "440.1-448" is given for the subdivisions of the French language. The range for standard subdivisions ("-05-08") is from Table 4.]
	-7 Education, research, related topics
	-71 Education
	-712 Secondary education
440.71273	United States
	[From Table 2. As instructed under standard subdivision "-0712," the number from Table 2 for "United States" (-73) is added to "-0712."]
	-7 North America
	Countries and localities
	[Centered heading: -71-79]
	-73 United States

35.   *Spanish words incorporated into the English language: an exhaustive list.*

422.461	*Index entry:* English language 420
	Etymology T4 -2
	Spanish language T6 -61

4	Language *[Class 400]*
	Specific languages
	[Centered heading: 420-490]
	Specific Indo-European languages
	[Centered heading: 420-491]
42	English and Old English (Anglo-Saxon) *[Class 420]*
	["42" is the base number for the English language.]
	Etymology and dictionaries of standard English
	[Centered heading: 422-423]
422.4	Foreign elements
	[From Table 4]
	-2 Etymology of the standard form of the language
	-24 Foreign elements
422.461	Spanish
	[From Table 6. As instructed under "-24" in Table 4, the number in Table 6 for the language of the foreign element (Spanish, (-61)) is added to "-24."]
	-6 Spanish and Portuguese
	-61 Spanish

36.   *The comprehensive French dictionary.*

443	*Index entry:* French language 440
	Dictionaries	*specific languages* T4 -3

4	Language *[Class 400]*
	Specific languages
	[Centered heading: 420-490]

	Specific Indo-European languages *[Centered heading: 420-491]*
44	Romance languages. French *[Class 440]* *["44" is the base number for the French language.]*
443	Dictionaries of the standard form of the language *[From Table 4. The number from Table 4 for "Dictionaries" (-3) is added to the base number for the French language. The standard subdivision "-03" should not be used in this situation.]*

37.   *German-English, English-German dictionary.*

433.31		*Index entry:* *German language 430* *Dictionaries	specific languages T4 –3* *English language T6 -21*

	4	Language *[Class 400]* Specific languages *[Centered heading: 420-490]* Specific Indo-European languages *[Centered heading: 420-491]*
	43	Germanic (Teutonic languages). German *[Class 430]* *[Classify a bilingual dictionary "with the language in which it will be the more useful."—1:440. "43" is the base number for the German language.]*
	433	Dictionaries of the standard form of the language *[From Table 4. The number from Table 4 for "Dictionaries" (-3) is added to the base number for the German language. The standard subdivision "-03" should not be used in this situation.]*
	433.21	English *[From Table 6. As instructed under "-32-39" in Table 4, the number in Table 6 for "English" (-21) is added to "3."]*
		-2 English and Old English (Anglo-Saxon) -21 English

38.   *German-Bulgarian, Bulgarian-German dictionary.*

491.81331		*Index entry:* *Bulgarian language 491.81* *Dictionaries	specific languages T4 -3* *German language T6 -31*

	4	Language *[Class 400]* Specific languages *[Centered heading: 420-490]* Specific Indo-European languages *[Centered heading: 420-491]*
	49	Other languages *[Class 490]*
	491	East Indo-European and Celtic languages *[Classify a bilingual dictionary "with the language in which it will be the more useful .... if classification with either language is equally useful, give priority to the language coming later in the sequence 420-490."—1:440.]*

491.8	Slavic languages
491.81	South Slavic languages. Bulgarian
	["491.81" is the base number for the Bulgarian language.]
491.813	Dictionaries of the standard form of the language
	[From Table 4. The number from Table 4 for "Dictionaries" (-3) is added to the base number for the Bulgarian language. The standard subdivision "-03" should not be used in this situation.]
491.81331	German
	[From Table 6. As instructed under "-32-39" in Table 4, the number for "German" in Table 6 (-31) is added to "3."]

-3   Germanic (Teutonic) languages
-31   German

39.   *Papers of the East Slavic Languages Association.*
[A bi-monthly publication of the international society]

491.700601   *Index entry: East Slavic languages   491.7*
                                               International organizations   T1 -0601

4	Language *[Class 400]*
	Specific languages
	[Centered heading: 420-490]
	Specific Indo-European languages
	[Centered heading: 420-491]
49	Other languages *[Class 490]*
491	East Indo-European and Celtic languages
491.7	East Slavic languages. Russian
491.700601	International organization
	[From Table 1. In the schedule ".7001-.7009" are given for the standard subdivisions of East Slavic languages. The standard subdivision for "international organizations" was assigned rather than the standard subdivision for "serial publications" because the former has a higher position in that table of preference for standard subdivisions (see 1:4).]

-06 Organizations and management
-0601 International organizations

G.   <u>800s and Tables 3-A, 3-B, and 3-C: Literature (Belles Lettres) and Subdivisions of Individual Literatures</u>.

*N.B. Although it is possible to find some complete class numbers for 810-890 in the schedules, generally it is easier to use the schedule **only** for determining the language's base number. then, proceed to Table 3-A or 3-B as required. Continue by following the step-by-step instructions for these tables.*

For titles 40-46 the following initial hierarchy applies:

Index entry: English literature   820

8	Literature (Belles-lettres) and rhetoric *[Class 800]*
82	English and Old English (Anglo-Saxon) literatures *[Class 820]*
	["82" is the base number for English literature.]
	Subdivisions of English literature
	[Centered heading: 820.1-828]

40.   *The encyclopedia of English literature.*

820.3   *Index entry: Encyclopedias   T1 -03*

Standard subdivisions; collections; history, description, critical appraisal of English literature
[Centered heading: -.1-.9]

820.3   Dictionaries, encyclopedias, concordances
[From Table 1. The range for standard subdivisions (-01-07) is given in Table 3-B. As instructed at the beginning of Table 3-B, the number from Table 1 for "Encyclopedias" (-03) is added to the base number "82."]

41.   *Pantheon anthology of English literature.*

820.8   *Index entry: Anthologies | literature | specific literatures*
                                     T3B -08

Standard subdivisions; collections; history, description, critical appraisal of English literature
[Centered heading: -.1-.9]

820.8   Collections of literary texts in more than one form
[From Table 3-B. As instructed at the beginning of Table 3-B, the number from that table for "Collections of literary texts in more than one form" (-08) is added to the base number "82."]

42.   *English fantasy.*
      [An anthology]

820.8015   *Index entry: Fantasy | literature | specific literatures*
                                     T3B -08015

Standard subdivisions; collections; history, description, critical appraisal of English literature
[Centered heading: -.1-.9]

820.8   Collections of literary texts in more than one form
[From Table 3-B. As instructed at the beginning of Table –3-B, the number from that table for "Collections of literary texts in more than one form" (-08) is added to the base number "82."]

820.8015   Symbolism, allegory, fantasy, myth
                                        [From Table 3-C. As instructed under "-080001-08099" in
                                        Table 3-B, the number from Table 3-C for "Fantasy" (-15) is
                                        added to "-080."]
                                            -1   Arts and literature displaying specific
                                                    qualities of style, mood, viewpoint
                                            -15   Symbolism, allegory, fantasy, myth

43.   *English literature for boys.*
       [A collection]

       820.8092826   *Index entry: Anthologies | literature | specific literatures*
                                                         T3B –08

                                        Standard subdivisions; collections; history, description,
                                        critical appraisal of English literature
                                        [Centered heading: -.1-.9]
       820.8   Collections of literary texts in more than one form
                                        [From Table 3-B. As instructed at the beginning of Table 3-B, the
                                        number from that table for "Collections of literary texts in more
                                        than one form" (-08) is added to the base number "82."]
       820.8092826   Boys
                                        [From Table 3-C. As instructed under "-080001-08099" in
                                        Table 3-B, the number from Table 3-C for "Boys." (-92826) is
                                        added to "-080."]
                                            -9   Literature for and by other specific kinds
                                                    of persons
                                            -92   Literature for and by persons of specific
                                                    classes
                                            -928   Persons of specific age groups and
                                                        sexes
                                            -9282   Children
                                            -92826   Boys

44.   *English literature of the pre-Elizabethan period: a criticism.*

       820.9002   *Index entry: Criticism | literature |specific literatures*
                                                         T3B -09

                                        Standard subdivisions; collections; history, description,
                                        critical appraisal of English literature
                                        [Centered heading: -.1-.9]
       820.9   History, description, critical appraisal of works in
                                        more than one form
                                        [From Table 3-B. As instructed at the beginning of Table 3-B, the
                                        number from that table for "Critical appraisal." (-09) is added to
                                        the base number "82."]
                                        Literature from specific periods
                                        [From Table 3-B: -09001-09009]

820.9002   1400-1558
                            [As instructed in Table 3-B, the number for "1440-1558"
                            from the "Period Table for "English" in the schedule (2) (see
                            3:755), is added to "-0900."]

45.   *English drama: a critical study.*

   822.009   *Index entry: Drama (Literature) | specific literatures*
                                           T3B -2

        822   Drama
                          [From Table 3-B. As instructed at the beginning of Table 3-B, the
                          number from that table for "Drama" (-2) is added to the base number
                          "82."]
                            Standard subdivisions; collections; history,
                            description, critical appraisal
                            [From Table 3-B:. -2001-2009]
        822.009   History, description, critical appraisal
                              [As instructed in Table 3-B under "-2001-2009," the number
                              for "Critical appraisal" under "-1-8" (see 1:419) (9) is added to
                              "-200."]

46.   *English drama of the Elizabethan period: a collection.*

   822.308   *Index entry: Drama (Literature) | specific literatures*
                                           T3B –2

        822   Drama
                          [From Table 3-B. As instructed at the beginning of Table 3-B, the
                          number from that table for 'Drama" (-2) is added to the base number
                          "82."]
                            Drama of specific periods
                            [From Table 3-B: -21-29]
        822.3   Elizabethan period, 1558-1625
                            [As instructed in Table 3-B, the number for the "Elizabethan
                            period, 1558-1625" from the "Period Table for English"
                            literature in the schedule (3) is added to "-2." The number
                            822.3 for "Drama of Elizabethan period, 1558-1625" does also
                            appear in the schedule but this number was develop following
                            the instructions is Table 3-B.]
        822.308   Collections of literary texts
                              [As instructed in Table 3-B under "-21-29," the number for
                              "Collections" under "-1-8" at the beginning of Table 3-B (8)
                              is added to "0"]

47.   *A collection of Welsh (Cymric) literature.*

891.6608   *Index entry:*   *Welsh literature* | *Welsh*   *891.66*

8   Literature (Belles-lettres) and rhetoric *[Class 800]*
89   Literatures of other specific languages and language families
               [Class 890]
891   East Indo-European and Celtic literatures
891.6   Celtic literatures
891.66   Welsh (Cymric) literature
                         [Base number for "Welsh literature" is "891.66"]
891.6608   Collections of literary texts in more than one form
                            [From Table 3-B. As instructed at the beginning of Table 3-B,
                            the number (from that table for "Collections of literary texts in
                            more than one form" (-08) is added to the base number
                            "891.66."]

48.   *Drama of the 1960's.*
      [A collection of Estonian plays]

894.5452208   *Index entry:*   *Estonian literature   894.545*
                                                 Drama (Literature) | *specific literatures*
                                                 T3B –2

8   Literature (Belles-lettres) and rhetoric *[Class 800]*
89   Literatures of other specific languages and language families
               [Class 890]
894   Altaic, Uralic, Hyperborean, Dravidian literatures
                   Uralic literatures
                   [Centered heading: 894.4-895.5]
894.5   Finno-Ugric literatures
894.54   Finnic literatures
894.545   Estonian literature
                            [Base number for "Estonian literature" is "894.545"]
894.5452   Drama
                               [From Table 3-B. As instructed at the beginning of Table
                               3-B, the number from that table for "Drama" (-2) is added
                               to the base number "894.545."]
                               Drama of specific periods
                               [From Table 3-B. -21-29]
894.54522   1861-1991
                                  [As instructed in Table 3-B, the number for the
                                  period that covers the 1960's from the period table
                                  for Estonian literature in the schedule (2) (see
                                  3:792), is added to "-2."]
894.5452208   Collections of literary texts
                                     [From Table 3-B. As instructed under "-21-29"
                                     the number for "Collections" under "-1-8" at the
                                     beginning of Table 3-B (8) is added to "-0." The
                                     result is added to "2."]

49.   *18th century French literature.*
      [A collection]

840.8005	*Index entry:* *French literature 840*
	Anthologies	*literature*	*specific literatures*
	T3B –08

8	Literature (Belles-lettres) and rhetoric *[Class 800]*
84	Literatures of Romance languages. French literature *[Class 840]*
	[Base number for French literature is "84"]
	Subdivisions of French literature
	[Centered heading: 840.1-848]
840.8	Collections of literary texts
	[From Table 3-B. As instructed at the beginning of Table 3-B, the number from that table for "Collections" (-08) is added to the base number "84."]
840.80	[Placeholder]
	[As instructed under "08" in Table 3-B, a "0" is added after "-08" followed by a number from Table 3-C.]
840.800	Specific periods
	[From Table 3-C]
840.8005	1715-1789
	[From Table 3-B. As instructed under "01-09", the time period for the "18th century" from the "Period Table for French" literature in the schedule (5) is used (see 3:766).]

50.   *19th century French poetry: a collection.*

841.708	*Index entry:* *French literature 840*
	Poetry	*specific literatures T3B -1*

8	Literature (Belles-lettres) and rhetoric *[Class 800]*
84	Literatures of Romance languages. French literature *[Class 840]*
	[Base number for French literature is "84"]
	Subdivisions of French literature
	[Centered heading: 840.1-848]
841	Poetry
	[From Table 3-B. As instructed at the beginning of Table 3-B, the number from that table for "Poetry" (-1) is added to the base number for French literature.]
841.7	Constitutional monarchy, 1815-1848
	[As instructed in Table 3-B, the number for the 19th century from the "Period Table for French" literature in the schedule (7), is added to "-1" (see 3:766).]
841.708	Collections of literary texts
	[From Table 3-B. As instructed under "-11-19" a "0" is added after the number for the specific time period (7). The number for collections under "-1-8" (8) is then added to "0."]

H.   900s: Geography, History, and Auxiliary Disciplines.

51.   *Geography of Martha's Vineyard, Massachusetts.*

917.4494   *Index entry: Geography   910*
                                          Martha's Vineyard   T2 -74494

9   Geography, history, and auxiliary disciplines *[Class 900]*
91   Geography and travel *[Class 910]*
                          Geography of and travel in ancient world and specific
                          continents, countries, localities in modern world;
                          extraterrestrial worlds
                          [Centered heading: 913-919]
917.4494   Dukes County
                          [From Table 2. As instructed under "913-919," the number from
                          Table 2 for "Dukes County" (-74494) is added to the base number
                          "91."]
                                  -7   North America
                                          Countries and localities
                                          [Centered heading: -71-79]
                                  -74   Northeastern United States (New England
                                              and Middle Atlantic states)
                                  -744   Massachusetts
                                  -7449   Counties bordering Nantucket Sound
                                  -74494   Dukes County
                                                  Including Elizabeth Islands,
                                                  Martha's Vineyard

52.   *Travel in the British Isles during the Roman occupation.*

913.61044   *Index entry: Travel   910*
                                          British Isles | Ancient   T2 -361

9   Geography, history, and auxiliary disciplines *[Class 900]*
91   Geography and travel *[Class 910]*
                          Geography of and travel in ancient world and specific
                          continents, countries, localities in modern world;
                          extraterrestrial worlds
                          [Centered heading: 913-919]
913.61   British Isles. Northern Britain and Ireland
                          [From Table 2. As instructed under "913-919," the number from
                          Table 2 for "British Isles" in the ancient world (-361) is added to the
                          base number "91."]
                                  -3   The ancient world
                                  -36   Europe north and west of Italian Peninsula
                                  -361   British Isles. Northern Britain and Ireland
913.6104   Travel
                          [As instructed under "913-919," the number from that table for
                          "Travel" (04) is added to the base number "913.61."]

913.61044	Roman period, 43-410
	[As instructed under "041-049," the number following "0" for the historical period for "British Isles" (936.204) (i.e., 4) is added to "04."]

53. *The exploration of Chile by Europeans.*

918.3042	*Index entry:* Explorations 910.9
	Chile T2 -83

9	Geography, history, and auxiliary disciplines *[Class 900]*
91	Geography and travel *[Class 910]*
	Geography of and travel in ancient world and specific continents, countries, localities in modern world; extraterrestrial worlds
	[Centered heading: 913-919]
918.3	Chile
	[From Table 2. As instructed under "913-919," the number from Table 2 for "Chile" (-8) is added to the base number "91."]
	-8 South America
	-83 Chile
918.304	Travel
	[As instructed under "913-919," the number from that table for "Travel" (04) is added to the base number "918.3."]
918.3042	Period of European discovery and conquest, 1535-1560
	[As instructed under "04," the number following "0" for the historical period for "Chile" (983.02) (i.e., 2) is added to "04."]

54. *The history of medieval Austria.*

943.602	*Index entry:* Austria 943.6

9	Geography, history, and auxiliary disciplines *[Class 900]*
	History of ancient world; of specific continents, countries, localities; of extraterrestrial worlds
	[Centered heading: 930-990]
	General history of modern world, extraterrestrial worlds
	[Centered heading: 940-990]
94	General history of Europe. Western Europe *[Class 940]*
943	Central Europe. Germany
943.6	Austria and Liechtenstein
943.602	Medieval period, 481-1500

55.   *The Spanish-American War: the American perspective.*

973.89   *Index entry:*   *Spanish-American War, 1898*   *973.89*

9   Geography, history, and auxiliary disciplines *[Class 900]*
             History of ancient world; of specific continents, countries,
             localities; of extraterrestrial worlds
             [Centered heading: 930-990]
                 General history of modern world, extraterrestrial worlds
                 [Centered heading: 940-990]
97   General history of North America *[Class 970]*
973   United States
973.8   Reconstruction period, 1865-1900
973.89   Spanish-American War, 1898

56.   *The history of Pawtucket, Rhode Island.*

974.51   *Index entry:*   *Rhode Island*   *974.5*

9   Geography, history, and auxiliary disciplines *[Class 900]*
             History of ancient world; of specific continents, countries,
             localities; of extraterrestrial worlds
             [Centered heading: 930-990]
                 General history of modern world, extraterrestrial worlds
                 [Centered heading: 940-990]
97   General history of North America *[Class 970]*
                         Countries and localities
                         [Centered heading: 971-979]
                             Specific States of the United States
                             [Centered heading: 974-979]
                                 Northeastern and southeastern United States
                                 [Centered heading: 974-975]
974   Northeastern United States (New England and
                                     Middle Atlantic states)
974.5   Rhode Island
974.51   Providence County
                                             [From Table 2. As instructed under "930-990," the
                                             number from Table 2 for "Providence County"
                                             (-7451) is added to the base number "9." This
                                             allows for specificity beyond the level of detail given
                                             in the schedule, (Rhode Island).]

57.   *Outline of Eastern European history.*

     947.000202   *Index entry:*   *Eastern Europe   947*
                                             Outlines   T1 -0202

         9   Geography, history, and auxiliary disciplines *[Class 900]*
                                  History of ancient world; of specific continents, countries,
                                  localities; of extraterrestrial worlds
                                  [Centered heading: 930-990]
                                    General history of modern world, extraterrestrial worlds
                                    [Centered heading: 940-990]
        94   General history of Europe. Western Europe *[Class 940]*
       947   Eastern Europe. Russia
      947.000202   Synopses and outlines
                                       [From Table 1. In the schedule the range ".0001-.0008" is
                                       given for the standard subdivisions of Eastern Europe.]
                                         02   Miscellany
                                        -0202 Synopses and outlines

58.   *History of the Burmese in New Zealand.*

     993.004958   *Index entry:*   *New Zealand   993*
                                              Burmese   T2 -958

         9   Geography, history and auxiliary disciplines *[Class 900]*
                                    History of ancient world; of specific continents, countries,
                                    localities; of extraterrestrial worlds
                                  [Centered heading: 930-990]
                                  General history of modern world, extraterrestrial worlds
                                  [Centered heading: 940-990]
        99   General history of other parts of world, of
                                extraterrestrial worlds. Pacific Ocean islands *[Class 990]*
       993   New Zealand
      993.004   Racial, ethnic, national groups
                                      [As instructed under "930-990," the number from that table for
                                    "Racial, ethnic, national groups" (004) is added to "993."]
      993.004958   Burmese
                                      [From Table 5. As instructed under "930-990," the number
                                    from Table 5 for "Burmese" (-958) is added to "004."]
                                       -9   Other racial, ethnic, national groups
                                       -95   East and Southeast Asian peoples;
                                             Mundas
                                       -958   Burmese

59.   *World history of the Irish people.*

       909.049162   *Index entry:*   *History | world   909*
                                                    Irish Gaels   T5 -9162

           9   Geography, history and auxiliary disciplines *[Class 900]*
           909   World history *[Class 900]*
           909.04   History with respect to racial, ethnic, national groups
           909.049162   Irish
                          [From Table 5. As instructed under "909.04," the number from
                          Table 5 for "Irish" (-9162) is added to the base number "909.04."]
                    -9   Other racial, ethnic, national groups
                    -91   Other Indo-European peoples
                    -916   Celts
                    -9162   Irish

I.   <u>Other Tables and "Add To" Directions.</u>

60.   *Customs of the Huguenots.*

       390.088245   *Index entry:*   *Customs (Social)   390*
                                                    Huguenots | religious group   T7 -245

           3   Social sciences *[Class 300]*
           39   Customs, etiquette, folklore *[Class 390]*
           390.08   History and description of customs with respect to kinds
                        of persons
                          [Although taken from the schedule, "390.08" is a standard subdivision
                          equivalent to "-08" in Table 1.]
           390.088   Religious groups
           390.088245   Huguenot churches
                          [From Table 7. As instructed under -08809-08899," the number
                          from Table 7 for "Huguenot churches" (-245) is added to "088."]
                    -2   Persons occupied with or adherent to
                          religion
                    -24   Persons occupied with Protestant churches
                          of Continental origin and related bodies
                    -245   Huguenot churches

61.   *The management of agricultural museums.*

       630.75   *Index entry:*   *Agriculture   630*
                                                    Museology   T1 -075

           6   Technology (Applied sciences) *[Class 600]*
           63   Agriculture and related technologies *[Class 630]*

630.7   Education, research, related topics
[The range for standard subdivisions of "630" is shown by the presence of some standard subdivisions in the schedule, i.e., 630.2, 630.7.]

630.75   Museum activities and services. Collecting
[From Table 1]

62.   *Visitor's guide to the Cobb Agriculture Museum, Butler County, Pennsylvania.*

630.7474891   *Index entry:*   *Agriculture   630*
                                             Museum catalogs   T1 -074
                                             Butler County (Pa.)   T2 -74891

6   Technology (Applied sciences) *[Class 600]*

63   Agriculture and related technologies *[Class 630]*

630.7   Education, research, related topics
[The range for standard subdivisions of "630" is shown by the presence of some standard subdivisions in the schedule, i.e., 630.2, 630.7.]

630.74   Museums, collections, exhibits
[From Table 1]

630.7474891   Butler County
[From Table 2. As instructed under "-0741-0749," the number from Table 2 for "Butler County" (-74891) is added to "-074."]

                       -7   North America
                               Countries and localities
                               [Centered heading:
                               -71-79]
                           -74   Northeastern United States (New England and Middle Atlantic states)
                                         Middle Atlantic states
                                         [Centered heading: -747-749]
                         -748   Pennsylvania
                         -7489   Northwestern counties
                         -74891   Butler County

63.   *The manufacture of football equipment.*
[This is American football]

688.76332   *Index entry:*   *Football | equipment technology   688.7633*
                                             American football   796.332

6   Technology (Applied sciences) *[Class 600]*

68   Manufacture of products for specific uses *[Class 680]*

688   Other final products, and packaging technology

688.7   Recreational equipment
                        Equipment for sports and games
                        [Centered heading: 688.74-688.79]

688.76   Equipment for outdoor sports and games

688.76332 American football
[*As instructed under "688.763," the numbers following "796" for "Football" (332) are added to the base number "688.76."*]

    3   Ball games
   33   Inflated ball driven by foot
  332 American football

[*Although the number "796.332" provides a further development of the number for "Auxiliary techniques and procedures; apparatus, equipment, materials" (796.33202028" this extended number is not used because the concept "equipment" has already been specified in "688.76."*]

64.   *Congenital diseases of the scalp.*

616.546043   *Index entry:*   *Scalp diseases   616.546*

6   Technology (Applied sciences) *[Class 600]*
61   Medical sciences. Medicine *[Class 610]*
616   Diseases
            Specific diseases
            [Centered heading: 616.1-616.9]
              Diseases of specific systems and organs
              [Centered heading: 616.1-616.8]
616.5   Diseases of the integument, hair, nails
616.54   Skin, hypertrophies, scalp diseases, related disorders
616.546   Diseases of scalp, hair, hair follicles
616.546043   Congenital diseases
                [As instructed under "616.1-616.9," the number from that table for "Congenital diseases" (043) is added to the base number "616.54."]
                  04   Special classes of diseases
                  043   Congenital diseases

65.   *Cheerleading at Indiana University basketball games.*
[Indiana University is located in Bloomington (Monroe County), Indiana]

791.64236309772255   *Index entry:*   *Cheerleading   791.64*
                                        Monroe County (Ind.)   T2 -772255

7   The arts. Fine and decorative arts *[Class 700]*
79   Recreational and performing arts *[Class 790]*
791   Public performances
791.6   Pageantry
791.64   Cheerleading

791.642363	College basketball
	[As instructed under "791.64," the numbers following "796.3"
	for "College basketball" (2363) are added to the base number
	"791.64."]

2	Inflated ball thrown or hit by hand	
23	Basketball	
236	Specific types of basketball	
2363	College basketball	

791.64236309	Historical, geographic, persons treatment
	[From Table 1]
791.64236309772255	Monroe County
	[From Table 2. As instructed under standard subdivision
	"-093-099," the number from Table 2 for "Monroe
	County" (-772255) is added to "-09."]

-7	North America	
	Countries and localities	
	[Centered heading: -71-79]	
-77		North Central United States.
		Lake states
		Lake states
		[Centered heading: -771-776]
-772		Indiana
-7722		South central counties
-77225		Brown and Monroe
		Counties
-772255		Monroe County

66.   *Materials for teaching science in elementary schools.*

372.35044	*Index entry: Science	elementary education*	*372.35*

3	Social sciences *[Class 300]*
37	Education *[Class 370]*
	Specific levels of education
	[Centered heading: 372-374]
372	Elementary education
	Elementary education in specific subjects
	[Centered heading: 372.3-372.8]
372.3	Computers, science, technology, health
372.35	Science and technology
372.35044	Teaching
	[As instructed under "372.3-372.8," the number from
	that table for "Teaching" (044) is added to "372.35."]

04	Special topics
044	Teaching

67.   *Stamps of Ghana: a collector's guide.*

| 769.569667 | | Index entry: | *Postage stamps | philately*   *769.56* |
| | | | *Ghana*   *T2 -667* |

	7	The arts. Fine and decorative arts *[Class 700]*
	76	Graphic arts. Printmaking and prints *[Class 760]*
		Printmaking and prints
		[Centered heading: 761-769]
	769	Prints
	769.5	Forms of prints
	769.56	Postage stamps and related devices
	769.569	Historical, geographic, persons treatment
	769.569667	Ghana

[From Table 2. As instructed under "769.5696," the number from Table 2 for "Ghana" (-667) is added to the base number "769.569."]

-6   Africa
-66   West Africa and offshore islands
-667   Ghana

68.   *Atlas of France.*

| 912.44 | | Index entry: | *Atlases*   *912* |
| | | | *France*   *T2 -44* |

	9	Geography, history, and auxiliary disciplines *[Class 900]*
	91	Geography and travel *[Class 910]*
	912	Graphic representation of surface of earth and of extraterrestrial worlds
	912.44	France and Monaco

[From Table 2. As instructed under "912," the number from Table 2 for "France" (-44) is added to the base number "912."]

-4   Europe. Western Europe
-44   France and Monaco

69.   *Seventeenth century bookbinding.*

| 686.3009032 | | Index entry: | *Bookbinding*   *686.3* |
| | | | *Historical periods*   *T1 –0901-0905* |

	6	Technology (Applied sciences) *[Class 600]*
	68	Manufacture of products for specific uses *[Class 680]*
	686	Printing and related activities
	686.3	Bookbinding
	686.3009032	17th century, 1600-1699

[From Table 1. In the schedule the range "686.3001-686.3009" is given for standard subdivisions.]

-09   Historical, geographic, persons treatment
-0903   Modern period, 1500-
-09032   17th century, 1600-1699

70.   *Ancient Roman coins: their description for collectors.*

    737.4937   *Index entry:*   Coins | numismatics   737.4
                                                      Roman Empire   T2 -37

7	The arts. Fine and decorative arts *[Class 700]*
73	Plastic arts. Sculpture *[Class 730]*
	Other plastic arts
	[Centered heading: 736-739]
737	Numismatics and sigillography
737.4	Coins
737.49	Of specific countries
737.4937	Italian Peninsula and adjacent territories

            [From Table 2. As instructed under "737.49," the number from Table 2 for "Ancient Rome" (-37) is added to the base number "737.49."]

                -3   The ancient world
                -37   Italian Peninsula and adjacent territories

71.   *Photography as a hobby: a guide for the amateur.*

    770.233   *Index entry:*   Photography   770

7	The arts. Fine and decorative arts *[Class 700]*
77	Photography and photographs *[Class 770]*
770.2	Miscellany
	[Although taken from the schedule, this is a standard subdivision equivalent to "-02" in Table 1.]
770.23	Photography as a profession, occupation, hobby
770.233	Photography as a hobby

72.   *Prospecting for gold in Colorado.*

    622.184109788   *Index entry:*   Gold-prospecting   622.1841
                                            Colorado   T2 -788

6	Technology (Applied sciences) *[Class 600]*
62	Engineering and allied operations *[Class 620]*
622	Mining and related operations
622.1	Prospecting
622.18	Prospecting for specific materials
622.1841	Gold

            [As instructed under "622.184," the numbers following "553" for "Gold" (41) are added to the base number "622.18."]

                4   Metals and semimetals
                41   Gold

622.184109	Historical, geographic, persons treatment
	[From Table 1]
622.184109788	Colorado

[From Table 2. As instructed under "-093-099," the number from Table 2 for "Colorado" (-788) is added "-09."]

-7	North America
-78	Western United States
-788	Colorado

73. *Flagstone sidewalks: illustrations of their design and construction.*

625.8810222	*Index entry:* *Sidewalks	road engineering* *625.88*
	Illustrations *T1 -022*

6	Technology (Applied sciences) *[Class 600]*
62	Engineering and allied operations *[Class 620]*
625	Engineering of railroads and roads
625.8	Artificial road surfaces
625.88	Sidewalks and auxiliary pavements
625.881	Flagstones

[As instructed under "625.881-.886," the number following "625.8" for "Flagstones" (1) is added to the base number "625.88."]

625.8810222	Pictures and related illustrations
	[From Table 1]

-02	Miscellany
-022	Illustrations, models, miniatures
-0222	Pictures and related illustrations

74. *Bibliography of folk literature.*

016.3982	*Index entry:* *Bibliography* *010*
	Folk literature *398.2*

0	Generalities *[Class 000]*
01	Bibliography *[Class 010]*
	Bibliographies and catalogs of individuals, of works by specific classes of authors, of anonymous and pseudonymous works, of works from specific places, of works on specific subjects or in specific disciplines
	[Centered heading: 012-016]
016	Bibliographies and catalogs of works on specific subjects or in specific disciplines
016.3982	Folk literature

[As instructed under "016," the number from the range "001-999" for "Folk literature" (398.2) is added to the base number "016."]

3	Social sciences
39	Customs, etiquette, folklore
398	Folklore
398.2	Folk literature

75. *Solar houses in Southern California: a guide to architectural design.*

728.370472097949   *Index entry: Solar houses | architecture   728.370472*
                                           California, Southern   T2 -7949

7	The arts. Fine and decorative arts *[Class 700]*
72	Architecture *[Class 720]*
	Specific types of structures
	[Centered heading: 725-728]
728	Residential and related buildings
728.3	Specific kinds of conventional housing
728.37	Separate houses
728.3704	Special topics

[As instructed under "721-729," the number for "Special topics" (04) is added to "728.37."]

728.370472   Energy resources

[As instructed under "04," the numbers following "720.4" for "Energy resources" (72) are added to "04."]

                              7   Architecture and the environment
                              72   Energy resources

728.37047209   Historical, geographic, persons treatment
                              [From Table 1]

728.370472097949   Southern counties (Southern California)
                              [From Table 2. As instructed under "-093-099," the number from Table 2 for "Southern California" (-7949) is added to "-09."]

                              -7   North America
                                     Countries and localities
                                     [Centered heading: -71-79]
                              -79   Great Basin and Pacific Slope
                                        region of United States.
                                        Pacific Coast states
                              -794   California
                              -7949   Southern counties
                                             (Southern California)

76. *The Holy Bible.*
     [A modern version in Japanese]

220.5956   *Index entry: Bible   220*
                                   Japanese   T5 -956

2	Religion *[Class 200]*
22	Bible *[Class 220]*
220.5	Modern versions and translations
220.5956	Japanese

[From Table 6. As instructed under "220.53-220.59," the number for "Japanese" (-956) is added to the base number "220.5."]

                              -9   Other languages
                              -95   Languages of East and Southeast Asia. Sino-
                                        Tibetan languages
                              -956   Japanese

77.   *The geography of Ethiopia.*

     916.3   *Index entry:*   *Geography   910*
                                                      Ethiopia   T2 -63

9	Geography, history, and auxiliary disciplines *[Class 900]*
91	Geography and travel *[Class 910]*
916.3	Ethiopia

            [From Table 2. As instructed under "913-919," the number from Table 2 for "Ethiopia" (-63) is added to the base number "91."]
                 -6   Africa
                 -63   Ethiopia and Eritrea
                       [Comprehensive works for Ethiopia are placed in "63" as instructed by the note under "-632-634."]

78.   *Design of interior furnishings for Glaxo-Wellcome, Inc., Research Triangle Park, North Carolina.*
    [A pharmaceutical firm in Durham County, North Carolina]

     747.875615109756563   *Index entry:*   *Interior furnishings | arts   747*
                                                        Research buildings | architecture   727.5
                                                        Pharmacology   615.1
                                                         Durham County (N.C.)   T2 -756563

7	The arts. Fine and decorative arts *[Class 700]*
74	Drawing and decorative arts *[Class 740]*
747	Interior decoration
747.8	Decoration of specific types of buildings
747.875	Research buildings

            [As instructed under "747.85-747.87," the numbers following "72" in the range "725-727" for "Research buildings" (75) are added to the base number "747.8."]
                 7   Buildings for educational and research purposes
                 75   Research buildings

     747.8756151   Drugs (Materia medica)
            [As instructed under "727.5", the number from the range "001"-"999" for "Pharmacology" (615.1) is added to the base number "727.5."]
                 6   Technology (Applied sciences)
                 61   Medical sciences. Medicine
                 615 Pharmacology and therapeutics
                 615.1 Drugs (Materia medica)

     747.875615109   Historical, geographic, persons treatment
            [From Table 1]

747.875615109756563   Durham County
[From Table 2. As instructed under "-093-099," the number from Table 2 for "Durham County" (-756563) is added to "-09."]

    -7   North America
         Countries and localities
         [Centered heading: -71-79]
    -75   Southeastern United States
          (South Atlantic states)
    -756   North Carolina
    -7565   Northeast Piedmont counties
    -75656   Durham and Orange
            Counties
    -756563   Durham County

79.   *The natural sciences.*
       [A programmed learning text]

507.7   *Index entry:* *Natural sciences*   *500*
                   Programmed instruction   *T1 -077*

   5   Natural sciences and mathematics *[Class 500]*
   507   Education, research, related topics *[Class 500]*
          [Although taken from the schedule, this is a standard subdivision equivalent to "-07" in Table 1.]
   507.7   Programmed texts
          [From Table 1]

80.   *The anatomy of snakes.*

571.31796   *Index entry:* *Anatomy*   *571.3*
                   Snakes   *597.96*

   5   Natural sciences and mathematics *[Class 500]*
   57   Life sciences. Biology *[Class 570]*
          General internal processes common to all organisms
          [Centered heading: 571-572]
   571   Physiology and related subjects
   571.3   Anatomy and morphology
   571.31   Animals
          [As instructed under "571-572", the number following "571" for "Animals" (1) is added to "571.3."]
   571.31796   Serpentes (Snakes)
          [As instructed under "571.1", the numbers following "59" for "Snakes" (796) are added to the "571.1."]
           -597   Cold-blooded vertebrates. Pisces
                (Fishes)
           -597.9   Reptilia
           -597.96   Serpentes (Snakes)

81.   *Research in medical toxicology.*

615.90072   *Index entry:*   *Toxicology* | *medicine*   *615.9*
                                               Research   *T1 -072*

       6   Technology (Applied sciences) *[Class 600]*
       61   Medical sciences. Medicine *[Class 610]*
       615   Pharmacology and therapeutics
       615.9   Toxicology
       615.90072   Research
                              *[From Table 1. In the schedule the range ".9001-.9009" is given
                              for standard subdivisions.]*
                                    -07 Education, research, related topics
                                    -072   Research; statistical methods

82.   *Travel in Trinidad today.*

917.298304   *Index entry:*   *Travel*   *910*
                                               Trinidad   *T2 -72983*

       9   Geography, history, and auxiliary disciplines *[Class 900]*
       91   Geography and travel *[Class 910]*
                          Geography of and travel in ancient world and specific
                          continents, countries, localities in modern world;
                          extraterrestrial worlds
                          [Centered heading: 913-919]
       917.2983   Trinidad and Tobago
                             *[From Table 2. As instructed under "913-919," the number from
                             Table 2 for "Trinidad" (-72983) is added to the base number "91."]*
                                    -7   North America
                                          Countries and localities
                                          [Centered heading: -71-79]
                                    -72   Middle America. Mexico
                                    -729   West Indies (Antilles) and Bermuda
                                    -7298   Windward and other southern islands
                                    -72983   Trinidad and Tobago
       917.298304   Travel
                             *[As instructed under "913-919," the number for "Travel" (04) is
                             added to the base number "917.2983."]*

83.   *The management of poplar forests.*

634.97232   *Index entry:*   *Poplars* | *forestry*   *634.9723*

       6   Technology (Applied sciences) *[Class 600]*
       63   Agriculture and related technologies *[Class 630]*
                          Specific plant crops
                          [Centered heading: 633-635]
       634   Orchards, fruits, forestry
       634.9   Forestry

634.97	Kinds of trees
634.972	Dicotyledons
634.9723	Poplar
634.97232	Forest management

[As instructed under "634.97," the number following "634.9" for "Forest management" (2) is added to the base number "634.9723."]

84.   *Books written by adolescents: a bibliography.*

013.055   Index entry: *Bibliography   010*
                                           Adolescents   T7 -055

0	Generalities *[Class 000]*
01	Bibliography *[Class 010]*
	Bibliographies and catalogs of individuals, of works by specific classes of authors, of anonymous and pseudonymous works, of works from specific places, of works on specific subjects or in specific disciplines *[Centered heading: 012-016]*
013	Bibliographies and catalogs of works by specific classes of authors
013.055	Young people twelve to twenty

[From Table 7. As instructed under "013," the number from Table 7 for "Adolescents," i.e., "Young people twelve to twenty" (-055) is added to the base number "013."]

-05 Persons by age
-055   Young people twelve to twenty

85.   *Crime in Brazil.*

364.981   Index entry: *Crime   364*
                                           Brazil   T2 -81

3	Social sciences *[Class 300]*
36	Social problems and services; association *[Class 360]*
364	Criminology
364.9	Historical, geographic, persons treatment of crime and its alleviation
364.981	Brazil

[From Table 2. As instructed under "364.9," the number from Table 2 for "Brazil" (-81) is added to the base number "364.9."]

-8   South America
-81   Brazil

86.   Norway's *participation in the Korean War.*
      [The contributions of Norway extend beyond military participation]

951.90420893982   *Index entry:*   *Korean War, 1950-1953*   *951.9042*
                                            Norway   *T2—481*

        9   Geography, history, and auxiliary disciplines *[Class 900]*
        95   General history of Asia. Orient. Far East *[Class 950]*
        951   China and adjacent areas
        951.9   Korea
        951.904   1945-
        951.9042   Korean War, 1950-1953
        951.90423   Participation of specific groups of countries, of
                                specific countries, localities, groups
                                *[As instructed under "940-990," the number for the
                                "Participation of specific groups of countries, of specific
                                countries, localities, groups" (3) is added to the base number
                                "951.9042."]*
        951.904234-39   Participation of specific countries and localities
        951.90423481   Norway
                                *[From Table 2. As instructed under "34-39" the
                                number from Table 2 for "Norway" (-481) is added to
                                the base number "951.90423."]*
                                    -4   Europe. Western Europe
                                    -48   Scandinavia
                                    -481   Norway

APPENDIX E

Answers to the
Library of Congress Classification Exercise

In the sections that follow, information enclosed within square brackets indicates that it was not derived directly from the classification schedules.

A.

1. *How to catalog a rare book,* by Duncan. 1973.

    Z695.74 .D8 1973   *Index entry:*   *Rare books | Libraries | Cataloging*
                                                Z695.74

Z	Bibliography and Library Science *[1995 ed]*
662-1000.5	Libraries
665-718.8	Library science. Information science
687-718.8	The collections. The books
693-695.83	Cataloging
695.2-695.83	By form
695.74	Rare books
.D8	[Duncan]
	[Cutter number for the personal name main entry]
1973	[Date]

2. *How to grow asparagus,* by Unwin. 1922.

    SB325 .U5 1922   *Index entry:*   *Asparagus | Vegetable culture*   *SB325*

S	Agriculture *[1996 ed.]*
SB	Plant culture
320-353.5	Vegetables
325-351	Culture of individual vegetables or types of vegetables
325	Asparagus
.U5	[Unwin}
	[Cutter number for the personal name main entry]
1922	[Date]

3.   *The woman's suffrage movement in the United States, 1870-1910,* by Sand. 1938.

   JK1896 .S2 1938   *Index entry: Women's suffrage | United States*
                                            JK1880+

          J   Political Science *[1997 ed.]*
            JK   Political institutions and public administration
              1-9593   United States
                1717-(2248)   Political rights. Practical politics
                  1846-(1936)   Suffrage. Right to vote
                    1880-1911   Women's suffrage. Women's right to vote
                      1896   General works
                        .S2   [Sand]
                                            [Cutter number for the personal name main entry]
                          1938   [Date]

4.   *The folklore of holy wells and springs,* by Ash. 1956.

   GR690 .A8 1956   *Index entry: Springs (Groundwater) | Folklore*
                                            GR690

                                            Wells (Folklore)   GR690

          G   Geography. Maps. Anthropology. Recreation *[4th ed.*
                              1976]
            GR   Folklore
              420-950   By subject
                650-690   Geographical topics
                  678-690   Waters
                    690   Springs. Wells
                      .A8   [Ash]
                                            [Cutter number for the personal name main entry]
                        1956   [Date]

5.   *How to train your homing pigeon,* by Walls. 1934.

   SF469 .W3 1934   *Index entry: Homing pigeons | Animal culture*
                                            SF469

          S   Agriculture *[1996 ed.]*
            SF   Animal culture
              460-473   Birds. Cage birds
                464.5-472   Pigeons
                  469   Homing, racing, and carrier pigeons
                    .W3   [Walls]
                                            [Cutter number for the personal name main entry]
                      1934   [Date]

6.   *The first book of astronomy*, by Clark. 1985.
      [A book for children]

      QB46 .C5 1985   *Index entry: Astronomy   QB1+*

             Q   Science *[1996 ed.]*
               QB   Astronomy
                46   Juvenile works
                  .C5   [Clark]
                                          [Cutter number for the personal name main entry]
                      1985   [Date]

7.   *The art of writing biographies*, by Queen. 1981.
      [A book of techniques]

      CT22 .Q4 1981   *Index entry: Biography   CT21+*

             C   Auxiliary sciences of history *[1996 ed.]*
               CT   Biography
                21-22   Biography as an art or literary form
                22   Technique
                  .Q4   [Queen]
                                            [Cutter number for the personal name main entry]
                      1981   [Date]

8.   *A manual of archeology for the amateur archaeologist*, by Biddle. 1979.

         CC75.5 .B5 1979   *Index entry: Amateurs' manuals | Archaeology*
                                                  CC75.5

             C   Auxiliary sciences of history *[1996 ed.]*
               CC   Archaeology
                72-81   Philosophy. Theory
                  73-81   Methodology
                    75.5   Amateurs' manuals
                      .B5   [Biddle]
                                              [Cutter number for the personal name main entry]
                        1979   [Date]

9.   *The chemical analysis of rocks*, by Hruska. 1979.

         QE438 .H7 1979   *Index entry: Chemical analysis | Rocks   QE438*

             Q   Science *[1996 ed.]*
               QE   Geology
                420-499   Petrology
                  438   Chemical analysis of rocks

.H7   [Hruska]
                             [Cutter number for the personal name main entry]
          1979   [Date]

10.   *Photography for children*, by Lytton. 1998.

       TR149 .L9 1998   *Index entry:*   Photography   TR1+

              T   Technology *[1995 ed.]*
              TR   Photography
              149   Popular works. Juvenile works
              .L9   [Lytton]
                             [Cutter number for the personal name main entry]
              1998   [Date]

11.   *Encyclopedia of science fiction*, by O'Rourke. 1996

       PN 3433.4 .O7 1996   *Index entry:*   *Science fiction* | *General* | *Literary history*
                                              PN3433+

              PN   Literature (General) *[1997 ed.]*
              3311-3503   Prose. Prose fiction
              3427-3448   Special kinds of fiction. Fiction genres
              3433-3433.8   Science fiction
              3433.4   Encyclopedias. Dictionaries
              .O7   [O'Rourke]
                             [Cutter number for the personal name main entry]
              1996   [Date]

12.   *Coins and coin collecting*, by Quiller. 1983.

       CJ76 .Q5 1983   *Index entry:*   *Numismatics and seals*   *CJ1+*
                                              Coins   *CJ1+*

              C   Auxiliary sciences of history *[1996 ed.]*
              CJ   Numismatics
              1-4625   Coins
              73-76   General works
              76   1971-
              .Q5   [Quiller]
                             [Cutter number for the personal name main entry]
              1983   [Date]

13. *Visiting Doctor Sue: A child's guide to what happens in an animal hospital,* by Ivers. 1986.

SF604.55 .I9 1986   *Index entry: Veterinary hospitals   SF604.4+*

S	Agriculture *[1996 ed.]*
SF	Animal culture
600-1100	Veterinary medicine
604.4-604.7	Veterinary hospitals
604.55	Juvenile works
.I9	[Ivers]
	[Cutter number for the personal name main entry]
1986	[Date]

14. *A history of 18th century astrology,* by Lewis. 1969.

BF1679 .L4 1969   *Index entry: Occult science   BF1403.2+*
                       [The index entry "History | Astrology BF
                       1729 .H57" does not lead to the history of
                       astrology but rather to the special topic of
                       history as addressed by Astrology]

B-BJ	Philosophy. Psychology *[1996 ed.]*
BF	Psychology
1404-2050	Occult sciences
1651-1729	Astrology
1671-1679	History
1674-1679	By period
1679	Modern
.L4	[Lewis]
	[Cutter number for the personal name main entry]
1969	[Date]

15. *The female worker: the vocational education for women,* by Tyrone. 1986.

LC1500 .T9 1986   *Index entry: Vocational education | Women*
                       LC7500+

L	Education *[1998 ed.]*
LC	Special aspects of education
1390-5160.3	Education of special classes of persons
1401-2572	Women
1500-1506	Vocational education
1500	General works
.T9	[Tyrone]
	[Cutter number for the personal name main entry]
1986	[Date]

16.   *A dictionary of philosophy,* by Ludlow. 1976.
       [In English]

       B41 .L8 1976   *Index entry:*   *Philosophy*   *B1+*

              B-BJ   Philosophy. Psychology *[1996 ed.]*
              B   Philosophy (General)
                  40-48   Dictionaries
                  41   English and American
                      .L8   [Ludlow]
                                                 [Cutter number for the personal name main entry]
                          1976   [Date]

17.   *"Bridge freezes before road": ice loads and bridge design,* by Womack. 1994.

       TG304 .W6 1994   *Index entry:*   *Snow and ice loads* | *Bridge design*
                                                           TG304

              T   Technology *[1995 ed.]*
                  TG   Bridge engineering
                  300-304   Bridge design and drafting
                  304   Snow and ice loads
                      .W6   [Womack]
                                                 [Cutter number for the personal name main entry]
                          1994   [Date]

B.   <u>A-Z directions.</u>

18.   *Life on the stage : the biography of Helen Hayes,* by Loy. 1982.
       [The American actress born in 1900]

       PN2287 .H3 L6 1982   *Index entry:*   *Dramatic representation*   *PN2000+*

              PN   Literature (General) *[1997 ed.]*
                  1600-3307   Drama
                  2000-3307   Dramatic representation. The Theater
                  2219.3-3030   Special regions or countries
                  2219.3-2554   America
                  2219.3-2440   North America
                  2220-2298   United States
                  2285-2287   Biography
                  2287.A-Z   Individual, A-Z
                      .H3   [Hayes]
                                                                   [Cutter number for "Hayes"]
                          L6   [Loy]
                                                                   *[Cutter number for the personal name main
                                                                   entry]*
                              1982   [Date]

19.   *The National League*, by Gregg. 1922.
      [A history of the professional baseball league]

      GV875 .A3 G7 1922   *Index entry:*   *National League of Professional Baseball*
                                                  Clubs   GV875

            G   Geography. Maps. Anthropology. Recreation *[4th ed.*
                                 1976]
                GV   Recreation. Leisure
            561-1198.995   Sports
               861-1017   Ball games
               862-881   Baseball
                  875   Leagues, clubs, etc.
                  875.A3A-Z   National League of Professional Baseball
                                                          Clubs
                        G7   [Gregg]
                                                               [Cutter number for the personal name main entry]
                           1922   [Date]

20.   *Go Cubs! a history of the Chicago Cubs*, by Rogers. 1994.
      [The professional baseball team]

      GV875 .C6 R6 1994   *Index entry:*   *Chicago Cubs   GV875 .C6*

            G   Geography. Maps. Anthropology. Recreation *[4th ed.*
                                 1976]
                GV   Recreation. Leisure
            561-1198.995   Sports
               861-1017   Ball games
               862-881   Baseball
                  875   Leagues, clubs, etc.
                     .A4-Z   Individual clubs. By name, A-Z
                        .C6   [Chicago Cubs]
                                                             [Cutter number from the list on p. 353]
                        R6   [Rogers]
                                                                 [Cutter number for the personal name main
                                                                 entry]
                           1994   [Date]

21.   *School architecture in California*, by Salten. 1996.

      LB3218 .C2 S2 1996   *Index entry:*   *Architecture, School   LB3201+*

            L   Education *[1998 ed.]*
                LB   Theory and practice of education
               3201-3325   School architecture and equipment. School physical
                                          facilities. Campus planning
               3218-3219   By region or country
                3218   United States

.A5-W	By state, A-W
.C2	[California]
	[Cutter number from SCM:SL Instruction G 302]
S2	[Salten]
	[Cutter number for the personal name main entry]
1996	[Date]

22.   *Witchcraft in Alabama*, by Shick. 1961.

BF1577 .A2 S5 1961   *Index entry:*   *Witchcraft*   BF1562.5+

B-BJ	Philosophy. Psychology *[1996 ed.]*
BF	Psychology
1404-2050	Occult sciences
1562.5-1584	Witchcraft
1573-1584	By region or country
1573-1578	United States
1577	Other regions, A-Z
.A2	[Alabama]
	[Cutter number from SCM:SL Instruction G 302]
S5	[Shick]
	[Cutter number for the personal name main entry]
1961	[Date]

23.   *Cheesebox on a raft: the Union ironclad Monitor*, by Carr. 1919.
      [Centers on the activities of this ship during the American Civil War]

E595 .M7 C3 1919   *Index entry:*   *Monitor (Ironclad)*   E595.M7

E-F	History: America *[1995 ed.]*
E	[America and United States (non-local)]
151-887	United States
456-655	Civil War period, 1861-1865
591-600	Naval history
591-595	General works. The Union Navy
595	Individual ships, A-Z
.M7	Monitor (Ironclad)
	[Cutter number from the list on p. 190]
C3	[Carr]
	[Cutter number for the personal name main entry]
1919	[Date]

24.   *The Hogarth Press: the history of a great private press,* by Hull. 1966.

Z232 .H73 H8 1966   *Index entry: Hogarth Press*

Z	Bibliography and Library Science *[1995 ed.]*
116-659	Book industries and trade
116.A5-265.5	Printing
231-232	Printers and printing establishments
232	Individual printers and establishments, A-Z
.H73	Hogarth Press
	[Cutter number from the list beginning on p. 15]
H8	[Hull]
	[Cutter number for the personal name main entry]
1966	[Date]

25.   *Techniques of writing mystery and detective stories,* by Fry. 1971.

PN3377.5 .D4 F7 1971   *Index entry: Detective and mystery stories | General |*
                                                Literary history | Technique
                                                PN3377.5.D4

PN	Literature (General) *[1997 ed.]*
3311-3503	Prose. Prose fiction
3355-3383	Technique. Authorship
3365-3377.5	Special forms, subjects, etc.
3377.5.A-Z	Other, A-Z
.D4	Detective and mystery stories
F7	[Fry]
	[Cutter number for the personal name main entry]
1971	[Date]

26.   *The Honda Accord repair manual: 1994-1996,* by Ferry. 1996.

TL215. H6 F4 1996   *Index entry: Gasoline automobiles   TL205+*

T	Technology *[1995 ed.]*
TL	Motor vehicles. Aeronautics. Astronautics
1-390	Motor vehicles
200-229	Special automobiles. By power
205-215	Gasoline automobiles
215.A-Z	Special makes, A-Z
	[Although not stated in the schedule, the Library of Congress places maintenance and repair manuals for specific makes of gasoline powered automobiles in TL 215 rather than in TL 152.]

.H6   [Honda]
                            *[Cutter number derived from the LC cutter table. LC
                            actually uses .H58" as the cutter number for
                            "Honda."]*
            F4   [Ferry]
                            [Cutter number for the personal name main entry]
                    1996   [Date]

27.   *A bibliography of articles on motorcycles,* by Jansen. 1978.

Z5173 .M58 J3 1978   *Index entry:*   Motorcycles | Bibliography   Z5173.M58

        Z   Bibliography and Library Science *[1995 ed.]*
        1001-8999   Bibliography
          5051-7999   Subject bibliography
            5170-5173   Automobiles. Automobile travel. Motor vehicles
              5173   Special topics, A-Z
                .M58   Motorcycles
                            [Cutter number from the list on p. 121]
                J3   [Jansen]
                            [Cutter number for the personal name main entry]
                    1978   [Date]

28.   *North American Indian embroidery,* by Llewellyn. 1947.

E98 .E5 L5 1947   *Index entry:*   Embroidery (Indian)   E98.E5

        E-F   History: America *[1995 ed.]*
        E   [America and United States (non-local)]
          75-99   Indians of North America
            98   Other topics, A-Z
              .E5   Embroidery
                            [Cutter number from the list beginning on p. 12]
              L5   [Llewellyn]
                            [Cutter number for the personal name main entry]
                    1947   [Date]

29.   *Flowers in literature: a perspective,* by Escher. 1949.

PN56 .F55 E8 1949   *Index entry:*   Flowers in literature | Literary history
                                             PN56.F55

        PN   Literature (General) *[1997 ed.]*
        45-57   Theory. Philosophy. Esthetics
          46-57   Relation to and treatment of special elements,
                                  problems, and subjects
            56-57   Other special

56.A-Z	Topics, A-Z
.F55	Flowers
E8	[Escher]
	[Cutter number for the personal name main entry]
1949	[Date]

30.   *How to win at the game Trivial Pursuit,* by Eastman. 1985.

GV1469 .T7 E15 1985   *Index entry:*   *Board games*   *GV1312+*
                                          Move games   *GV1312+*

G		Geography. Maps. Anthropology. Recreation *[4th ed. 1976]*
GV		Recreation. Leisure
1199-1570		Games and amusements
1221-1469		Indoor games and amusements
1312-1469		Board games. Move games
1469		Other board games, A-Z
.T7		[Trivial pursuit]
		[Cutter number derived from the LC cutter table]
E15		[Eastman]
		[Cutter number for "Eastman" developed by expanding on the decimal number .1. This was done because the cutter table provides for the use of ".E2" for words beginning with "Eb."]
1985		[Date]

31.   *Modern paper manufacture in Japan,* by Ervin. 1980.

TS1095 .J3 E7 1980   *Index entry:*   *Paper manufacture*   *TS1080+*

T		Technology *[1995 ed.]*
TS		Manufactures
1080-1268		Paper manufacture and trade
1090-1096		History
1094-1096		Modern
1095		Special countries, A-Z
.J3		[Japan]
		[Cutter number from SCM:SL Instruction G 300]
E7		[Ervin]
		[Cutter number for the personal name main entry]
1980		[Date]

C.   Fixed Successive Cutter Numbers.

32.   *Kew Gardens: the British Royal Botanic Gardens,* by Mayfield. 1983.

QK73 .G72 K4 1983   *Index entry: Botanical gardens | Botany   QK71+*

Q	Science *[1996 ed.]*
QK	Botany
63-73	Botanical gardens
73.A-Z	By region or country, A-Z
.G7	[Great Britain]
	[Cutter number from SCM:SL Instruction G 300[JS1]]
.G72	Individual. By name, A-Z
	[Successive cutter number "2" from the table on p. 257]
K4	[Kew Gardens]
	[Cutter number derived from the LC cutter table]
1983	[Date]

Note: *No cutter number could be provided for "Mayfield" because 2 cutter numbers were used as part of the subject classification.*

33.   *Weighted in the balance: a history of the "Laboratory of the Government Chemist" an Australian institution,* by Blunt. 1992.

QD51.5 .A82 L3 1992   *Index entry: Laboratories | Chemistry   QD51+*

Q	Science *[1996 ed.]*
QD	Chemistry
51-54	Laboratories
51.5.A-Z	By region or country, A-Z
.A8	[Australia]
	[Cutter number from SCM:SL Instruction G 300[JS2]]
.A82	Individual laboratories. By name, A-Z
	[Successive cutter number "2" from the table on p. 145]
L3	[Laboratory of the Government Chemist]
	[Cutter number derived from the LC cutter table]
1992	[Date]

Note: *No cutter number could be provided for "Blunt" because 2 cutter numbers were used as part of the subject classification.*

34.   *Great buildings, great food: the architecture of the great restaurants of France,* by Marchand. 1989.

NA7858 .F8 M2 1989   *Index entry: Restaurants | Architecture   NA7855+*

N	Fine Arts *[1996 ed.]*
NA	Architecture
4100-8480	Special classes of buildings
4170-8480	Classed by use

7855-7858		Restaurants. Coffee houses
7858		Other regions or countries, A-Z
.F8		[France]
		[Cutter number from SCM:SL Instruction G 300
		General works
		[Successive cutter number ".x" from the table on p.
		180]
	M3	[Marchand]
		[Cutter number for the personal name main
		entry]
	1989	[Date]

35.   *Brasserie France: architecture with a Mediterranean flair,* by Bates. 1996.
      [This restaurant is in Marseilles]

NA7858 .F82 M3 1996   *Index entry: Restaurants | Architecture   NA7855+*

N		Fine Arts *[1996 ed.]*
NA		Architecture
4100-8480		Special classes of buildings
4170-8480		Classed by use
7855-7858		Restaurants. Coffee houses
7858		Other regions or countries, A-Z
.F8		[France]
		[Cutter number from SCM:SL Instruction G 300
.F82		Special restaurants or coffeehouses
		[Successive cutter number ".x2" from the table on p.
		180]
		By place, A-Z
	M3	[Marseilles]
		[Cutter number for derived from the LC cutter
		table]
	1996	[Date]

Note: *No cutter number could be provided for "Bates" because 2 cutter numbers were used as*
        part of the subject classification.

36.   *Latvian book publishing directory,* compiled by Solowicz. 1998.

Z375 .L35 S6 1998   *Index entry: Bookselling and publishing   Z278+*

Z	Bibliography and Library Science *[1995 ed.]*
116-659	Book industries and trade
278-549	Bookselling and publishing
289-544	By region or country
291-447	Europe
375	Baltic States
.L3	Latvia
.L35	Directories
	[Successive cutter number ".x5" from Table Z9 on
	p. 375]

S6   [Solowicz]
                *[Cutter number for the personal name main
                entry]*
        1998   [Date]

37. *Walking tour of the bookdealers of Riga*, by Litinski. 1997.
     [Riga, Latvia]

     Z375 .L386 R5 1997   *Index entry: Bookselling and publishing   Z278+*

            Z   Bibliography and Library Science *[1995 ed.]*
         116-659   Book industries and trade
         278-549   Bookselling and publishing
         289-544   By region or country
         291-447   Europe
            375   Baltic States
            .L3   Latvia
                                            Local
            .L386   By city, A-Z
                                *[Successive cutter number ".x86" from Table Z9
                                on p. 375]*
            R5   [Riga]
                                *[Cutter number derived from the LC cutter
                                table]*
              1997   [Date]

     *Note: No cutter number could be provided for "Litinski" because 2 cutter numbers were used as
     part of the subject classification.*

38. *Philadelphians to the rescue: Philadelphia's volunteer fire companies of the early 19th
     century*, by Chestnut. 1984.

     TH9505 .P4074 C4 1984   *Index entry: Fire departments, City   TH9500+*

            T   Technology *[1995 ed.]*
            TH   Building construction
         9111-9599.A6-Z   Protection from fire. Fire prevention and extinction
         9500-9599.A6-Z   Protection from fire in special countries and cities
                                City fire departments. Firemen's associations
         9502-9507   North America (United States and Canada)
         9503-9505   United States
         9505.A-Z   Special cities, A-Z
            .P4   [Philadelphia]
                                [Cutter number derived from the LC cutter table]

	.P4074	Volunteer companies. Constitution, by-laws, history, etc.

.P4074   Volunteer companies. Constitution, by-laws, history, etc.
[Successive cutter number .x047" from Table T3 on p. 438]

Fire companies.
Conventions, etc.
.x074   Volunteer companies. Constitution, by-laws, history, etc.

C4   [Chestnut]
[Cutter number for the personal name main entry]

1984   [Date]

39. *Firehouse: the firehouses of Illinois,* by Barnard. 1999.

TH9504 .I38 B3 1999   *Index entry: Firemen's associations   TH9500+*
[Although this is not a good index entry for this concept it is the best that appears in the index.]

T   Technology *[1995 ed.]*
TH   Building construction
9111-9599.A6-Z   Protection from fire. Fire prevention and extinction
9500-9599.A6-Z   Protection from fire in special countries and cities
                      City fire departments. Firemen's associations
9502-9507   North America (United States and Canada)
9503-9505   United States
9504.A-W   Special states, A-W
.I3   [Illinois]
                  [Cutter number from SCM:SL Instruction G 300
.I38   Local fire equipment. Engines, enginehouses, etc.
                  [Successive cutter number .x08" from Table T3 on p. 438. As instructed on p. 184 this number from Table T3 is added to the cutter number for "Illinois" without the use of "0".]
B3   [Barnard]
                  [Cutter number for the personal name main entry]
1999   [Date]

D.   Tables within the text. Double Cutter Numbers.

40.   *Directory of school officials in Kentucky*, issued by the Kentucky Department of
Public Instruction. 1977.

LB2803 .K4 K4 1977   *Index entry:*   *School administration*   LB2801+
                                              [Although there is an index entry "School
                                              administrators LB1777.5" that entry leads
                                              to works that address the topic of the
                                              education and training of school
                                              administrators and supervisors rather
                                              works that are directories of these officials.]

L   Education *[1998 ed.]*
  LB   Theory and practice of education
    2801-3095   School administration and organization
      2801-2865   General
        2803   Directories and lists of school officials
          2803.A2-Z   United States
            A4-Z   Regions or states, A-Z
              .K4   [Kentucky]
                                  [Cutter number from SCM:SL Instruction G 302]
                                  General
                                  [Successive cutter number ".x" from the table
                                  "Under each state" on p. 95]
                K4   [Kentucky Department of Public
                                  Instruction]
                                  [Cutter number for "Kentucky" (the corporate
                                  name main entry) from SCM:SL Instruction G
                                  302]
                  1977   [Date]

41.   *Directory of school officials in Preston County, W. Va.*, issued by the Preston
County Board of Education. 1980.

LB2803 .W42 P7 1980   *Index entry:*   *School administration*   LB2801+
                                              [See the comment to the index entry for item
                                              40]

L   Education *[1998 ed.]*
  LB   Theory and practice of education
    2801-3095   School administration and organization
      2801-2865   General
        2803   Directories and lists of school officials
          2803.A2-Z   United States
            A4-Z   Regions or states, A-Z
              .W4   [West Virginia]
                                  [Cutter number from SCM:SL Instruction G 302]
                .W42   Counties, A-Z
                                  [Successive cutter number ".x2" from the table
                                  "Under each state" on p. 95]

	P7	[Preston County]
		[Cutter number derived from the LC cutter table]
	1980	[Date]

42. *Examination of the British drug scene,* by Hunter. 1971.

HV5840 .G7 H8 1971   *Index entry:*   *Drug abuse | Social pathology*
                                             HV5800+

                                             Drug habits | Social pathology
                                             HV5800+

H		Social sciences *[1997 ed.]*	
	HV	Social pathology. Social and public welfare. Criminology	
	5800-5840	Drug habits. Drug abuse	
	5825-5840	By region or country	
	5840	Other regions or countries, A-Z	
	.G7	[Great Britain]	
		[Cutter number from SCM:SL Instruction G 300]	
		General Works	
		[".xA1-xZ" from the Table on p. 542]	
	H8	[Hunter]	
		[Cutter number for the personal name main entry]	
	1971	[Date]	

43. *Psychedelic drug use in Vancouver,* by Steele. 1982.

HV5840 .C22 V3 1982   *Index entry:*   *Drug abuse | Social pathology*
                                             HV5800+

                                             Drug habits | Social pathology
                                             HV5800+

H		Social sciences *[1997 ed.]*	
	HV	Social pathology. Social and public welfare. Criminology	
	5800-5840	Drug habits. Drug abuse	
	5825-5840	By region or country	
	5840	Other regions or countries, A-Z	
	.C2	[Canada]	
		[Cutter number from SCM:SL Instruction G 300]	
	.C22	Local, A-Z	
		[Successive cutter number "x2A-Z" from the table on p. 542]	
	V3	[Vancouver]	
		[Cutter number derived from the LC cutter table]	
	1982	[Date]	

Note: *No cutter number could be provided for "Steele" because 2 cutter numbers were used as part of the subject classification.*

44. *The history of Brazil's libraries,* by Louis. 1955.

Z769 .A1 L6 1955   *Index entry:*   *History | Libraries*   *Z721+*

Z   Bibliography and Library science *[1995 ed.]*
    662-1000.5   Libraries
        729-871   Library reports. History. Statistics
            735-871   Other regions or countries
                763-786   South America
                    769-770   Brazil
                        769.A1   General works. History
                            L6   [Louis]
                                                  [Cutter number for the personal name main entry]
                                1955   [Date]

45. *Libraries in the Tolna region of Hungary: a history,* by Case. 1952.

Z794.3 .A2 T6 1952   *Index entry:*   *History | Libraries*   *Z721+*

Z   Bibliography and Library science *[1995 ed.]*
    662-1000.5   Libraries
        729-871   Library reports. History. Statistics
            735-871   Other regions or countries
                789-841.8   Europe
                    794.3   Hungary
                        .A2A-Z   By region, state or place
                            T6   [Tolna]
                                                  [Cutter number derived from the LC cutter table]
                                1952   [Date]

Note: *No cutter number could be provided for "Case" because 2 cutter numbers were used as part of the subject classification.*

46. *The Srečko Vilhar Public Library: an illustrated history,* by Smolič. 1994.
     [Located in Koper, Slovenia]

Z841.8 .A3 S6 1994   *Index entry:*   *History | Libraries*   *Z721+*

Z   Bibliography and Library science *[1995 ed.]*
    662-1000.5   Libraries
        729-871   Library reports. History. Statistics
            735-871   Other regions or countries
                789-841.8   Europe
                    841.8   Slovenia
                        .A3   Individual libraries. By name, A-Z
                            S6   [Srečko Vilhar]
                                                  [Cutter number for the name of the library]
                                1994   [Date]

Note: *No cutter number could be provided for "Smolič" because 2 cutter numbers were used as part of the subject classification.*

47.   *Caves of Scotland*, by MacDonald. 1977.

GB608.45 .M3 1977   *Index entry: Caves | Geomorphology   GB601+*

G   Geography. Maps. Anthropology. Recreation *[4th ed. 1976]*
    GB   Physical geography
        400-649   Geomorphology. Landforms. Terrain
            561-649   Other natural landforms
                599-649   Karst landforms
                    601-649   Caves. Speleology
                        603-608   By region or country
                            608   Other
                                608.45   Scotland
                                            [From Table I on p. 380. As instructed the number from that Table for Scotland (.45) is appended to the existing number.]

                    .M3   [MacDonald]
                                            [Cutter number for the personal name main entry]
                1977   [Date]

48.   *Made by ice: Wisconsin landforms created by the glaciers*, by Edison. 1946.

GB585 .W6 E3 1946   *Index entry: Glacial landforms   GB581+*

G   Geography. Maps. Anthropology. Recreation *[4th ed. 1976]*
    GB   Physical geography
        400-649   Geomorphology. Landforms. Terrain
            561-649   Other natural landforms
                581-588   Glacial landforms
                    585   By state, A-W
                                            [The table below "Other natural landforms" on p. 245 provides a number range from "(1)" to "(8)". The fifth number in the range for "Glacial landforms" (585) is used to express "By state, A-W."]
                    .W6   [Wisconsin]
                                            [Cutter number from SCM:SL Instruction G 302]
                E3   [Edison]
                                            [Cutter number for the personal name main entry]
                1946   [Date]

49.   *The beautiful valleys of Scotland*, by Lutz. 1981.

GB568.45 .L8 1981   *Index entry: Valleys (Natural landforms)   GB561+*

G   Geography. Maps. Anthropology. Recreation *[4th ed. 1976]*
    GB   Physical geography
        400-649   Geomorphology. Landforms. Terrain
            561-649   Other natural landforms

561-568   Floodplains, river channels, valleys, watersheds
568   Other countries
                 [The table below "Other natural landforms" on p. 245
                 provides a number range from "(1)" to "(8)". The eighth
                 number in the range for "Floodplains, river channels,
                 valleys, watersheds (568) is used to express "Other
                 countries."]
568.45   Scotland
                 [From Table I on p. 380. As instructed the number
                 from that Table for Scotland (.45) is appended to the
                 existing number.]
.L8   [Lutz]
                 [Cutter number for the personal name main entry]
1981   [Date]

50.   *The handbook for publishers in France,* by La Mont. 1974.

Z308 .L3 1974   *Index entry: Bookselling and publishing   Z278+*

Z   Bibliography and Library Science *[1995 ed.]*
116-659   Book industries and trade
278-549   Bookselling and publishing
289-549   By region or country
291-447   Europe
303-310   France
308   Handbooks, manuals, etc.
                 [In Table Z7, a number range from "0" to "7" is
                 provided. As instructed at the beginning of this table
                 on p. 373, the appropriate number in the table is added
                 to the first number in the number range for the
                 country. Thus, the number in the table for
                 "Handbooks, manuals, etc." (5) is added to the first
                 number (303) in the range for France.]
.L3   [La Mont]
                 [Cutter number for the personal name main entry]
1974   [Date]

51.   *The history of publishing in Czechoslovakia,* by Zdarsky. 1984.

Z301.3 .Z3 1984   *Index entry: Bookselling and publishing   Z278+*

Z   Bibliography and Library Science *[1995 ed.]*
116-659   Book industries and trade
278-549   Bookselling and publishing
289-549   By region or country
291-447   Europe
301   Czechoslovakia

	301.3	History. Biography
		[In Table Z8, a number range from "0" to "0.86" is provided. As instructed at the beginning of this table on p. 374, the appropriate number in the table is added to the first number in the number range for the country. Thus, the number in the table for "History. Biography" (0.3) is added to the first number, and in this case the only number, (301) in the range for Czechoslovakia.]
	.Z3	[Zdarsky]
		[Cutter number for the personal name main entry]
	1984	[Date]

52.   *Publishers and booksellers in Turkey: a comprehensive directory,* by Land. 1985.

Z464 .T895 L3 1985   *Index entry: Bookselling and publishing   Z278+*

Z		Bibliography and Library Science *[1995 ed.]*
116-659		Book industries and trade
278-549		Bookselling and publishing
289-549		By region or country
448-464		Asia
464		Other, A-Z
.T89		Turkey
.T895		Directories
		[In Table Z9, a number range from ".x" to ".x86" is provided. The "x" represents the cutter number for Turkey (.T89). The successive cutter number for "Directories" (5) is appended to the cutter number for Turkey.]
	L3	[Land]
		[Cutter number for the personal name main entry]
	1985	[Date]

E.   <u>Tables within the text</u>.

For titles 53-59 the following initial hierarchy and index entry applies:

Index entry: Sports | Modern History (By region or country   GV581+

G		Geography. Maps. Anthropology. Recreation *[4th ed. 1976]*
GV		Recreation. Leisure
561-1198.995		Sports
571-688		History

53.   *The history of sports in Texas,* by Connelly. 1964.

    GV584 .T4 C6 1964

581-601	America
583-584.5	United States
584	By state, A-W
.T4	[Texas]
	[Cutter number from SCM:SL Instruction G 302]
L6	[Connelly]
	[Cutter number for the personal name main entry]
1964	[Date]

54.   *The history of sports in Baton Rouge, La.,* by Quentin. 1921.

    GV584.5 .B3 Q4 1921

581-601	America
583-584.5	United States
584.5	By city, A-Z
.B3	[Baton Rouge]
	[Cutter number derived from the LC cutter table]
Q4	[Quentin]
	[Cutter number for the personal name main entry]
1921	[Date]

55.   *The history of sports in Ontario Province, Canada,* by Stone. 1932.

    GV585.3 .O6 S7 1932

581-601	America
585-585.5	Canada
585.3	By province, A-Z
.O6	[Ontario]
	[Cutter number from SCM:SL Instruction G 302]
S7	[Stone]
	[Cutter number for "Stone"]
1932	[Date]

56.   *The history of sports in Mexico City, Mexico,* by Squires. 1970.

    GV588.5 .M4 S6 1970

581-601	America
586-601	Latin America
587-588.5	Mexico

588.5	By city, A-Z
	[Using the column for 2 no. countries in the table on p. 343, the 2.5th number in the number range for Mexico (588.5) is used to express "By city, A-Z."]
.M4	[Mexico City]
	[Cutter number derived from the LC cutter table]
S6	[Squires]
	[Cutter number for the personal name main entry]
1970	[Date]

57. *The history of sports in Bogota,* by Lares. 1968.
[The city in Colombia, South America]

GV601 .C75 B6 1968

581-601	America
586-601	Latin America
601	Other South American regions or countries, A-Z
.C7	[Colombia]
	[Cutter number from SCM:SL Instruction G 300]
.C75	By city, A-Z
	[Using the column for Cutter no. countries in the table on p. 343, the successive cutter number ".x5" is used to express "By city, A-Z."]
B6	[Bogata]
	[Cutter number derived from the LC cutter table]
1968	[Date]

Note: *No cutter number could be provided for "Lares" because 2 cutter numbers were used as part of the subject classification.*

58. *The history of sports in Ireland,* by O'Brien. 1949.

GV606.5 .O2 1949

605-648	Europe
606.5-606.55	Ireland
606.5	General works
	[Using the column for 1 no. countries in the table on p. 343, the 1st number in the number range for Ireland (606.5) is used to express "General works."]
.O2	[O'Brien]
	[Cutter number for the personal name main entry]
1949	[Date]

59.   *The history of sports in Dublin*, by McCaffrey. 1976.

GV606.55 .D8 M3 1976

605-648	Europe
606.5-606.55	Ireland
606.55	By city, A-Z
	[Using the column for l no. countries in the table on p. 343, the 1.5th number in the number range for Ireland(606.55) is used to express "By city, A-Z."]
.D8	[Dublin]
	[Cutter number derived from the LC cutter table]
M3	[McCaffrey]
	[Cutter number for the personal name main entry]
1976	[Date]

F.   <u>Class H</u>.

For titles 60-62 the following initial hierarchy and index entry applies:

Index entry: Police   HV7551+

H	Social Sciences *[1997 ed.]*
HV	Social pathology. Social and public welfare. Criminology
7231-9920.5	Criminal justice administration
7551-8280.7	Police. Detectives. Constabulary
	Police.
8130-8280.7	By region or country
8157-8280.7	Other regions or countries

60.   *The municipal police of Buenos Aires*, by Edwards. 1981.

HV8180 .B8 E3 1981

8180	Argentina.
	By city, A-Z
	[In Table H5, the number range for Argentina is 27- -30. Thus, Argentina is a 4 number country. These numbers are added to 8150 (i.e., 8177-8180) as instructed on p. 573. Using the section for "4 nos." on p. 573, the 4th number in the number range for Argentina (8180) is used to express "By city, A-Z."]
.B8	[Buenos Aires]
	[Cutter number derived from the LC cutter table]
E3	[Edwards]
	[Cutter number for the personal name main entry]
1981	[Date]

61.   *The accountability of the English constable,* by Marshall. 1973.

    HV8196 .A2 M3 1973

8196	England and Wales *[In Table H5, the number for England and Wales is 46. Thus, England and Wales is a 1 number country. This number is added to 8150 (i.e., 8196) as instructed on p. 573.]*
.A2	General works. History and description *[Using the section for "1 no." countries on p. 573, the reserve cutter number ".A2" is used to express "General works. History and description."]*
M3	[Marshall] *[Cutter number for the personal name main entry]*
1973	[Date]

62.   *The national police in Bulgaria,* by Raible. 1961.

    HV8241.5 .A2 R3 1961

8241.5	Bulgaria *[In Table H5, the number for Bulgaria is 91.5. Thus, Bulgaria is a 1 number country even thought that number is a decimal number. This number is added to 8150 (i.e., 8241.5) as instructed on p. 573.]*
.A2	General works. History and description *[Using the section for "1 no." countries on p. 573, the reserve cutter number ".A2" is used to express "General works. History and description."]*
R3	[Raible] *[Cutter number for the personal name main entry]*
1961	[Date]

For titles 63-70 the following hierarchy and index entry applies:

           Index entry: [No useful index entry was identified]

H	Social sciences *[1997 ed.]*
HN	Social history and conditions. Social problems. Social reform
50-981	By region or country
101-942.5	Other regions or countries

63.   *The 20th century: a century of social reform in India*, by Natira. 1949.

      HN683.N3 1949

683		India
		History and description
		[In Table H8, number range for India is 581-590. Thus, India is a 10 number country. These numbers are added to 100 (i.e., 681-690) as instructed on p. 428. Using the section for "10 nos." beginning on p. 428, the 3rd number in the number range for India (683) is used to express "History and description."]
	.N3	[Natira]
		[Cutter number for the personal name main entry]
	1949	[Date]

64.   *A study of life in a Devonshire community*, by White. 1976.

      HN398 .D4 W4 1976

398		Great Britain
		Local, A-Z
		[In Table H8, the number range for Great Britain is 281-300. Thus, Great Britain is a 20 number country. These numbers are added to 100 (i.e., 381-400) as instructed on p. 428. Using the section for "20 nos." on p. 428, the 18th number in the number range for Great Britain (398) is used to express "Local, A-Z."]
	.D4	[Devonshire]
		[Cutter number derived from the LC cutter table]
	W4	[White]
		[Cutter number for the personal name main entry]
	1976	[Date]

65.   *Social problems in the Arab countries: a statistical report*, by Azeno. 1983.

      HN766 .A85 A9 1983

766		Arab countries (Collective)
		[In Table H8, the Arab countries are expressed by "666". Thus the Arab countries are treated is a 1 number country. This number is added to 100 (i.e., 766) as instructed on p. 428.]
	.A85	Statistics. Social indicators
		[Using the section for "1 no." on p. 429, the reserve cutter number ".A85" is used to express "Statistics. Social indicators."]
	A9	[Azeno]
		[Cutter number for the personal name main entry]
	1983	[Date]

66.   *A social history of 19th century Europe*, by Hill. 1935

   HN373 .H5 1935

373	Europe
	History and description
	[In Table H8, the number range for Europe is 271-280.
	Thus, Europe is treated as a 10 number country. These
	numbers are added to 100 (i.e., 371-380) as instructed on
	p. 428. Using the section for "10 nos." beginning on p.
	428, the 3rd number in the number range for Europe
	(373) is used to express "History and description." 19th
	century cannot be expressed.]
.H5	[Hill]
	[Cutter number for the personal name main entry]
1935	[Date]

67.   *Power in Ica: the social structure of a Peruvian community*, by Lyle. 1966.

   HN350 .I2 L9 1966

350	Peru
	Local, A-Z
	[In Table H8, the number range for Peru is 241-250.
	Thus, Peru is a 10 number country. These numbers are
	added to 100 (i.e., 341-350) as instructed on p. 428.
	Using the section for "10 nos." beginning on p. 428, the
	10th number in the number range for Peru (350) is used
	to express "Local, A-Z."]
.I2	[Ica}
	[Cutter number derived from the LC cutter table]
L9	[Lyle]
	[Cutter number for the personal name main entry]
1966	[Date]

68.   *Social mobility in Gibraltar*, by Wherry. 1981.

   HN590.5 .Z9 S65 1981

590.5	Gibraltar
	[In Table H8, Gibraltar is expressed by the number 490.5.
	Thus, Gibraltar is a 1 number country. This number is
	added to 100 (i.e., 590.5) as instructed on p. 429.]
.Z9	Special topics (not otherwise provided for),
	A-Z
	[Using the section for "1 no." on p. 429, the reserve
	cutter number ".Z9" is used to express "Special topics
	not otherwise provided for."]

S65	Social mobility

[As instructed by the note under ".Z9A-Z Special topics, A-Z" for "1 no.," the list of special topics under number 20 in the section for "20 nos. on p. 428 is used to express special topics. Thus, , ".S6" is used for "Social mobility."]

1981	[Date]

Note: *No cutter number could be provided for Wherry because 2 cutter numbers were used as part of the subject classification.*

69.   *The literature of social reform in China, 1830-1853,* compiled and translated by Ogden. 1927.

HN735 .L5 1927

735	China
	Social reform literature
	Early through 1850

[In Table H8, the number range for China is 631-640. Thus, China is a 10 number country. These numbers are added to 100 (i.e., 731-740) as instructed on p. 428. Using the section for "10 nos." beginning on p. 428, the 5th number in the number range for China (735) is used to express "Social reform literature. Early through 1850."]

.L5	[Literature of social reform]

[Cutter number for the first non-article word of the title main entry]

1927	[Date]

70.   *Continuity and change: the social history of Spain since World War II,* by Ilian. 1978.

HN583.5 .I4 1978

583.5	Spain
	History and description, 1945-

[In Table H8, the number range for Spain is 481-490. Thus, Spain is a 10 number country. These numbers are added to 100 (i.e., 581-590) as instructed on p. 428. Using the section for "10 nos." beginning on p. 428, the 3.5th number in the number range for Spain (583.5) is used to express "History and description, 1945-   ."]

.I4	[Ilian]

[Cutter number for the personal name main entry]

1978	[Date]

For titles 94-97 the following initial hierarchy and index entry applies:

Index entry: Banks and banking   HG1501+

H		Social sciences *[1997 ed.]*
HG		Finance
1501-3550		Banking
2401-3550		By region or country
2701-3542.7		Other regions or countries

71.   *La Banque de France: its history and influence,* by Andre. 1989.

HG3034 .A5 1989

> 3034 —— France
> Central Bank. National Bank. Banks of issue
> General Works. History and description
> *[In Table H8, the number range for France is 321-340. Thus, France is a 20 number country. These numbers are added to HG2700 (i.e., HG2981-HG3000) as instructed on p. 317. Using the section for "20 nos." on p. 317, the 14th number in the number range for France (3034) is used to express "Central bank. National Bank. Banks of issue. General works. History and description."]*
>
> .A5 —— [Andre]
> *[Cutter number for the personal name main entry]*
>
> 1989 —— [Date]

72.   *Banking and monetary control in South Africa,* by Koster. 1978.

HG3401 .A6 K6 1978

> 3401 —— South Africa
> *[In Table H8, South Africa is expressed by the number 701. Thus, South Africa is a 1 number country. This number is added to HG2700 (i.e., HG3401) as instructed on p. 318.]*
>
> .A6 —— History and policy
> *[Using the section for "1 no." on p. 318, the reserve cutter number ".A6" is used to express "History and policy."]*
>
> K6 —— [Koster]
> *[Cutter number for the personal name main entry]*
>
> 1978 —— [Date]

73. *Annual report of the Banco de los Andes.*
     [Located in Bogata, Colombia]

     HG2910 .B64 B3

       2910   Colombia
                                By city, A-Z

[In Table H8, the number range for Colombia is 201-210. Thus, Colombia is a 10 number country. These numbers are added to HG2700 (i.e., HG2901-HG2910) as instructed on p. 317. Using the section for "10 nos." beginning on p. 317, the 10th number in the number range for Colombia (2910) is used to express "By city, A-Z."]

      .B6   [Bogata]
[Cutter number derived from the LC cutter table]

      .B64   Individual banks, A-Z.
[Successive cutter number ".x4" under 10 on p. 318 is used to express "Individual banks, A-Z."]

      B3   [Banco de los Andes]
[Cutter number for the corporate name main entry]

Note: *SCM:SL Guideline G 820 indicates that no date should be provided for serials.*

74. *Banking in Barcelona, Spain: 1840 to 1920,* by Voltes. 1962.

     HG3190 .B32 V6 1962

       3190   By city, A-Z
[In Table H8, the number range for Spain is 481-490. Thus, Spain is a 10 number country. These numbers are added to HG2700 (i.e., HG3181-HG3190) as instructed on p. 317. Using the section for "10 nos." beginning on p. 31, the 10th number in the number range for Spain (3190) is used to express "By city, A-Z."]

      .B3   [Barcelona]
[Cutter number derived from the LC cutter table]

      .B32   General works
[Successive cutter number ".x2" under 10 on p. 317 is used to express "General works."]

      V6   [Voltes]
[Cutter number for the personal name main entry]

      1962   [Date]

G.   Class P: Forty-Nine Number Author.

For titles 75-81 the following initial hierarchy and index entry applies:

Index entry:	*[No useful index entry was identified]*
	[Although there is no index entry for this author or the time period in which he wrote, there is an entry for "American literature PS" but that is considered too general to be of any help in classifying the works that follow.]

PS	American literature *[1998 ed.]*
700-3576	Individual authors
991-(3390)	19th century
1300-1348	Clemens, Samuel Langhorne ("Mark Twain")
	[Table P-PZ31 (Table for Authors (49 nos.)) in the P-PZ Tables [1998 ed.] is used for Twain. Numbers from this table are added successively to the base number "13."]

75.   *The writings of Mark Twain* (Samuel Langhorne Clemens). Autographed [unedited] edition. 1899.

PS1300 .E99

1300	Collected works
	Original editions and reprints. By date
	[Number "0" from P-PZ31]
.E00-E99	1800-1899
	[Date letters. "E" represents the 19th century]
.E99	[1899]
	[Date letter for 1899]

76.   *Huckleberry Finn,* by Mark Twain. London. 1844.

PS1305 .A1 1844

1305-1322	Separate works
1305	Adventures of Huckleberry Finn
0.A1-A3	Texts
	[From Table P-PZ41 (Table for Separate Works (1 no.)). The "0" before this cutter number range is added arithmetically to "1305."]
.A1	By date
1844	[Date]

77. *Le avventure di Tom Sawyer,* par Mark Twain ; traduzione di T. Orsi. 1930.
     [A translation into Italian]

    PS1306 .A66 1930

1305-1322	Separate works
1306	Adventures of Tom Sawyer
0.A31-69	Translations
	[From P-PZ41 (Table for Separate Works (1 no.))]
0.A6-69	Other. By language
	[The "0" before this cutter number range is added arithmetically to "1306."]
.A66	[Italian]
	["Italian" is represented by the second 6]
1930	[Date]

78. *Interpretations of The Adventures of Huckleberry Finn: a collection of essays,* edited by Abbott. 1938.

    PS1305 .I5 1938

1305-1322	Separate works
1305	Adventures of Huckleberry Finn
0.A7-Z	Criticism
	[From Table P-PZ41 (Table for Separate Works (1 no.)). The "0" before this cutter number range is added arithmetically to "1305."]
.I5	[The Adventures of Huckleberry Finn]
	[Cutter number for "Interpretations," the first non-article word of the title main entry.]
1938	[Date]

79. *Twain's The mysterious stranger and the critics,* by Tuckey. 1968.
     [A criticism]

    PS1322 .M93 T8 1968

1305-1322	Separate works
1322	Other, A-Z
.M9	[Mysterious stranger]
	[Cutter number derived from the LC cutter table]
.M93	Criticism
	[From P-PZ43 (Table for Separate Works (Successive Cutter Nos.)). The successive cutter number ".x3" expresses "Criticism."]
T8	[Tuckey]
	[Cutter number for the personal name main entry]
1968	[Date]

80.   *Mark Twain: a profile,* by Kaplan. 1967.
       [A biography]

    PS1331 .K3 1967

1329-1335		Biography, criticism, etc.
		[Numbers "29"-"35" from Table P-PZ31 (Table for Authors (49 nos.))]
1331.A5-Z		General works
		[The number for "General works" (31) and its cutter number extensions is added successively to the base number "13" (1331).]
.K3		[Kaplan]
		[Cutter number for the personal name main entry]
1967		[Date]

81.   *Mark Twain's letters,* arranged with commentary by Paine. 1917.

    PS1331 .A4 1917

1329-1335		Biography, criticism, etc.
		[Numbers "29"-"35" from Table P-PZ31 (Table for Authors (49 nos.))]
1331.A2-.A49		Autobiographical works
		[The number for "Autobiographical works" (31) and its cutter number extensions is added successively to the base number "13" (1331).]
.A4		Letters (Collections). By date
1917		[Date]

H.   Class P: Nineteen Number Author.

      For titles 82-89 the following initial hierarchy and index entry applies:

    Index entry: [No useful index entry was identified]
    [Although there is no index entry for this author or the time period in which he wrote, there is an entry for "American literature PS" but that is considered too general to be of any help in classifying the works that follow.]

PS	American literature *[1998 ed.]*
700-3576	Individual authors
991-(3390)	19th century
2380-2388	Melville, Herman *School administration LB2801+* (Table P-PZ33)
	[Table P-PZ33 (Table for Authors (9 nos.)) in the P-PZ Tables [1998 ed.] is used for Melville. Numbers from this table are added arithmetically to the first number in the range for Melville (2380).]

82.   *The works of Herman Melville*, edited by Winchester.   London, 1922-1924.

     PS2381 .W5 1922

	Collected works.
2381	By editor, if given
	[From Table P-PZ33 (Table for Authors (9 nos.)). The
	"1" from this table is added arithmetically to "3280."]
.W5	[Winchester]
	[Cutter number for "Winchester"]
1922	[Date]

83.   *Typee, or, A peep at Polynesian life*, by Herman Melville. 1957.

     PS2384 .T9 1957

2384A-Z	Separate works. By title
	[From Table P-PZ33 (Table for Authors (9 nos.)). The "4"
	from this table is added arithmetically to "3280."]
.T9	[Typee]
	[Cutter number derived from the LC cutter table]
.T9	Texts. By date
	[From Table P-PZ43 (Table for Separate Works
	(Successive Cutter nos.)). The ".x" for the cutter
	number for the title expresses "Texts."]
1957	[Date]

84.   *Typee*, roman traduit de L'anglois par Verdier, Paris. 1945.
      [A translation into French]

     PS2384 .T9 F7 1945

2384	Separate works. By title
	[From Table P-PZ33 (Table for Authors (9 nos.)). The "4"
	from this table is added arithmetically to "3280."]
.T9	[Typee]
	[Cutter number derived from the LC cutter table]
.T9	Texts. By date
	[From Table P-PZ43 (Table for Separate Works
	(Successive Cutter nos.)). The ".x" for the cutter
	number for the title expresses "Texts."]
A4-Z	Translations. By language
	[The successive cutter number ".xA4-.xZ" is used to
	express the language into which the work has been
	translated.]
F7	[French]
	[Cutter number derived from the LC cutter table]
1945	[Date]

85.   *Rebel genius, the life of Herman Melville,* by Bixby. 1970.

   PS2386 .B5 1970

2386	Biography, criticism, etc.
	[From Table P-PZ33 (Table for Authors (9 nos.)). The "6"
	from this table is added arithmetically to "3280."]
.A5-Z	General works
.B5	[Bixby]
	[Cutter number for the personal name main entry]
1970	[Date]

86.   *Studies in the minor and later works of Melville,* by Hull. 1970.

   PS2387 .H8 1970

2387-2388	Criticism
	[From Table P-PZ33 (Table for Authors (9 nos.)). The "7"
	or "8" from this table are added arithmetically to "3280."]
2387	General works
.H8	[Hull]
	[Cutter number for the personal name main entry]
1970	[Date]

87.   *Melville's use of the Bible,* by Wright. 1949.

   PS2388 .B52 W7 1949

2387-2388	Criticism
	[From Table P-PZ33 (Table for Authors (9 nos.)). The "7"
	or "8" from this table are added arithmetically to "3280."]
2388	Special, A-Z
.B52	Bible
	[Cutter number from the list in Table P-PZ33 under
	the number "8."]
W7	[Wright]
	[Cutter number for the personal name main entry]
1949	[Date]

88.   *Melville's Israel Potter,* by Keyssar. 1969.
   [A criticism of that work]

   PS2384 .I83 K4 1969

2384	Separate works. By title
	[From Table P-PZ33 (Table for Authors (9 nos.)). The "4"
	from this table is added arithmetically to "3280."]
.I8	[Israel Potter]
	[Cutter number derived from the LC cutter table]

	.I83		Criticism

.I83   Criticism
                            [From Table P-PZ43 (Table for Separate Works
                            (Successive Cutter nos.)). The successive cutter
                            number "x3" expresses "Criticism."]
         K4   [Keyssar]
                            [Cutter number for the personal name main entry]
                1969   [Date]

89.   *The letters of Herman Melville,* edited by Davis. 1960.

       PS2386 .A4 1960

            2386   Biography, criticism, etc.
                            [From Table P-PZ33 (Table for Authors (9 nos.)). The "6"
                            from this table is added arithmetically to "3280."]
            .A4   Letters (Collections). By date
            1960   [Date]

I.   <u>Class P: Cutter Number Author.</u>

       For titles 90-93 the following initial hierarchy and index entry applies:

                Index entry: *[No useful index entry was identified]*
                                  [Although there is no index entry for this
                                  author or the time period in which he wrote,
                                  there is an entry for "American literature
                                  PS" but that is considered too general to be
                                  of any help in classifying the works that
                                  follow.]

            PS   American literature *[1998 ed.]*
          700-3576   Individual authors
          3500-3549   1900-1960
            3511   F
            .A86   [aulkner]
                            [Cutter number for the remaining part of the author's
                            surname. Using the LC cutter table this cutter would
                            normally be ."A9." In order to fit Faulkner into its proper
                            alphabetical location in the LC shelf list, LC uses the cutter
                            number ".A86." This places Faulkner after "Fast, Howard"
                            (.A784) and before "Faust, Frederick" (.A87) names that
                            appears in the list of cuttered names under PS 3511.]
                            [Table P-PZ40 (Table for Authors (Cutter no.)) in the P-PZ
                            Tables [1998 ed.] is now used for those authors.]

90.   *The Faulkner reader: selections from the works of William Faulkner.* 1954.

    PS3511 .A86 A6 1954

.A6	Selected works. Selections. By date
	[From Table P-PZ40]
1954	[Date]

91.   *The sound and the fury,* by William Faulkner. 1961.

    PS3511 .A86 S6 1961

.xA61-Z458	Separate works. By title
	[From Table P-PZ40]
S6	[Sound and the fury]
	[Cutter number derived from the LC cutter table]
S6	Texts. By date
	[From Table P-PZ43 (Table for Separate Works (Successive Cutter nos.)). The ".x" for the cutter number for the title expresses "Texts."]
1961	[Date]

92.   *Faulkner's The sound and the fury,* by Gold. 1964.
    [A criticism]

    PS3511 .A86 S633 1964

.xA61-Z458	Separate works. By title
	[From Table P-PZ40]
S6	[Sound and the fury]
	[Cutter number derived from the LC cutter table]
S63	Criticism
	[From Table P-PZ43 (Table for Separate Works (Successive Cutter nos.)). The successive cutter number "x3" expresses "Criticism."]
S633	[Gold]
	[A second successive cutter number is added to express the main entry of the criticism. Based on the range "1"-"9," the letter "G" for the main entry "Gold" is assigned the number "3." See SCM:SL Instruction G 340.]
1964	[Date]

93.　*Requiem pour une Nonne,* by William Faulkner; translated by Coindreau. 1957.
　　[A translation into French of *Requiem for a nun*]

　　PS3511 .A86 R44 1957

.xA61-Z458	Separate works. By title
	[From Table P-PZ40]
R4	[Requiem for a nun]
	[Cutter number derived from the LC cutter table]
R4	Texts. By date
	[From Table P-PZ43 (Table for Separate Works (Successive Cutter nos.)). The ".x" for the cutter number for the title expresses "Texts."]
.xA-Z	Translations. By language
.xA4-.xZ	Other languages, A-Z
R44	[French]
	[Because two cutter numbers have already been used, the second "4" is used to express a translation into French. This number is derived from the Translation Table in SCM:SL Instruction G 150.]
1957	[Date]

94.　*Four studies of Faulkner,* by Overton. 1980.
　　[A criticism]

　　PS3511 .A86 Z78 1980

.xZ4581-.xZ999	Biography and criticism
	[From Table P-PZ40]
.xZ5-.xZ999	General works
Z78	[Overton]
	[Because all criticisms of Faulkner are confined to the small cutter range of Z5-999 it is common in situations such as this to express the second letter of the name in the cutter number. In this case the "7" represents "O" and the "8" represents "v."]
1980	[Date]

APPENDIX F

Answers to the
Library of Congress Subject Headings Exercise

The second indicator in all subject fields identifies the subject authority on which the subject entry is based. Since all of the answers that follow are LCSH headings, they all have a second indicator of "0"

The majority of these subject headings are topical in nature and as such appear in the following OCLC/MARC Field

Field 650 -- Subject Added Entry–Topical Term

There are, however, a number of subject headings that are other than topical. These include personal names, corporate names and geographical names. The following OCLC/MARC Fields and indicators are used for those types of subject headings:

Field 600 -- Subject Added Entry–Personal name
 1st Indicator 0 -- Forename
 1st Indicator 1 -- Surname*
 1st Indicator 3 -- Family name

Field 610 -- Subject Added Entry–Corporate Name
 1st Indicator 1 -- Jurisdiction name
 1st Indicator 2 -- Name in direct order

Field 651 -- Subject Added Entry–Geographic Name

A. Simple Subject Headings.

1. *Plea Bargaining: is it fair?*

  650 0 Plea bargaining.

2. *An introduction to machine-shop mathematics.*

  650 0 Shop mathematics.

3. *Water-borne power projection: naval policy and a nation's destiny.*

  650 0 Sea-power.

---

* See the N.B. comment at the beginning of Chapter 3 for the change in OCLC/MARC coding practice for the first indicator which changes the wording for value "1" from "Single surname" to "Surname."

4.   *Ocean drilling vessels.*

     650   0   Deep-sea drilling ships.

5.   *What are the effects of agricultural chemicals on plants?*

     650   0   Plants, effect of agricultural chemicals on.

6.   *Windmills: the clean, free power source.*

     650   0   Windmills.

7.   *Your solar heated home.*

     650   0   Solar houses.

8.   *An introduction to industrial psychology.*

     650   0   Psychology, Industrial.

9.   *The story of orchestration.*

     650   0   Instrumentation and orchestration.

10.   *The Sopwith Camel.*
      [A type of fighter plane]

     650   0   Camel (Fighter planes)

11.   *Danish Christmas carols.*

     650   0   Carols, Danish.
                    *[Although not listed specifically in LCSH the instruction under
                    "Carols" provides for qualifying by the name of the language.]*

     650   0   Christmas music.
                    *[This second subject heading is used to bring out the Christmas
                    aspect of the work. The term "Carols" does not exclusively apply to
                    Christmas music. "Christmas music" cannot be subdivided
                    geographically.]*

12.   *Rats and the diseases they carry.*

     650   0   Rats as carriers of disease.

13. *The Battle for Guadalcanal.*
     [A World War Two series of battles]

     651   0   Guadalcanal (Solomon Islands), Battle of, 1942-1943.
                [See SCM:SH Instruction H 1285.]

14. *Requirements for controlled atmospheres in space.*

     650   0   Artificial atmospheres (Space environment)

15. *Infant welfare.*

     650   0   Maternal and infant welfare.

B.   Subject Headings with Topical Subdivisions.

16. *The 1956 Anglo-French intervention in Egypt.*

     651   0   Egypt ‡x History ‡y Intervention, 1956.

17. *Ride down that road again: recycling road building materials.*

     650   0   Road materials ‡x Recycling.

18. *How to breed roses.*

     650   0   Roses ‡x Breeding.

19. *When did Buddha die? The controversy continues.*

     600 0 0   Gautama Buddha ‡x Date of death.

20. *Gasoline pipelines.*

     650   0   Gasoline pipelines.

21. *Light filters in photography.*

     650   0   Photography ‡x Light filters.

22. *Crabgrass, dandelions, and other green lawn disasters: weed control in the lawns of suburbia.*

     650   0   Lawns ‡x Weed control.

23.   *Aircraft collision avoidance systems: the state of the art.*

650   0   Airplanes ‡x Collision avoidance.

24.   *Quality processing for top quality photos.*

650   0   Photography ‡x Processing.

25.   *Operation Overlord: D-Day, 1944.*
       [Accounts of the invasion]

650   0   World War, 1939-1945 ‡x Campaigns ‡z France ‡z Normandy.
            [The subject heading "Operation Overlord" would be inappropriate
            because its use is limited by its scope note to documents that deal
            with the "military planning and diplomatic negotiations for the
            Normandy Invasion."]

C.   Subject Headings with Geographic Subdivisions.

26.   *The courts of Scotland.*
       [Addresses the legal courts]

650   0   Courts ‡z Scotland.

27.   *Taxation of artists in the Republic of Ireland: the laws and commentary.*

650   0   Artists ‡x Taxation ‡x Law and legislation ‡z Ireland.
            [Although the country is known as the Republic of Ireland the
            authorized form of name is "Ireland." That term is used for both the
            republic and for the island of the British Isles called Ireland. The
            country created by the Government of Ireland Act of 1920 uses the
            term "Northern Ireland."]

28.   *Children of working parents: the Minneapolis experience.*

650   0   Children of working parents ‡z Minnesota ‡z Minneapolis.
            [SCM:SH Instruction H 830 indicates that for geographic
            subdivisions states within the United States are not to be entered
            under the country first but rather under the state, i.e., not ‡z United
            States ‡z Minnesota. That instruction also states that only two
            levels of geographic subdivision are to be used. Thus the country
            level has not been included.]

29.   *Crack abuse in Cleveland: the report of the 1989 survey.*

      650   0   Crack (Drug) ‡z Ohio ‡z Cleveland
                  [The use of this subject heading is called for by the scope note under the subject heading "Drug abuse surveys."]

      650   0   Drug abuse surveys ‡z Ohio ‡z Cleveland.
                  [This subject heading is assigned to bring out the survey aspect of the work.]

30.   *Electronic spying by the United States.*
      [The collection of foreign non-communication electromagnetic radiations by agencies of the U.S. government]

      650   0   Electronic intelligence.
                  [Geographic subdivision is not allowed for this subject heading.]

31.   *Labor unions in the tire industry of Akron, Ohio.*

      650   0   Trade unions ‡x Tire industry workers ‡z Ohio ‡z Akron.

32.   *Political activities of artisans in Mexico City.*

      650   0   Artisans ‡z Mexico ‡z Mexico City ‡x Political activity.
                  [The subdivision "Political activity" cannot be subdivided geographically. Accordingly, the geographic subdivision is located after the subject heading which is able to be geographically divided (see SCM:SH 860).]

33.   *The pre-Lenten carnivals of Baton Rouge, Louisiana.*

      650   0   Carnival ‡z Louisiana ‡z Baton Rouge.
                  [See the scope notes under "Carnival" and "Carnivals" for the differences in meanings of these two subject headings.]

34.   *Dog laws of Washington, D.C.*

      650   0   Dogs ‡x Law and legislation ‡z Washington (D.C.)
                  [SCM:SH Instruction H 830 indicates that the city Washington, D.C. is to be entered directly as a geographic subdivision. The form of name for the city was derived from the LC Name Authority File.]

35.   *Bog men of England and Denmark.*

      650   0   Bog bodies ‡z England.

      650   0   Bog bodies ‡z Denmark.

36.   *The new way to get the job done in the U.S.: contracting for services.*

    650   0   Contracting out ‡z United States.

                [When the geographic subdivision is for the United States rather than for a political unit lower than the country level the name of the country is used as the geographic subdivision.]

37.   *Nineteenth century magazine illustration in Great Britain.*

    650   0   Magazine illustration ‡y 19th century ‡z Great Britain.

                [Both "Magazine illustration" and "19th century" can be divided geographically. Accordingly, the geographic subdivision is placed after the subdivision (see SCM:SH 860).]

38.   *Costume in 17th and 18th century France: a definitive history.*

    650   0   Costume ‡z France ‡x History ‡y 17th century.

    650   0   Costume ‡z France ‡x History ‡y 18th century.

                [Two subject headings need to be assigned to adequately cover the time span of the document. These time periods cannot be combined by the cataloger.]

                [The free-floating subdivision "History" and the time periods cannot be subdivided geographically. Accordingly, the geographic subdivision is located after the subject heading which is able to be geographically divided (see SCM:SH Instruction H 860).]

39.   *Mandatory retirement laws in Georgia.*

    650   0   Retirement, Mandatory ‡x Law and legislation ‡z Georgia.

40.   *Depression glass of East Liverpool, Ohio.*

    650   0   Depression glass.

                [This subject heading cannot be subdivided geographically.]

41.   *What family? The problem of family abandonment in Indiana.*

    650   0   Desertion and non-support ‡z Indiana.

D.   Subject Headings with Form and Topical Free-Floating Subdivisions.

42.   *The history of the Dewey Decimal Classification.*

    650   0   Classification, Dewey Decimal ‡x History.

                [See SCM:SH Instructions H 1095 and H 1647 for the use of the free-floating subdivision "History."]

43.   *Soil density in Zurich, Switzerland: a bibliography.*

       650   0   Soils ‡z Switzerland ‡z Zurich ‡x Density ‡v Bibliography.
                   *[The subdivision "Density" and the free-floating subdivision
                   "Bibliography" cannot be subdivided geographically. Accordingly,
                   the geographic subdivision is located after the subject heading which
                   is able to be geographically divided (see SCM:SH 860).]*

                   *[See SCM:SH Instruction H 1095 for the use of the free-floating
                   subdivision "Bibliography."]*

44.   *The effects of drugs on the newborn: a compilation of essays.*

       650   0   Infants (Newborn) ‡x Effect of drugs on.
                   *[There is no subdivision that expresses "essays." See SCM:SH
                   Instruction H 1210.]*

45.   *Minority employment in the states of California and New York: a comparative statistical report.*

       650   0   Minorities ‡x Employment ‡z California ‡v Statistics.

       650   0   Minorities ‡x Employment ‡z New York (State) ‡v Statistics.
                   *[The form of name for the State of New York was derived from the
                   LC Name Authority File.]*

                   *[See SCM:SH Instructions H 1095 and H 2095 for the use of the
                   free-floating subdivision "Statistics."]*

46.   *U. S. copyright law for musical works: abstracts.*

       650   0   Copyright ‡x Music ‡z United States ‡v Abstracts.
                   *[See SCM:SH Instructions H 1095 and H 1205 for the use of the
                   free-floating subdivision "Abstracts."]*

47.   *Fox hunting in Albemarle County, Virginia: an historical view.*

       650   0   Fox hunting ‡z Virginia ‡z Albermarle County ‡ x History.
                   *[See SCM:SH Instruction H 1095 for the use of the free-floating
                   subdivision "History."]*

48.   *Fire towers and fire spotters of North and South Carolina: a directory.*

       650   0   Fire lookout stations ‡z North Carolina ‡v Directories.

       650   0   Fire lookout stations ‡z South Carolina ‡v Directories.
[Continued on next page]

650   0   Fire lookouts ‡z North Carolina ‡v Directories.

650   0   Fire lookouts ‡z South Carolina ‡v Directories.
> *[The free-floating subdivision "Directories" cannot be subdivided geographically. Accordingly, the geographic subdivision is located after the subject heading which is able to be geographically divided (see SCM:SH 860).]*
>
> *[See SCM:SH Instructions H 1095 and H 1558 for the use of the free-floating subdivision "Directories."]*

49.   *Physics: a basic textbook.*

650   0   Physics.
> *[The free-floating subdivision "Textbooks" is not used for books that are textbooks on the subject except in very limited instances. See SCM:SH Instructions H 1095 and H 2187 for guidance on its use.]*

50.   *Macroeconomics for the layman.*

650   0   Macroeconomics ‡v Popular works.
> *[See SCM:SH Instructions H 1095 and H 1943.5 for the use of the free-floating subdivision "Popular Works."]*

51.   *Railroad collisions in late 19th century Pennsylvania.*

650   0   Railroad accidents ‡z Pennsylvania ‡x History ‡x 19th century.
> *[The free-floating subdivision "History" and the time period cannot be subdivided geographically. Accordingly, the geographic subdivision is located after the subject heading which is able to be geographically divided (see SCM:SH Instruction H 860).]*
>
> *[See SCM:SH Instructions H 1095 and H 1647 for the use of the free-floating subdivision "History ‡y 19th century."]*

52.   *Zeppelins: an illustrated history.*
[The text of this work is richly illustrated with photographs. They constitute approximately two-thirds of this work. This work deals with airships throughout the world rather than being limited to German zeppelins.]

650   0   Airships ‡x History.
> *[See SCM:SH Instructions H 1095 and H 1647 for the use of the free-floating subdivision "History."]*

650   0   Airships ‡x History ‡v Pictorial works.
> *[See SCM:SH Instructions H 1095 and H 1935 for the use of the free-floating subdivision "Pictorial works." Note the requirement for this second subject heading when the work that consists of text and illustrations and the illustrations constitute more than half the work and the illustrations are emphasized.]*

53.   *Yearbook of industrial mental health.*

    650   0   Industrial psychiatry ‡v Periodicals.
              *[There is no subdivision that expresses "yearbook." (see SCM:SH
              Instruction H 2400). See Instructions H 1095 and H 1927 for the
              use of the free-floating subdivision "Periodicals."]*

54.   *Tennessee's campsites: a directory.*

    650   0   Camp sites, facilities, etc. ‡z Tennessee ‡v Directories.
              *[See SCM:SH Instructions H 1095 and H 1558 for the use of the
              free-floating subdivision "Directories."]*

55.   *Nursing home care and the Federal commitment*

    650   0   Nursing home care ‡x Government policy ‡z United States.
              *[See SCM:SH Instructions H 1095 and H 1642 for the use of the
              free-floating subdivision "Government policy." The subject heading
              "Federal aid to nursing homes ‡z United States" is somewhat
              narrower in scope than the topic implied by the title in that that
              subject heading is confined to Federal aid for nursing home care
              rather than the Federal government's policy to nursing home care in
              general.]*

56.   *Japanese history, 1919 to 1945: a source book.*

    650   0   Japan ‡x History ‡y 1912-1945 ‡v Sources.
              *[See SCM:SH Instructions H 1095 and H 2080 for the use of the
              free-floating subdivision "Sources."]*

57.   *House repair for the homeowner.*

    650   0   Dwellings ‡x Maintenance and repair ‡v Amateurs' manuals.
              *[You may wish to refer to SCM:SH Instruction H 1943.5 to see the
              difference between the subdivision "Amateurs' manuals" and the
              free-floating subdivision "Popular works."]*

E.   Subject Headings with Pattern and Other Free-Floating Subdivisions.

58.   *Thomas Alva Edison: a definitive biography.*

    600 1 0   Edison, Thomas A. (Thomas Alva), ‡d 1847-1931.
              *[The form of name for Edison was derived from the LC Name
              Authority File.]*

              *[Unless otherwise indicated, the free-floating subdivision
              "Biography" is not added to the name heading for the biography of
              an individual (see SCM:SH Instructions H 1110 (Names of Persons)
              and H 1330).]*

[Continued on next page]

650   0   Inventors ‡z United States ‡v Biography.

> *[See SCM:SH Instruction H 1330 for the provision of a second subject heading for the class of persons of which an individual was a member. In this situation the free-floating subdivision "Biography" is used.]*

> *[The free-floating subdivision "Bibliography" cannot be subdivided geographically. Accordingly, the geographic subdivision is located after the subject heading which is able to be geographically divided (see SCM:SH Instruction H 860).]*

59.   *The travelers' guide to Peru.*
       [Provides information on facilities, accommodations and items of interest]

651   0   Peru ‡v Guidebooks.

> *[See SCM:SH Instructions H 1095 and H 1645 for the use of the free-floating subdivision "Guidebooks. The free-floating subdivision "Description and travel" would not be appropriate given the guidance of H 1530. The free-floating subdivision "Tours" was not assigned because nothing indicated that this work dealt with planned itineraries for travelers.]*

60.   *Genealogy of the Carpenter family of Massachusetts.*

600 3 0   Carpenter family.

> *[See SCM:SH Instruction H 1631 for an explanation of why the free-floating subdivision "Genealogy" is not used with a family name.]*

651   0   Massachusetts ‡v Genealogy.

> *[See SCM:SH Instructions H 1631 and H 1845 for the use of "[local place] ‡v Genealogy" as a second subject heading.]*

61.   *Control of the color fading of apples.*

650   0   Apples ‡x Color ‡x Fading ‡x Control.

> *[See SCM:SH Instruction H 1180 (Pattern Heading: Plants and Crops) for the use of the free-floating subdivision "Color ‡x Fading ‡x Control."]*

62.   *Edgar Allan Poe as a character in mystery novels: review essays.*

600 1 0   Poe, Edgar Allan, 1809-1849 ‡x In literature.

> *[The form of name for Poe was derived from the LC Name Authority File.]*

> *[See SCM:SH Instruction H 1110 (Names of Persons) for the use of the free-floating subdivision "In literature." under the names of persons. The free-floating subdivision "‡v Fiction" would only be assigned if this were a work in which Poe appeared as a character or in belles lettres about him.]*

63. *Camping and backpacking in the Great Lakes area.*

    650   0   Camping ‡z Great Lakes Region.

    650   0   Backpacking ‡z Great Lakes Region.
          [See SCM:SH Instruction H 760 for the naming of geographic
          regions. The form of name for the region was derived from the LC
          Name Authority File.]

64. *Japan and France: a review of their foreign relations.*
    [The foreign relations between these two countries primarily from the Japanese perspective]

    651   0   Japan ‡x Foreign relations ‡z France.

    651   0   France ‡x Foreign relations ‡z Japan.
          [See SCM:SH Instruction H 1629 for the provision of a second
          subject heading with the two places reversed.]

65. *At the tip of the continent: the Strait of Magellan along the Chilean coast.*
    [A general geography text not a work designed for travelers]

    651   0   Magellan, Strait of (Chile and Argentina) ‡x Description and travel.
          [See SCM:SH Instructions H 1140 (Names of Places) and H 1530
          for the use of the free-floating division "Description and travel."]

66. *They fell for the Union: Pennsylvanian's who died for their country in the Civil War.*
    [A listing]

    651   0   United States ‡x History ‡y Civil War, 1861-1865 ‡v Registers of dead.
          [See SCM:SH Instruction H 1200 (Pattern Headings: Wars) for the
          use of the free-floating subdivision "Registers of dead." See also
          SCM:SH Instruction 1845 (Historical Materials, Including Local
          Historical Materials).]

    651   0   Pennsylvania ‡x History ‡y Civil War, 1861-1865 ‡v Registers of dead.
          [See SCM:SH Instruction H 1200 (Pattern Headings: Wars) for the
          provision of a second subject headings for a subordinate jurisdiction
          when that work discusses a subordinate jurisdiction and the name of
          the war has been established under a place.]

67. *Lord Peter: English dilettante or true detective?*
    [A character created by Dorothy L. Sayers]

    600 1 0   Sayers, Dorothy L. ‡q (Dorothy Leigh), ‡d 1893-1957 ‡x Characters ‡x
          Lord Peter Wimsey.
                  [Continued on next page]

650   0   Wimsey, Peter, Lord (Fictitious character)

[The provision of this second subject heading for the name of the fictitious character is called for by SCM:SH Instruction H 1110 (Names of Persons) under the free-floating subdivision "Characters ‡x [name of individual character]."]

[As a fictitious character the name "Wimsey, Peter, Lord" is considered a topical subject heading rather than a personal name heading and is thus coded "650." See SCM:SH Instruction H 1610 for further guidance on entry under the name of a fictitious character.]

68.   *Tunnel vision: innovations in the diagnosis of retinitis pigmentosa in the United States.*

650   0   Retinitis pigmentosa ‡x Diagnosis ‡z United States.

[See SCM:SH Instruction H 1150 (Pattern Headings: Diseases) for the use of the free-floating subdivision "Diagnosis."]

69.   *The incidence of diseases in lambs in Greene County, Pennsylvania: a statistical evaluation.*

650   0   Lambs ‡x Diseases ‡z Pennsylvania ‡z Greene County ‡v Statistics.

[See SCM:SH Instruction H 1147 (Pattern Headings: Animals) for the use of the free-floating subdivision "Diseases."]

[See Instructions H 1095 and H 2095 for the use of the free-floating subdivision "Statistics." Note that because this is a work of statistics rather than a work about statistics it receives the subfield code "v" rather than "x."]

[The free-floating subdivisions "Diseases" and "Statistics" cannot be subdivided geographically. Accordingly, the geographic subdivision is located after the subject heading which is able to be geographically divided (see SCM:SH Instruction H 860).]

70.   *Lost with the Titanic.*
[A novel about the loss of the R.M.S. Titanic in 1912]

610 2 0   Titanic (Steamship) ‡v Fiction.

[The form of name for the Titanic was derived from the LC Name Authority File.]

[See SCM:SH Instructions H 1105 (Corporate Bodies) for the use of the free-floating subdivision "Fiction" and H 1790 for its use with historical fiction including works about corporate bodies.]

71.   *Henry Ford's contributions to the automobile industry.*
      [This work concentrates on his contributions to the U.S. auto industry rather than his life or the Ford Motor Company.]

    600 1 0   Ford, Henry, ‡d 1863-1947.

> *[The form of name for Ford was derived from the LC Name Authority File.]*
>
> *[See SCM:SH Instruction H 1110 (Names of Persons) for the use of the free-floating subdivision 'Contributions to [specific field or topic]". For this work, the subdivision "Contributions to the automobile industry" was not used because it is considered the primary field with which Ford was associated.]*

    650   0   Automobile industry and trade ‡z United States ‡x History.

> *[The free-floating subdivision "History" cannot be subdivided geographically. Accordingly, the geographic subdivision is located after the subject heading which is able to be geographically divided (see SCM:SH Instruction H 860).]*
>
> *[The free-floating subdivision "Biography" was not added because this work is not primarily biographical, rather it examines Ford's contributions from an historical perspective. See SCM:SH Instructions H 1095 and H 1647 for use of the free-floating subdivision "History." The more detailed free-floating subdivision "History ‡y 20th century" was not used because the history of this industry is essentially confined to the current century.]*
>
> *[If a significant part of the book dealt with the Ford Motor Company a third subject heading "Ford Motor Company ‡x History" would also have been assigned.]*

72.   *The West Virginia University: pictorial views of campus.*

    610 2 0   West Virginia University ‡v Pictorial works.

> *[The form of name for West Virginia University was derived from the LC Name Authority File.]*
>
> *[Although "Pictorial works" is not listed as a free-floating subdivision under SCM:SH Instruction H 1151 (Pattern Headings: Individual Educational Institutions) that instruction also states that the free-floating subdivisions under SCM:SH Instruction H 1105 (Corporate Bodies) can also be used for individual educational institutions. The free-floating standard subdivision "Pictorial works" is listed there. See SCM:SH Instruction 1935 for the use of the free-floating subdivision "Pictorial works."]*

73.   *Women in the fiction of Ernest Hemingway.*

    600 1 0   Hemingway, Ernest, ‡d 1899-1961 ‡x Characters ‡x Women.

> *[The form of name for Hemingway was derived from the LC Name Authority File.]*
>
> *[See SCM:SH Instruction H 1110 (Names of Persons) for the use of the free-floating subdivision "Characters ‡x Children [Jews, Physicians, etc."]*

[Continued on next page]

650   0   Women in literature.

> *[An instruction to add a second subject heading for the "[group of category] in literature" appears under SCM:SH Instruction H 1110 (Names of Persons) "Characters ‡x Children [Jews, Physicians, etc."]*

74.   *Recruiting practices of the Central Intelligence Agency.*

610 1 0   United States. ‡b Central Intelligence Agency ‡x Officials and Employees ‡x Recruiting.

> *[Despite the fact this subject headings begins with "United States," because those words are part of a heading for a corporate name the subject heading is coded "610" (Subject Added Entry–Corporate Name) rather than "651" (Subject Added entry–Geographic Name). The form of name for the Central Intelligence Agency was derived from the LC Name Authority File.]*

> *[See SCM:SH Instruction H 1140 (Names of Places) for the use of the free-floating subdivision "Officials and employees." The reference under "Officials and employees" provides for the use of free-floating subdivisions appearing under SCM:SH Instruction H 1100 (Classes of Persons). This is the source of the free-floating subdivision "Recruiting."]*

> *[Geographic subdivision, although allowed, would be inappropriate given the use of "United States" in the corporate name. See SCM:SH Instruction H 830.]*

F.   <u>Miscellaneous Subject Heading Situations</u>. Assign the most appropriate subject heading(s) for the following titles.

75.   *How to catalog a rare book.*

650   0   Cataloging of rare books.

76.   *How to grow asparagus.*

650   0   Asparagus.

77.   *The conservation of museum collections.*

650   0   Museum conservation methods.

78.   *Sacred waters: the folklore of holy wells and holy springs in Europe.*

    650   0   Holy wells ‡z Europe ‡v Folklore.

          [The free-floating subdivision "Folklore" cannot be subdivided geographically. Accordingly, the geographic subdivision is located after the subject heading which is able to be geographically divided (see SCM:SH Instruction H 860).]

          [See SCM:SH Instruction H 1627 for the use of the free-floating subdivision "Folklore."]

    650   0   Springs ‡z Europe ‡x Religious aspects ‡v Folklore.

          [The subdivision "Religious aspects" also cannot be subdivided geographically. Accordingly, the geographic subdivision is located after the subject heading which is able to be geographically divided (see SCM:SH Instruction H 860).]

79.   *How to train your homing pigeon.*

    650   0   Homing pigeons ‡x Training.

          [See SCM:SH Instruction H 1147 (Pattern Headings: Animals) for the use of the free-floating subdivision "Training."]

80.   *The first book of astronomy.*
    [A book for children]

    650   0   Astronomy ‡v Juvenile literature.

          [See SCM:SH Instructions H 1095 and H 1690 for the use of the free-floating subdivision "Juvenile literature."]

81.   *The art of writing biographies.*
    [A book of techniques]

    650   0   Biography as a literary form.

          [The free-floating subdivision "Technique" was not added to this subject heading because the heading "Biography ‡x Technique" is a UF reference under "Biography as a literary form" indicating that "Technique" is implied in the meaning of the subject heading. See SCM:SH Instruction H 1095 for uses of the free-floating subdivision "Technique."]

82.   *The essential manual of archeology for the amateur archaeologist.*

    650   0   Archaeology ‡v Amateurs' manuals.

          [See SCM:SH Instruction H 1943.5 for the use of the free-floating subdivision "Amateurs' manuals" and the difference between it and the free-floating subdivision "Popular works."]

83.   *The chemical analysis of rocks.*

       650   0   Rocks ‡x Analysis.

84.   *Photography for children.*

       650   0   Photography ‡v Juvenile literature.
                   [See SCM:SH Instruction H 1690 for the use of the free-floating
                   subdivision "Juvenile literature."]

85.   *Lawyers as characters in modern fiction.*

       650   0   Lawyers in literature.

86.   *Coins and coin collectors.*

       650   0   Coins.

       650   0   Coins ‡x Collectors and collecting.
                   [Both subject headings were assigned in order to present both the
                   coins and the collectors aspects.]

87.   *Veterinary hospitals: a survey.*

       650   0   Veterinary hospitals.

88.   *The history of 18th century astrology.*

       650   0   Astrology ‡x History ‡y 18th century.
                   [See SCM:SH Instructions H 1095 and H 1647 for the use of the
                   free-floating subdivision "History ‡y 18th century."]

89.   *Vocational education for women.*

       650   0   Women ‡x Vocational education.

90.   *The complete dictionary of philosophy.*
       [In English]

       650   0   Philosophy ‡v Dictionaries.
                   [See SCM:SH Instruction H 1540 for the use of the free-floating
                   subdivision "Dictionaries."]

91. *Children's furniture building for the home craftsman.*

     650   0   Furniture making ‡v Amateurs' manuals.
          [See SCM:SH Instruction H 1943.5 for the use of the free-floating subdivision "Amateurs' manuals" and the difference between it and the free-floating subdivision "Popular works."]

     650   0   Children's furniture ‡v Amateurs' manuals.

92. *Life on the stage: the biography of Helen Hayes.*
[The American actress born in 1900]

     600 1 0   Hayes, Helen, ‡d 1900-
          [The form of name for the Hayes was derived from the LC Name Authority File.]

          [Unless otherwise indicated, the free-floating subdivision "Biography" is not added to the name heading for the biography of an individual (see SCM:SH Instruction H 1110 (Names of Persons).]

     650   0   Actors ‡z United States ‡v Biography.
          [See SCM:SH Instruction H 1330 for the provision of a second subject heading for the class of persons of which an individual was a member. In this situation the free-floating subdivision "Biography" is used. The subject heading "Actresses" is used only for works on female actresses collectively. Works about individual male or female actors use the subject heading "Actors." See the scope note under "Actors," "Actresses," and SCM:SH Instruction 1330.]

          [The free-floating subdivision "Biography" cannot be subdivided geographically. Accordingly, the geographic subdivision is located after the subject heading which is able to be geographically divided (see SCM:SH Instruction H 860).]

          [A third subject heading "Motion picture actors and actresses ‡y United States ‡v Biography" was not used because the title implies that this work concentrates on her theatrical career. If it had not, then that subject heading would also have been assigned. See SCM:SH Instruction H 1330.]

93. *The National League.*
[A history of the professional baseball league]

     610 2 0   National League of Professional Baseball Clubs ‡x History.
          [The form of name for the National League was derived from the LC Name Authority File.]

          [See SCM:SH Instructions H 1105 (Corporate Bodies) and H 1647 for the use of the free-floating subdivision "History."]

94. *Go Cubs! a history of the Chicago Cubs.*
    [The professional baseball team]

       610 2 0   Chicago Cubs (Baseball team) ‡x History.
                     [The form of name for the Chicago Cubs was derived from the LC Name Authority File.]

                     [See SCM:SH Instructions H 1105 (Corporate Bodies) and H 1647 for the use of the free-floating subdivision "History."]

95. *School architecture in California.*

       650   0   School buildings ‡z California.

96. *Witchcraft in Alabama.*

       650   0   Witchcraft ‡z Alabama.

97. *Cheesebox on a raft: the Union ironclad Monitor.*
    [Centers on the activities of this ship during the Civil War]

       610 2 0   Monitor (Ironclad)
                     [The form of name for the Monitor was derived from the LC Name Authority File.]

       651   0   United States ‡x History ‡y Civil War, 1861-1865 ‡x Naval operations.
                     [If this work were limited to the Monitor's battle with the Merrimac in 1862 it would have been assigned the subject heading "Hampton Roads (Va.), Battle of, 1862" rather than this heading.]

98. *The Hogarth Press: the history of a great private press.*

       610 2 0   Hogarth Press ‡x History.
                     [The form of name for the Hogarth Press was derived from the LC Name Authority File.]

                     [See SCM:SH Instructions H 1105 (Corporate Bodies) and H 1647 for the use of the free-floating subdivision "History."]

99. *Techniques of writing mystery and detective stories.*

       650   0   Detective and mystery stories ‡v Technique.
                     [See SCM:SH Instruction H 1095 for uses of the free-floating subdivision "Technique."]

100.   *A repair manual for the Buick automobile.*

    650   0   Buick automobile ‡x Maintenance and repair.
                    [See SCM:SH Instruction H 1095 for the use of the free-floating
                    subdivision "Maintenance and repair." Note the difference between
                    "Maintenance and repair" and "Repairing."]

101.   *"The open road": A bibliography of articles on motorcycles.*

    650   0   Motorcycles ‡v Bibliography.
                    [See SCM:SH Instruction H 1095 for the use of the free-floating
                    subdivision "Bibliography."]

102.   *North American Indian embroidery.*

    650   0   Indian embroidery ‡z North America.

103.   *Flowers in literature.*

    650   0   Flowers in literature.

104.   *How to win at the game Trivial Pursuit.*

    650   0   Trivial Pursuit (Game)

105.   *Modern paper manufacture in Japan: the industry and the craft.*

    650   0   Paper industry ‡z Japan.

    650   0   Papermaking ‡z Japan.